MW00352946

MAKING AND FAKING KINSHIP

MAKING AND FAKING KINSHIP

*Marriage and Labor Migration between
China and South Korea*

CAREN FREEMAN

CORNELL UNIVERSITY PRESS
ITHACA AND LONDON

Korea Foundation

한국국제교류재단

The Korea Foundation has provided financial assistance for the undertaking of this publication project.

Copyright © 2011 by Cornell University

All rights reserved. Except for brief quotations in a review, this book, or parts thereof, must not be reproduced in any form without permission in writing from the publisher. For information, address Cornell University Press, Sage House, 512 East State Street, Ithaca, New York 14850.

First published 2011 by Cornell University Press
Printed in the United States of America

Library of Congress Cataloging-in-Publication Data

Freeman, Caren, 1968–
  Making and faking kinship : marriage and labor migration between China and South Korea / Caren Freeman.
      p. cm.
  Includes bibliographical references and index.
  ISBN 978-0-8014-4958-1 (alk. paper)
  1. Intercountry marriage—Korea (South)   2. Intercountry marriage—China.   3. Women immigrants—Korea (South)   4. Foreign workers, Chinese—Korea (South)   5. Rural families—Korea (South)   6. Family policy—Korea (South)   I. Title.
  HQ1032.F74   2011
  306.85'2095195—dc23   2011022279

Cornell University Press strives to use environmentally responsible suppliers and materials to the fullest extent possible in the publishing of its books. Such materials include vegetable-based, low-VOC inks and acid-free papers that are recycled, totally chlorine-free, or partly composed of nonwood fibers. For further information, visit our website at www.cornellpress.cornell.edu.

Cloth printing   10 9 8 7 6 5 4 3 2 1

For my parents

Contents

ACKNOWLEDGMENTS

This book was more than a decade in the making. Over this long period, I received a tremendous amount of support—financial, intellectual, logistical, emotional, and familial—from many different sources. The people to whom I owe the greatest thanks remain anonymous in order to protect their privacy: the Chosŏnjok and South Korean families and individuals who gave so generously of their time and let me into their hearts and homes. I am especially grateful to my host families in Harbin, Mudanjiang, and Creek Road Village who cared for me as if I were one of their own. Without them this project would not have been possible.

While in the field, I was sustained by many friendships, new and old. I thank Shin Seungnam ("Ŏnni") for sharing her home with me in Seoul, answering my incessant questions, and helping me track down information related to my research. Jung Hyeouk assisted me in countless ways as a close friend and confidante. I am also grateful to Shin Jongjin for his readiness to help me, whether in Seoul or in Charlottesville. I could not have secured and carried out interviews with dozens of South Korean farmers and their Chosŏnjok brides without the assistance of my patient and intrepid research assistants, Kim Kyŏngŭn and Kim Chiyŏng, and, on my first rural excursion, Kim Hyunjoo.

I am grateful to the granting agencies that provided the funding I needed to conduct eighteen months of field research. USIA Fulbright generously funded my first year of research in South Korea. The executive director of Fulbright, Horace H. Underwood, eased my entry into the field and facilitated communication and camaraderie among the Fulbright Junior Researchers in Seoul. Support from Fulbright-Hays, SSRC-IDRF, and the Wenner-Gren Foundation enabled me to carry out the second phase of research in Heilongjiang, China, and a follow-up study in South Korea. Keith Clemenger of the SSRC was instrumental in helping me obtain sponsorship from the Chinese Academy of Social Sciences (CASS) in Beijing after I was rebuffed by Yanbian University officials. CASS in turn helped me establish an affiliation with the Heilongjiang Provincial Academy of Social Sciences in Harbin. Professors Liu Shuang and Bu Ping of the Heilongjiang Academy of Social Sciences extended a warm welcome and helped me get acclimated in Harbin.

For the formative stages of this project, I am indebted to advisers at University of Virginia. Susan McKinnon first inspired me to write about transnational kinship. She has challenged me every step of the way to deepen my analysis and sharpen the theoretical basis of my arguments. For his exacting readings of the earliest drafts of each chapter, I am grateful to John Shepherd whose encouragement has kept me focused over the years. I also thank Fred Damon who lent his enthusiasm to my research in East Asia. I always take to heart his thought-provoking queries, even if I fall short in my responses to them. Finally, I posthumously recognize Dell Hymes for his expert editorial assistance and warm encouragement.

Throughout the process of writing and revision, I benefited from the opportunity to present my ideas and receive critical feedback as a participant on numerous conference panels. Sections of this book were presented at the 2001, 2002, 2005, 2007, and 2008 meetings of the American Anthropological Association and the 2001 and 2010 meetings of the Association for Asian Studies. These forums helped me crystallize my thoughts for chapters 2 through 5. Some of the ethnographic vignettes in this book were published earlier in Nicole Constable's edited volume *Cross-Border Marriages: Gender and Mobility in Transnational Asia* (2005), which grew out of the 2001 conference panels. Nicole's enthusiastic interest in my work and the inspiring example of her own research and writing fueled my determination to turn this project into a book. Her careful reading of an early draft contributed greatly to the final version.

I also acknowledge the immensely helpful comments provided by one anonymous reviewer and Nancy Abelmann. Nancy's editorial insight resulted in a more tightly constructed, ethnography-centered book with more suggestive titles and subheadings. Thanks also go to Nancy for coming up with the book's evocative title. Clark Sorensen helped me track down details on Chosŏnjok settlement patterns and handed me an interesting question to ponder: How does a researcher define what is "old" and "new" when studying a population as complexly positioned between the currents of "Korean" and "Chinese" history? Further reflection must await future publication. At Cornell University Press, I am extremely thankful to Roger Haydon for his lightning-quick feedback, persistent encouragement, and editorial expertise throughout revision and publication. I am also grateful to Candace J. Akins and Martha Walsh.

I began what turned out to be an inordinately long, drawn-out process of writing by giving birth to my son, Benhui. Along the way my daughter, Sohie, was born. With their boundless desire for my undivided attention, they constituted the greatest obstacle in the timely completion of this project but also my greatest joy in life. A number of friends provided moral support, proofreading, and/or childcare assistance at various stages: Holly Lord, Tania Grasso, Emily Snelling, Robin Edwards, Karen Rifkin, Sivan Sherman, Hilary Steinitz, Rachel Miller, and my sister, Cyndilee Kosloff. For making sure I got a minimum dose of exercise and fresh air each day, I thank Chula and Cecil (both of whom I miss profoundly) and Meimei. I never could have managed to see this project to the end without the expert childcare and nutritious Korean meals provided by my parents-in-law, Hyunjung and Keysun Ryang. Eugene Ryang tolerated our transnational relationship through nearly two years of fieldwork and has stood by me throughout the travails of writing and parenting. With his constant exhortations to rest, exercise, and strive for a "balanced life," I emerged from the writing phase much healthier and more spiritually centered than I might otherwise have been. Most of all, I thank my parents, Stanton and Rita Freeman, to whom this book is dedicated. They encouraged and enabled me to pursue my wanderlust early on, which eventually led me to the study of anthropology.

Notes on Language and Translations

Romanization

I have followed the McCune-Reischauer system of romanization for Korean words and names. Chinese terms and names are romanized in pinyin. For the names of authors, I use the romanization that appears in their publications. I render the names of friends according to their preferred method of romanization. Names appear according to the Korean and Chinese practice of putting the family name before the first name, except where individual preference dictates the English convention of surname last.

Translations

Translations of native terms appear in either Korean or Chinese, reflecting the language that was used by my research subjects. Most Chosŏnjok employed a mixture of both languages when speaking to me, and thus

Chinese and Korean terms may alternately appear in passages attributed to a single individual. In referring to concepts that are used by both Korean and Chinese speakers, I provide translations in both languages. All translations are my own unless otherwise noted.

Korea and Koreans

While some scholars use the term "Korean Chinese" to refer to Koreans who reside in the People's Republic of China, I follow the subjective naming practices of my research subjects who refer to themselves as Chosŏnjok (Chaoxianzu in Chinese). When referring to the Republic of Korea (ROK), I am careful to use "South Korea" rather than simply "Korea." I follow this practice to help bear in mind that North Korea (DPRK), as a political and geographic territory, stands between the nations of China and South Korea. Only when the context makes it clearly unambiguous, do I drop the geopolitical modifier and refer to South Korea as Korea.

Making and Faking Kinship

Introduction

I first learned about transnational marriages between Chosŏnjok women and South Korean men in 1995 while reading the *Korea Times* one morning on the subway in Seoul. I had been casting about for some time for a research topic that would allow me to draw upon my decade-long acquaintance with China, further explore a newfound interest in South Korea, and build on theoretical interests in kinship, gender, and transnationalism I had been cultivating. The editorial I read that morning struck me as a winning lottery ticket, the prize being a project ideally suited to this particular combination of personal and academic interests.

The article was written by David Steinberg, a scholar of South Korean society whose insightful commentaries appeared in a weekly editorial column. In this particular essay, Steinberg described a "quiet rural social crisis" under way in the South Korean countryside concerning the inability of hundreds of thousands of rural bachelors across the country to find marriage partners. South Korean women en masse, like their counterparts in

Japan[1] and Taiwan and even outside the continent in Ireland,[2] have largely rejected rural matrimony and the drudgery of rural living presumed to go along with it, setting their sights instead on city-dwelling husbands. What was unique to the situation in South Korea, and what I was most surprised to learn from the article, were the measures being taken by the South Korean government to redress the shortage of rural brides: government-funded matchmakers were leading groups of farmers on week-long "marriage tours" to northeastern China where they were expected to fare better in the competition for local brides.

Home to nearly two million ethnic Koreans or Chosŏnjok[3] (*Chaoxianzu*), northeastern China was viewed in the early 1990s as an ideal source of potential brides for South Korea's bachelor farmers and, as I would later discover, for other men on the margins of South Korea's marriage market, including unskilled workers, divorcees, widowers, and the disabled. Between 1990—when marriages between women in China and men in South Korea first began—and 1998 when I set out to do the research for this project, tens of thousands of Chosŏnjok women had stepped forward to fill the vacancies in South Korean households in villages, small towns, and cities throughout the peninsula (Kang 1998).[4] By the time I arrived in the field, the project of supplying Chosŏnjok brides for South Korean men was no longer primarily a government-funded initiative. A host of profit-seeking marriage brokers had come to dominate the business of leading marriage tours to northeastern China.[5]

South Korea has since witnessed an extraordinary rise in the number of foreign brides entering the country, not just from China but from other

---

1. Kelsky 2001, 1–2; Burgess 2004.

2. Gilot 1998; "Irish Farmers' Need for Wives Becomes Calendar Fodder," *Korea Times,* February 4, 1999, p. 10.

3. "Chosŏn" derives from the name of the last dynasty on the Korean peninsula before Japanese colonization. Ethnic Koreans who migrated to northeastern China as early as the late seventeenth century and throughout the early twentieth century were officially recognized in 1945 as an ethnic minority in the People's Republic of China under the name of Chosŏnjok or "the Chosŏn nationality." North Koreans also use *Chosŏn* to refer to their country, while South Koreans use the term *Han'guk*.

4. By the end of 1999 the number of marriages between Chinese (predominantly Chosŏnjok) women and South Korean men totaled 37,171; by 2005 the figure had nearly doubled to reach 70,163 (Lim 2010, 65).

5. In 2009 more than 1,200 agencies were officially registered as international marriage brokers (Kwon 2010).

countries in the region, including Vietnam, the Philippines, Thailand, Mongolia, Cambodia, and Russia. By 2005, thirty-six percent of South Korean men in rural areas were reportedly married to foreign brides (HK Lee 2007, 9).[6] Amid predictions that households with migrant women will comprise twenty percent of the total number of South Korean households by the year 2020 (HM Kim 2007, 101), the "multicultural family" as it is now called in South Korea is a rapidly escalating social and political issue, spawning a broad-based public debate as well as myriad popular culture representations[7] and legislative initiatives. This book documents the first spate of international marriages that grew out of the evolving political, economic, and demographic circumstances within and between China and South Korea during the 1990s. An in-depth ethnographic look at the complex cultural logics surrounding this earlier wave of migrant brides will enable us to understand the historical precedents of what has become a steadily growing and contentious phenomenon in South Korea today.

Looked at from the Chinese side, the exodus of Chosŏnjok brides to South Korea emerged in the broader context of rapid marketization and globalization of the national economy and the increasing opportunities for spatial mobility that accompanied these twin processes. Anthropologists have examined patterns of domestic and transnational mobility among diverse segments of the population in China's post-1978 economic reform period, including overseas Chinese entrepreneurs shuttling across the Pacific (Ong 1997, 1999), migrant workers moving to special economic zones within China (CK Lee 1997, 1998), Chinese scholars sojourning abroad (Liu 1997), and the vast "floating population" (*liudong renkou*) of peasant migrants moving to cities throughout China (Zhang 2001a, 2001b; Solinger 1999). Less attention has been paid to how the new and increasingly transnational dimensions of social and spatial mobility have affected the lives of China's minority nationalities. The popular perception that China's minorities live in isolated enclaves on the political, social, and economic periphery of the Han Chinese world, presumably far removed from regional

---

6. Cho Uhn (2005) puts the proportion of rural households with foreign brides in 2005 at 27.2 percent, or 11.7 percent of *all* marriages in South Korea (28). Tim Lim (2010), citing South Korean government statistics, asserts that "multicultural marriages" comprised 13.6 percent of all marriages in South Korea in 2005, dropping to 11.9 percent in 2006 (65).

7. See Epstein 2009.

and transnational networks of mobility, makes it perhaps startling to note that in the late 1990s, the Chosŏnjok had higher rates of mobility than any other nationality in the People's Republic of China (PRC), including the Han Chinese (Zheng 1998, 74).

The unique opportunities for geographic mobility open to the Chosŏnjok in the 1990s were to a large extent created by the restructuring of political and economic relations between the Chinese and South Korean nations and their complementary economic requirements. The opening of China's doors to the global economy in the post-Mao period coincided with the emergence of labor shortages in the rapidly industrializing South Korean economy as well as bride shortages in the South Korean countryside, itself a consequence of earlier migrations by women to South Korean cities. In response, South Korean capitalists have invested heavily in China's northern and northeastern provinces, and China's Chosŏnjok population has helped redress the shortage of both wives and workers in South Korea. By 2001, it is estimated that there were 200,000 Chosŏnjok migrants living, either legally or illegally, in South Korea (J Lee 2001, 129).

Although the symbiotic needs served by the back-and-forth movement of people between the two countries were clearly important in explaining the surge of Chosŏnjok brides (and other migrants) into South Korea, some empirical questions prompted me to undertake this research. What exactly was entailed in a "marriage tour," and why would the South Korean government promote and facilitate this type of transnational matchmaking? Even more perplexing, why would large numbers of Chosŏnjok women opt to marry South Korean farmers and poor workers when few South Korean women would deign to marry them? The sudden appeal of foreign brides for South Korean farmers and blue-collar workers could be understood in light of their widespread marital predicament, but it was less clear what motivated women from China to venture so far from home and across national borders to marry into the lowest rungs of South Korean society. Were Chosŏnjok women being coerced into transnational unions by impoverished families who could not afford to support them? Or was northeastern China such a dreary place compared to the South Korean countryside that women themselves were actively seeking South Korean marriage partners as a pathway to upward mobility? With respect to the business of matchmaking, how did commercial marriage brokers and their clientele differ from the matchmakers dispatched with government funding to northeastern China?

Aside from the potential economic factors driving the migration of women out of China and into South Korea, were there also particular gendered imaginings that Chosŏnjok women and South Korean men produced and consumed about one another which might explain the female-dominated migration pattern between the two countries?[8] If so, how did these gendered expectations and stereotypes play out in the course of actual marital relationships? Migrant brides from China presumably brought with them models of gender, family, and nationality/ethnicity that differed from those of South Korean husbands and their families. I wondered what sort of cultural contradictions these differences posed for married couples in their everyday lives, and what sort of strategies couples devised to overcome or make sense of them.

I set about designing a project that would enable me to address these questions. I sought first and foremost to document the motivations and experiences of individual brides, grooms, their family members, and marriage brokers on either end of the marriage exchange, paying special attention to the potentially divergent cultural meanings Chosŏnjok and South Koreans ascribed to categories of kinship, gender, and nationality/ethnicity. I devoted the first portion of my fieldwork to exploring the effects of the influx of Chosŏnjok brides on South Korean family and social life. The second phase involved investigating how the exodus of brides from northeastern China was affecting families and communities left behind.

When it came time for me to relocate to northeastern China, it was immediately apparent that the marriages of Chosŏnjok women to South Korean men were but one type of migration strategy and one type of transnational conjugality that that had emerged amid the new opportunities for travel between the two countries. The pattern of already-married Chosŏnjok men and women performing long stints of migrant labor in South Korea, either with or without their spouses and leaving children behind, constituted another equally pervasive form of "transnational family"

---

8. Of the thousands of Chosŏnjok-Korean marriages each year throughout the 1990s, only an estimated ten such marriages were between Chosŏnjok men and Korean women (Kang 1998, 10). According to statistics released by the Ministry of Justice in June 2009, the total number of female marriage migrants of diverse national origins to South Korea outnumbered male marriage migrants seven to one, with 110,000 foreign brides and 15,000 foreign grooms (Female Foreign Spouses Outnumber Males 7 to 1. *Chosunilbo,* August 7, 2009, available at http://english.chosun.com/site/data/html_dir/2009/08/07/2009080700468.html).

that had developed alongside, and was intertwined with, the movement of Chosŏnjok brides into South Korea.

The migration strategies enacted by already-married Chosŏnjok couples were directly linked to the demand for Chosŏnjok brides in South Korea in two important respects. First, at the turn of the millennium, would-be migrants to South Korea faced a limited range of options for legally crossing the border into South Korea. Unlike migrant brides who could acquire citizenship and with it the chance to live and work in South Korea indefinitely, migrant workers, as in the United States and other wealthy nations around the globe, were treated as a cheap and disposable labor force despite the urgent need for their unskilled labor. They were legally denied the rights of long-term, let alone permanent, settlement as well as rights of family reunification. Arranging a paper marriage to a South Korean man (after filing a paper divorce with her Chosŏnjok husband) was a common way for Chosŏnjok women of diverse socioeconomic backgrounds to circumvent South Korea's restrictive immigration laws and acquire lifelong access to South Korea's labor market. I use the terms "paper," "fraudulent," "sham," "counterfeit," and "fake" interchangeably throughout the book to describe marriages contracted for the instrumental purpose of gaining access and residency rights to South Korea (for a fuller explanation of fake marriage terminology see chapter 2). Amid South Korea's enthusiastic embrace of Chosŏnjok brides for the nation's farmers, fraudulent marriage schemes initially went undetected or ignored by immigration officials. (Later, due to the high incidence of paper marriages, government officials in both countries would come to view them as the norm rather than the exception.)

Second, because South Korean immigration law permitted Chosŏnjok parents to visit a married-out daughter in South Korea on the occasion of her wedding and other officially recognized life-cycle events, every Chosŏnjok–South Korean marriage created an opportunity for two other Chosŏnjok migrants to cross the border: either the legitimate parents of the bride, or one man and one woman masquerading as the parents of the bride. Middle-aged Chosŏnjok men and women routinely used the family visitation visa, whether acquired legally or through the purchase of forged documents, to work illegally in South Korea for years at a time.[9]

---

9. There had been no age limit on the family visitation visa until 1992, when the Korean government set a minimum age limit of sixty to stem the flow of Chosŏnjok migrants into the

To take into account these complex exchanges and counterfeit kinship practices, I expanded the focus of the book from "transnational marriage" to a broader examination of "transnational kinship." Bringing the transnational family-making practices of migrant brides and laborers together in one ethnographic frame allows us to explore the interconnections and challenge the dichotomies between marriage and labor migration, nation-building and kinship-making projects, legal and illegal border crossings. It also enables us to observe the role of migrants' agency in negotiating such processes and discursive constructions depending on where they are positioned along the spectrum of legal, political, and social inclusion/exclusion from the nation. The unequal status of Chosŏnjok migrant brides and laborers vis-à-vis the South Korean state provides a unique window on the gendered and kinship-based nature of immigration processes; it demonstrates how a single diasporic ethnic group from a single nation-state is stratified in accordance with the nation-building goals of the imagined "homeland." And it sheds light on gendered assumptions about how family and national belonging are defined, how migrants and their families grapple with the complex decisions involved in forming transnational households, and how definitions of responsible parenting and conjugal relations are confronted and altered in the course of splitting the family across national borders.

Border Crossing and the Global Economy

Though serendipitous encounters in the field brought me to the specific topic of transnational kinship between South Korea and China, the general phenomenon of flows across national borders, whether of people, information, goods, ideas, or capital, was making its debut in the mid-1990s as a central focus of academic study.[10] As scholars across the disciplines

---

country. The government lowered the age limit to fifty-five in 1994 and forty-five in 2002 (HK Lee 2007, 6fn6). The age limitations did not stop younger Chosŏnjok from inventing clever ways of looking older by, for example, dying their hair grey, donning old-style clothing, and even undergoing reversible surgical procedures to appear wrinkled.

  10. While the term *transnationalism* is typically used to describe the intensification of cross-border activities under contemporary conditions of late capitalism, Immanuel Wallerstein pioneered a transnational framework for understanding the evolution of the European-centered modern capitalist system. I am grateful to Frederick Damon for calling my attention to scholarship

became increasingly aware of the unprecedented speed, frequency, and pervasiveness of border-crossing movements under conditions of late capitalism, they began to envision and speak about the globe as having entered an era of transnationalism. At the inception of this project, an emergent body of anthropological research had just begun to introduce concepts such as transnational social spaces, diasporic identities, and multilocal affiliations (Glick-Schiller et al. 1992; Gupta and Ferguson 1992; Rouse 1995), raising important theoretical concerns regarding the articulation of localized cultural expressions with global social and economic processes as well as questions about the significance and meaning of territorial borders and boundaries. While this emergent body of work was a source of inspiration, at the time there were very few fine-grained ethnographic analyses (with the exception of the articles in Glick-Schiller et al. 1992 and Rouse 1995) capable of moving the discussion of global-local interconnections beyond the level of abstract formulations and evocative imagery.

Many ethnographically grounded studies have since appeared, which influenced the way I interpret the data I had collected. Thematically and theoretically, I divide the literature that relates most closely to my understanding of the marriage and mobility stories presented here into three main categories: ethnographies of migration, ethnographies of nationalism, and ethnographies of kinship. The next three sections are devoted respectively to: a brief discussion of the mechanisms of power that enable, channel, and control flows of labor and marriage migration; the production of altered concepts of the nation-state and national belonging as a result of increased migration flows across national borders; and finally, how transnational movement leads to reconfigured definitions and practices of kinship.

Gender, Agency, and Transnational Migration

The growth of new and globalizing markets in capital, labor, and information has drawn women in increasing numbers into circuits of transnational

that predated the language of "transnationalism" but was nevertheless concerned with mapping flows across national borders and understanding the cultural logics behind them. These foundational texts include Wallerstein (1974, 1980, 1989), Wolf (1982), Mintz (1985) and *American Ethnologist* 5(3) (1978), special issue on political economy.

mobility. In terms of global labor markets, scholars have noted that it is increasingly women in poorer, less-developed regions and countries who fill the growing demand for low-wage service labor—in occupations such as domestic work, nursing, and the sex industry—in wealthier, postindustrial cities (see Ehrenreich and Hochschild 2003; Piper and Roces 2003; Sassen 2003; Lan 2006). Most recently, scholars have noted that similar patterns of gender and geography also dominate global patterns of marriage migration. Like the movement of female migrant workers, the movement of migrant brides across national borders does not reflect, in the words of Nicole Constable, a "global free-for-all in which all combinations—regardless of class, nationality, ethnicity, or gender, for example—are possible" (2005, 3). Rather, contemporary marriage migrations tend to form "marriage-scapes" shaped by multiple and intersecting structures of inequality, including economic geographies as well as culturally constructed notions about gender and desirability (Constable 2005, 3–10).

Piper and Roces (2003) draw further connections between the feminization of work-related and marriage-related migration, enumerating the potential ways the two trends might be directly linked. A woman who marries across national borders may subsequently enter the labor market, for example. Or, alternatively, a woman who takes up temporary employment overseas may end up meeting and marrying a man in the country where she works. Piper and Roces break down the distinction between migrant wife and migrant worker in a third sense, pointing out that women may engage in migrant labor in their capacity as wives and mothers to men and children who remain at home or accompany them abroad. All three possibilities can be observed in the case of Chosŏnjok migrant brides and workers in South Korea.

Having mapped the multiple and intersecting forms of female mobility that crisscross the globe, scholars could turn their attention to exploring the implications of these trends for the key actors involved in the processes. Of particular interest to me is how these patterns operating on a global level are played out in the lives of individual migrant women in the context of their families (natal and marital), communities (home and host), and nations (of origin and settlement). There is broad consensus among anthropologists working on gender and migration that migrant women workers/brides/wives are not just passive pawns in a game of international labor and marriage exchange, propelled across the globe by structural inequalities in the world system. The question then is whether and in what sense female mobility reproduces or reworks (or both) the hierarchies of power (gender, class, nationality/ethnicity, etc.) that structure transnational space. Only an ethnographically grounded study of women's labor/marriage migration has the potential to illuminate both how social relations of inequality are reproduced or reconfigured at a broader level across transnational space as well as how they are negotiated, contested, and reconfigured in individual experience.

Existing ethnographies have produced tools with which to analyze the scope of women's agency with respect to circuits of transnational mobility, including Gardner's (1995) "geography of power," Doreen Massey's (1994) "power geometry," Smith and Guarnizo's (1998) concept of "transnational-ism from below," and Mahler and Pessar's (2001) "gendered geographies of power." What I emphasize here, and what the stories of Chosŏnjok wom-en's transnational mobility contained in this book point to, is the paradoxi-cal nature of the way power operates across and within the shifting terrain of the global economy. On the one hand, I argue that Chosŏnjok women were enabled by their marriageability and employability in feminized niches of the South Korean labor and marriage markets to expand their opportunities overseas and potentially improve their social and economic circumstances. On the other hand, contrary to their expectations of mov-ing "up" the imagined geographic ladder of nations, Chosŏnjok women's dreams of upward mobility were paradoxically constrained by the hierar-chies of gender, class, and nationality/ethnicity they confronted once they arrived in South Korea. One of my main objectives is to examine the var-ied ways in which individual Chosŏnjok women received, negotiated, and potentially reworked or reproduced the dominant cultural meanings and practices that stood in their way of achieving the upward mobility they were seeking.

Nationalism/Transnationalism

The intensity and seeming unruliness of transnational flows that bypass government rules and political boundaries have prompted anthropologists to contemplate the effects of transnational processes on the power and in-tegrity of the nation-state. The social imaginaries of transnationalism with their associated images of cultural hybridity, deterritorialization, and fluidity appear to threaten the "imagined communities" (Anderson 1983) of nation-states that are based on claims of cultural and territorial boundedness (see Jacobson 1997; Sassen 1998, 1999). While the cultural and political integrity of nation-states has indeed come under pressure as a result of globalizing forces, there is widespread consensus among scholars that transnational processes not only pose a challenge to state control and models of nationalism but paradoxically at the same time serve to strengthen them. The challenge for anthropologists is to describe and capture the complex ways in which the tensions between nationalist regimes and diasporic processes play out in the shifting dynamics of global capitalism.

There are two approaches to studying this complex interaction. One is to examine the ways transnational processes are embedded in the institution of the nation-state with its programs and policies of advocating connections with particular populations and political regimes overseas. South Korean government policies are critical to determining whether and under what conditions Chosŏnjok are permitted to visit, work in, or live in South Korea. In this study I focus on the regulatory role of South Korean political elites as "gate keepers" of the nation-state, as they selectively admit certain categories of Chosŏnjok migrants and then attempt to regulate and control the scope of their activities after they arrive. While the South Korean state imposes rigid immigration restrictions on Chosŏnjok migrants, I emphasize the creative ways would-be migrants manipulate official categories and manufacture counterfeit identities to elude state control and gain entry to South Korea. These manipulations in turn shape the laws and policies that the South Korean state enacts in its attempt to regulate and stem the flow of Chosŏnjok migrants into the country. Thus, though the state plays an important role in creating the conditions that enable and constrain border-crossing activities, the migrants themselves, operating with different and often subversive agendas, succeed (to a certain extent) in exploiting state-level policies designed to exclude them and bend them to their own advantage. This give-and-take relationship between the South Korean state and Chosŏnjok migrants is clearly reflected in South Korea's ever-changing immigration laws as South Korean lawmakers equivocate over how best to protect their territorial interests without cutting off strategically important access to overseas sources of Korean capital, labor, and brides.

The second approach to studying the tensions between "nation making" and "un-making" is thus to focus on the alternative constructions and definitions of belonging that emerge out of the encounter between nationalist regimes and transnational migrants. Aihwa Ong describes how the encounter with global capitalism has prompted the Chinese state to promote a new vision of transnational Chinese solidarity (based on older notions of Chinese racial homogeneity) as a way of attracting offshore Chinese investment. As Ong shows, while crucial for the development of the PRC, the influx of overseas Chinese has engendered a "crisis of cultural identity" as the Chinese state struggles to balance its political and territorial interests against "the promiscuous opportunism of overseas-Chinese capitalism" (1999, 60). Other scholars have described similar disjunctures between nationalist (or regionalist) models of ethnic identity and deterritorialized notions of ethnic solidarity from the point of view of return migrants and their (re)encounter with their imagined homelands (Long and Oxfeld 2004; Louie 2004). The growing ethnographic literature on the experience of Brazilian Japanese and their "return" migration to Japan as unskilled laborers over the last few decades, for example, vividly illustrates how diasporic encounters in the "homeland" at once destabilize and reinforce existing ideas about Japaneseness that equate "race," culture, and membership in the nation (see Linger 2001; Roth 2002; Tsuda 2003). Encounters between transnational adoptees and their countries of birth provide another emotionally charged site from which to observe the tensions and contradictions inherent in these interactions (see Dorrow 2006; Kim 2003, 2007, 2010; Yngvesson 2005).

The combined ethnographic record suggests that returnees often feel ambivalent about their homecoming, reflecting divergent cultural expectations of citizenship, ancestral obligations, kinship roles, and gender between diasporic communities and their "homeland." As the literature on Korean transnational adoption reveals, experiences of reunion and "return" open up the possibility for the production of alternative, sometimes counterhegemonic political and cultural subjectivities (Kim 2007, 2010). At the same time, the influx of "outsiders" has the potential to revive or strengthen nationalist identity within the "homeland." In this book, I examine how the tensions between imagined and actual experiences of "ethnic reunification" are played out in state-level discourses and immigration policies, in the marital homes of transnationally married couples, in the illicit immigration strategies of migrant mothers, and in the context of home communities upended by soaring rates of outward migration.

New Kinship in a Transnational World

Alongside and intertwined with the question of how definitions and practices of the nation-state are being transformed by unprecedented patterns of transnational mobility is the question of how kinship relations are being redefined and experienced in this new transnational milieu. In South Korea, the linkages between the processes of nation making and kin making are especially pronounced since notions of Koreanness are constructed through metaphors of kinship or blood ties. As I explore in chapters 1 and 2, South Korea conceives of itself as a divided nation, and the restoring of kinship ties severed as a result of national division operates not only as a powerful symbol of national reunification but as an explicit goal of South Korea's immigration policies toward the Chosŏnjok. Specifically, marriages between Chosŏnjok women and South Korean men on the one hand and family reunions between Chosŏnjok and their consanguineal family members in South Korea on the other constituted two primary sites where the South Korean government projected its hope for the resuscitation of divided families and, by extension, the divided nation-state. This emphasis on the importance of embracing Chosŏnjok "relatives" and Chosŏnjok-Korean marriages, promoted in state-level discourses and codified in immigration law, turned kinship into a key signifier for the inclusions and exclusions that define national membership.

The open-door kin policies, however, confronted South Koreans with the challenge of putting their ideology of "blood equals nationality" into practice. The situation is analogous in many ways to the ambivalences surrounding kinship categories in the former East and West Germany as the two states oscillated between separation and reunification. As John Borneman writes:

> At the political level, both states looked to kinship categories as a quasi-natural model for the structuring of nationality and citizenship. Because the two states publicly contested each other's membership categories, Berliners were quite aware of the arbitrary, political nature of belonging and therefore active in manipulating the official classifications." (1992, 19–20)

Like East Berliners who desired entry into West Berlin, Chosŏnjok who desired entry into South Korea also learned to manipulate kinship categories in order to take advantage of the travel privileges that South Korea's kin-focused immigration policies allowed. As I examine in detail in the second half of the book, the instrumental uses of genealogy and marital relationships that Chosŏnjok resorted to in order to cross the border often had little or nothing to do with connectedness to blood relatives or genuine conjugal commitment, thereby casting doubt and suspicion on the meaning of both kinship and Koreanness.

The German and the South Korean examples as well as the Chinese cases alluded to in the section above suggest that contemporary practices of transnational mobility potentially reinforce connections between kin making and nation making even as they destabilize the meaning of what it is to belong to a family or nation. Put another way, Janet Carsten observes that reckoning kinship relations (like the project of nation building) necessarily involves making inclusions and exclusions. Yet, as she points out, "what is most striking about the cases of 'new kinship' "[11] she examines "is not so much the newness of the kinship that results, but the very explicitness of the moves by which people are able to define who is kin and who is not, and what kinds of kinship count and what kinds do not" (2004, 180). Anthropological and folk models of kinship that define kinship as a pregiven matter of nature/blood/biology rather than a matter of choice are becoming increasingly difficult to uphold given the multiplicity and malleability of what might count as kinship under contemporary conditions (see Modell 1994 on adoption reunions; Weston 1991 on gay American kinship ideology; Franklin and McKinnon 2001).

The experiences of migrant brides who crossed the border in South Korea also had the unintended effect of unsettling the myth of "ethnic homogeneity" as well as expectations about the kind of wives Chosŏnjok women would make. When migrant brides from China arrived in their South Korean marital households, they brought with them alternative models of kinship and gender which had been shaped in the context of the

---

11. The term "new kinship" was coined by anthropologists to refer to the new family formations that have arisen in the context of the global economy, biogenetics, and cyberspace, as well as to the analytic strategies deployed by lay persons and anthropologists alike to make sense of them (see chapter 1 of Carsten 2004; Franklin and McKinnon 2001, introduction).

PRC and which in certain respects, as I explore in chapter 3, collided with South Korean norms and social practices. The process of marrying across borders, initially envisioned as bridging the "unnatural" political boundaries dividing two populations linked by immutable ties of blood, in many cases paradoxically ends up "denaturalizing" kinship and drawing more distinct lines of separation between the two populations of Koreans.

This unease about what kinship is, what it should mean, and how it should be practiced across the emergent "transnational social field" connecting China and South Korea was also at play in the transnational life strategies of Chosŏnjok mothers and fathers who sought to make money as unskilled workers in South Korea. In the second part of the book, I explore the legally transgressive strategies and range of geographically dispersed family configurations that Chosŏnjok migrants pursued in exchange for the chance to live and work in South Korea. I depict widespread practices such as fake marriages and divorces, illegal border crossings, forging of identity papers, extramarital romance, and the leaving behind of children and spouses as part of a wider logic of mobility and family flexibility that grew out of the sociopolitical and economic changes occurring within and between China and South Korea.

The creative maneuvering of migrants in the search for opportunities overseas is well documented and appreciated, yet scholars have paid less attention to the agency exercised by women and men left behind by migrant spouses and their efforts to create new life chances for themselves back home. Though denied a ticket to the cosmopolitan pleasures and financial rewards imagined to exist overseas and possessing little leverage to ensure the sexual fidelity of their migrant spouses, these "left behind" wives and husbands were not necessarily just waiting around for spouses to return and remittances to arrive. Rather than simply "left behind" and left out of an overseas adventure, Chosŏnjok spouses who remained in China dared to transcend conventional expectations of middle-aged gender and sexuality as they searched for urban pleasures of their own. The case of Chosŏnjok "split transnational families," I argue, illustrates the ability of migrants *as well as* those left behind to creatively work within constraints and expand their existing life chances. And in so doing, they negotiate and rework existing gender, marital, and intergenerational ideals.

While I show that flexible family and gender norms constitute a defining feature of "split transnational families," the ethnographic material

I present also underscores the cultural and practical limits of such flexibility. Oftentimes Chosŏnjok strategies for accumulating capital proved to be more flexible than the actual families, and "split transnational families" became simply "split families," sometimes accompanied or followed by the formation of new transnational family relations. The pervasiveness of marital infidelity, estranged spouses, abandoned children, and the public anxieties surrounding them point to the emotional and moral costs involved in transnational family making.

This focus on the moral conundrums and high-risk stakes involved in the making (and breaking) of split transnational families contrasts with an emphasis in the migration literature on the durability of familial and community relationships despite the strain of long-term spatial and temporal separation (Glick-Schiller et al. 1992, 1994). I should point out that in highlighting the resilience of cross-border relationships, researchers were responding to earlier models of migration which emphasized the gradual assimilation of the migrant worker or migrant family unit into the host society in a one-way process that was presumed to culminate in the complete severing of ties to the country of origin. Anthropologist Roger Rouse (1991), for example, in his work on Mexican migration to the United States describes the tying together of sending and receiving communities into a singular transnational community through the continuous back and forth movement of people, money, goods, and information. Similarly, Rhacel Salazar Parreñas (2001a) describes the formation of multinational household structures among Filipino labor migrants that link multiple communities of Filipinos across the globe.

While circuitous patterns of migration such as Rouse describes sometimes do occur in the case of Chosŏnjok migrants to South Korea, I emphasize a range of transnational family arrangements, some of which lead, intentionally or unintentionally, to the disbanding of relationships to kin and community left behind in China. The stories I recount suggest that stretching ties across borders sometimes leads to the breaking of ties, and the breaking of ties in turn can lead to new transnational family formations. Thus, rather than celebrate transnational family ties as a largely stable and harmonious stretching of kinship relations to form a larger transnational community, I stress the dynamic and often conflict-ridden processes involved in making and unmaking of kinship. I examine how individuals on the move as well as those who stay put negotiate these processes. I also describe how they unfold in the intimate domain of the family as well as in the broader discursive fields in which families were forced to operate.

Research Methods

The ethnographic data for this book are based on nineteen months of fieldwork I conducted while living in South Korea and northeastern China from 1998 to 2000. The project was carried out in three phases: ten months in South Korea, six months in northeastern China, and a return to South Korea for a final three months of follow-up research. The research methods I employed varied according to the vicissitudes of each particular field site. In South Korea, I had to craft a research strategy that would enable me to trace geographically dispersed marriage and migration patterns while at the same time allow me to enter the daily lives of a significant number of transnationally married couples. I solved this dilemma by basing myself in Seoul and making periodic visits to rural areas to conduct structured interviews with Chosŏnjok brides, their marital families, and, when present, natal family members who had accompanied them to South Korea.

Living in Seoul enabled me to participate in a range of networks that catered to Chosŏnjok migrants, including church-related organizations, private clubs, and social gatherings. One such gathering was a weekly English class that I taught, on and off throughout the duration of my stay in Seoul, to a small but eclectic group of Chosŏnjok migrants I had assembled through the assistance of a South Korean activist with contacts in the Chosŏnjok migrant community. The group was composed of two sisters from Mudanjiang who had contracted marriages (one genuine and one sham) to South Korean men, a young unmarried couple who resided together in Seoul as migrant laborers, two middle-aged men from Mudanjiang who had entered Seoul on business visas, and a twenty-eight-year-old woman from Harbin whose parents had sent her to South Korea to further her studies and in the process find a South Korean husband. Though they differed greatly in terms of age, background, and motivations for coming to South Korea, they all shared an interest in bettering their lives through their experiences abroad and a view of the English language as conferring important cosmopolitan capital they would require along the way. While the students' commitment to studying English and my style of teaching both lacked the intensity and focus needed to attain even a modicum of linguistic competence, our weekly meetings, and the dinners and socializing that regularly followed, satisfied our mutual desire for cross-cultural interaction and exploration. My relationships with nearly all the migrants in the class evolved into long-lasting friendships; my ongoing conversations with each and their willingness to put me in touch with other members of their social networks in South Korea, and later in China, played a significant role in shaping the contours and content of my field research.

Government-funded and private matchmaking agencies were also crucial in providing me with introductions to transnationally married couples in rural and urban areas across South Korea. I spent several months interviewing dozens of marriage brokers, mostly in Seoul, whose businesses I located the old-fashioned way—through the telephone book.[12] After a face-to-face meeting, nearly every broker I met agreed to put me in contact with farmers they had successfully matched with Chosŏnjok brides. Once contacted, the rural couples were equally willing to host my research assistant and me during overnight stays in their villages.

I hired thirty-year-old Kim Kyŏng'ŭn and later Ewha University senior Kim Chiyŏng to help me request interviews by phone, accompany me on visits to the countryside, and transcribe taped interviews. Because of the unusual nature of my cold-call requests and my yet-to-fully-evolve Korean telephone skills, I found it more effective to have a native Korean speaker make the initial telephone calls to potential interviewees. Many of the people I met in the countryside had never had face-to-face contact with a white American, and so it also helped to have a friendly Korean face alongside me to ease any initial feelings of nervousness or suspicion on the part of my research subjects. Having a female traveling companion also served to head off potential concerns about the safety and social acceptability of an unmarried woman traveling alone and in a foreign country. The companionship of a fellow traveler was a comfort to me as well on the long train and bus trips into the countryside.

The linguistic "safety net" provided by my native-speaking research assistants was especially helpful during the early months of fieldwork before

---

12. By 2007 160 websites specializing in matching South Korean men with foreign brides had appeared (Hye-kyung Lee 2007, 9). There were few if any at the time of my field research.

I had developed an ear for the Korean *topolect(s)*[13] spoken in northeastern China. Chosŏnjok speech patterns, accents, and expressions were generally perceived by South Koreans as bearing close resemblance to those of North Korea. This can be attributed in part to Zhou Enlai's designation in 1962 of Pyŏngyang "topolect" as the standard language of instruction in Chosŏnjok schools in northeastern China. The total ban on communication between China and South Korea throughout the cold war period coupled with the ongoing ties of travel and communication between Chosŏnjok residents and their North Korean relatives may have served to preserve and deepen the imprint of North Korea on Chosŏnjok language patterns. At the same time, historical patterns of migration and settlement within China have given rise to regional linguistic differences between Chosŏnjok communities. A team of South Korean anthropologists conducting surveys in Heilongjiang Province immediately recognized the pervasive influence of topolects spoken in southern Korea, primarily Kyŏngsang but also Chŏlla and Ch'ungch'ong (K Kim 1998).

I should also mention here the multiple uses of Chinese while conducting fieldwork among the Chosŏnjok in both China and South Korea. For one thing, Chosŏnjok speech patterns are peppered with literal translations of Chinese expressions that are difficult for non-Chinese-speaking South Koreans to comprehend. To give one example, the Chosŏnjok have adopted the expression *il opsŭmnida,* a direct translation of the Chinese term *meishi,* meaning "no problem" or "no worries." This simple utterance would most likely be unintelligible to South Koreans who use the term *kwenchanda.* Second, Chinese served as a "secret language" on occasions when a Chosŏnjok bride wished to communicate something to me in confidence while in earshot of South Korea family members. Finally, while many of the Chosŏnjok I encountered in South Korea and China were fluent speakers of Korean, some had little or no knowledge of their ancestral tongue. This was especially true of members of the younger generation (under thirty years old) who had attended Han Chinese schools in urban areas. The daughters in my host family in Harbin, for example had attended mainstream schools since early childhood. Now in their twenties, they were unable to speak any Korean, though their parents spoke it at home.

---

13. Victor Mair (1991) proposed adopting the term "topolect" rather than "dialect" as a more accurate and less value-laden translation of the Chinese word *fangyan.* The same Chinese-derived word *bang-eon* is used in Korea, in addition to the native term *saturi.*

The majority of couples I interviewed permitted me to tape record our conversations. Several husbands and wives I visited were accustomed to the attention of outsiders, having already been interviewed by local journalists at the time of their weddings. One couple's story was the subject of a nationally televised documentary on Chosŏnjok–South Korean marriages (*Takkyu: I Saram* [Documentary: this person]. SBS Broadcasting, October 18, 1998). A few welcomed a chance to tell their stories and voice their concerns to someone from a larger world who they perceived might be able to advocate on their behalf. Still others were simply motivated to help a foreign student pursue her graduate studies.

I usually began by asking them to describe how they came to consider the possibility of a transnationally brokered marriage, how they met and decided to marry their spouse, how their geographically separated families proceeded through the rites of marriage, and what, if any, challenges they faced in forging a transnational conjugal relationship. Though I relied on a similar set of informational questions to jump start the interview, I allowed my interviewees the space, if they were so inclined (and the majority of them were), to take the conversational lead and set the agenda for our discussions in accordance with what they felt was most important for me to understand about their transnational conjugal experiences. When possible, I sought to interview family members separately, but given the brevity of our time together and in some cases the rigors of their farming or work schedules, I often had little choice but to interview couples, and sometimes entire extended families, together in the same room. In situations where the husband worked long hours and the wife stayed at home, I had to settle for interviewing the wife only.

I realized that the success of my research strategy hinged on the seemingly unreasonable expectation that the couples I visited reveal, upon meeting me for the first time, information about intimate matters such as their thoughts and feelings toward one another and close family members, and their expectations, conflicts, and disappointments with respect to their marital lives. Initially I had feared that concerns with social face (*mianzi/ myŏn*) and privacy would inhibit people from sharing their innermost feelings and experiences with a complete stranger, as I had been forewarned by a South Korean ethnographer who had worked among the Chosŏnjok in China. To my surprise and delight, however, the couples I interviewed expressed themselves with such candor that at times I was the one left feeling embarrassed or caught off guard. One husband asked me in front of his wife and three daughters, with an earnest expression upon his face, why I had not bothered to ask him about his level of sexual satisfaction in his marriage. In the course of another interview, a wife spoke bluntly in front of her husband of her loveless marriage, her husband's inability to understand her way of thinking, and the lack of sensitivity on the part of her in-laws. The husband listened unflinchingly, sometimes chuckling good-naturedly, sometimes asking me to comment on the irrational nature of his wife's assertions. The general outspokenness of my interviewees on matters of marital harmony and strife leads me to believe that my foreignness and outsider status served as an asset, rather than a liability. My being completely removed from their social and familial networks inside South Korea may have given my informants the security of imagining that their secrets would be safely carried out of the community and out of the country.

During the second period of my fieldwork (December 1999 to May 2000), I traveled to Heilongjiang Province in northeastern China to investigate the ways the exodus of young women from this region to South Korea was affecting kin and communities left behind. I had initially hoped to conduct fieldwork in Yanbian/Yŏnbyŏn, the Korean Autonomous Prefecture of Jilin/Killim Province[14] where the Chosŏnjok, in certain towns and counties, still constitute the majority of the population. My application for official permission to conduct fieldwork there, however, was declined by the local government without explanation, much to my disappointment. A friend and professor at Yanji University in Yŏnbyŏn tried to no avail to find an academic department willing to take responsibility for sponsoring my research. In the end, I secured the nominal institutional affiliation required under the terms of my sponsoring organizations with the Chinese Academy of Social Sciences (CASS) in Beijing, which was more open to hosting foreign researchers interested in minority affairs. CASS in turn helped me establish an affiliation with the Heilongjiang Provincial Academy of Social Sciences in Harbin, which proved equally warm and receptive. While Chosŏnjok settlement patterns in Heilongjiang are not as

---

14. Following Lenin's precepts on how to secure the allegiance of national minorities in a socialist state, the Chinese Communist Party permitted the establishment of autonomous regions in areas where there was a concentrated pattern of minority settlement. The Yŏnbyŏn Korean Autonomous Prefecture was established in 1955, giving the Chosŏnjok direct involvement in lower-level politics (Beijing still retained tight centralized control) as well as the freedom to preserve and develop their own linguistic and cultural practices (Olivier 1995, 63–64).

densely clustered as in Yŏnbyŏn, I had little difficulty locating villages and urban districts where Chosŏnjok residents made up a significant portion of the population.[15]

I had mistakenly assumed that Yŏnbyŏn, because of its status as an autonomous region, was the only respectable location to conduct ethnographic research on the Chosŏnjok of China. As Olivier observes, "[T]he other Koreans, who also reside permanently in China, tend to be somewhat overshadowed by the publicity given to Yŏnbyŏn, and many non-specialists do not realize that only about half of the Koreans of China live in Yŏnbyŏn" (1995, 54). Heilongjiang Province indeed proved to be an ideal field site owing to the unrestricted freedom of movement I enjoyed while conducting my research as well as the high rates of outward migration among the Chosŏnjok living there. With their direct and relatively recent ancestral ties to southern Korea, the Chosŏnjok in Heilongjiang Province were the first to take advantage of South Korea's family visitation provisions in the 1990s (K Kim 1998, 16).[16] Most Heilongjiang residents, with the exception of those in Mudanjiang City, trace their ancestry to one of the three southern provinces on the Korean peninsula: Kyŏngsang, Chŏlla, or Ch'ungch'ŏng (K Kim 1998, 16).[17] Between 1990 and 2000, over fourteen percent of the Chosŏnjok population in Heilongjaing Province, a total of 63,940 people, left the region for South Korea or industrial cities within China (Ehlert 2008, 23).

---

15. While the Chosŏnjok in Heilongjiang Province were too widely dispersed to justify the creation of a Yŏnbyŏn-style autonomous region, they were given five small Korean autonomous districts and 101 Korean autonomous villages (Olivier 1995, 63–64).

16. The first settlements in Heilongjiang appeared after the Japanese annexation of Korea in 1910, when Korean farmers pushed northward, above Jilin and Liaoning provinces where the land had already been claimed by earlier waves of northern Korean migrants. Other Koreans fled to Manchuria during the colonial period with the goal of joining the anti-Japanese independence movement and setting up a Korean government in exile (Lee 2002, 119; HO Park 2005; Seol and Skrentny 2009, 152). After the Manchukuo government was established in 1931, entire villages from southern Korea were uprooted and forcibly deported to Heilongjiang Province to satisfy the colonial regime's need for labor in the remote areas of Japanese-controlled Manchuria (Lee 2002, 119).

17. By contrast Jilin and Liaoning provinces were settled principally by Korean farmers from the northern part of the Korean peninsula, Hamkyŏng Province and Pyŏngan Province respectively (K Kim 1998, 16). The first northern Korean migrants to China were peasants driven by seasonal droughts, who crossed the border beginning in the late seventeenth century in defiance of the official ban on migration upheld by both the Qing and the Chosŏn courts (Lee 2002, 119). The number of migrants increased significantly following a severe famine in northern Korea in 1869 (118).

I spent the first three months in the city of Harbin, living with the family of a Chosŏnjok woman named Hyejin, whom I had met and befriended through the English classes I offered to Chosŏnjok migrants in Seoul. Hyejin had returned to Harbin from South Korea just weeks before my arrival, and she implored her parents to allow me to stay as a boarder in her home. Hyejin's family was initially uneasy about a foreigner living on their premises. Not only was it illegal to house a foreigner without first registering with the local police, but the family found my motives for wanting to participate in and observe their everyday lives, no matter how I tried to explain them, inscrutable at best and highly suspect at worst. Fortunately for my sake, the family was reluctant to cast me out on the ice-encrusted streets with Chinese New Year around the corner. We agreed that after the holiday I would search for other accommodations.

Two weeks later I mentioned a desire to gather materials related to the history of Chosŏnjok immigration from the Korean peninsula to China. At last, I had offered up what seemed to be a worthy subject of study and overnight the suspicions surrounding my activities evaporated. Hyejin's mother proudly took to introducing me to friends and relatives as researching the history of their immigrant ancestors. Whereas before there had been awkwardness and silence between us, Hyejin's mother now seized every opportunity to regale me with childhood memories and stories of her grandfather's resistance against the Japanese colonial occupation. Overnight, it seemed, I had been transformed from persona non grata into distinguished houseguest. It was with a certain amount of guilt that I allowed her to believe that I was an immigration historian rather than a cultural anthropologist. In reality, I was far more interested in understanding and documenting the family crisis surrounding Hyejin's younger sister whose South Korean husband had recently confessed to having a romantic affair with a "bar girl" (*sulchip agasi*) from Yŏnbyŏn. The sister's predicament had the effect of drawing me deeper into the family circle as a source of moral support and potential advice. Ironically, it also deepened my sense of guilt as I converted the family discord surrounding the sister's transnational marriage into "data" for my research.

Having gained their acceptance, I was graciously allowed to stay with them for a full three months. During this time, aside from intimate glimpses into the social life of Hyejin's family and their extended circle of friends and relatives, I also took the opportunity while living in the provincial capital to examine local media sources, particularly back issues of the

Korean-language *Hŭknyonggang sinmun* (hereafter, *Heilongjiang News*), which were useful in understanding the public discourse and debate surrounding Chosŏnjok-Korean marriages and, more broadly, the large-scale exodus of Chosŏnjok migrants to South Korea.

In March 2000, I relocated to a Chosŏnjok village outside the city of Mudanjiang where I hoped I would be able to identify and interview potential brides who were contemplating or pursuing marriages to South Korean men. When I arrived, however, I was startled to discover that nearly all the daughters in this particular village, which I refer to as Creek Road Village,[18] had already migrated out in search of employment and/or marriage partners. So pervasive was "Korea Fever" (*han'guk yŏl*) that the question "When are you going to Korea?" was rapidly replacing the conventional greeting of "Have you eaten yet?" Most of the adults, young and old, who remained in the village had either been to South Korea and back or were yearning to capitalize on their ethnic ties to South Korea and its labor market. My host "mother," a poor widow who fed, sheltered, and warmed me on the *kang* (fire-heated platform) of her one-room, mud-thatch (*hŭkch'ip*) home throughout the still-frigid springtime, was one of many people I met in the village who were desperately casting about for a means of gaining (illicit) entry to work in South Korea. My rural host mother intended to purchase the identity papers and visitation rights of a neighbor whose daughter had married to South Korea.[19]

The practice of purchasing fictitious kinship identities to bypass South Korea's restrictive immigration laws was not confined to the poorest segments of Chosŏnjok society. A close relationship I cultivated with an urban, educated mother in Mudanjiang City, who also took me into her home and her confidence, opened the doors for me to observe firsthand the prevalence and social acceptability of counterfeit kinship practices among her more privileged circle of family members and friends. Shuttling back and forth between the homes of my urban and rural families enabled me

---

18. All of the names of places and people, aside from the names of provinces and large cities, are pseudonyms to protect the anonymity of my research subjects.

19. By 2001, it is estimated that there were 150,000 illegal Chosŏnjok sojourners in South Korea who had entered the country with either genuine or fake documentation and overstayed their visas to work for extended periods (JY Lee 2002, 131).

to document and describe reconfiguration of everyday norms of family and conjugal life according to the new logics of flexibility and family dispersal that were taking hold across the region.

I used the final three months of my fieldwork (June to August 2000) to return to South Korea to pay follow-up visits to rural and urban families I had interviewed during the first phase of the project and to pursue new contacts I had made during my stay in China. I found it very useful to experience reentry into the metropolis of Seoul after living in northeastern China, following the route of the migrants I studied. It heightened my awareness of the extent to which uneven economic development can be viscerally and immediately experienced, even in the air one breathes. Adjusting physically to the move from northeastern China to Seoul also deepened my appreciation of the tensions and disjunctures that Chosŏnjok migrants experienced when they made the journey themselves.

Overview of the Book

Part I, "Migrant Brides and the Pact of Gender, Kinship, Nation" (chapters 1–3), looks at the social conditions that gave rise to transnational marriages between China and South Korea and the often contradictory logics of kinship, gender, and ethnonationalism these unions entailed. Chapter 1 describes the government-endorsed marriage tours for South Korean rural bachelors as a form of rural "family welfare" that relies on the imported labor of coethnic women to achieve two important state goals: the rehabilitation of the rural sector and the restoration of "ethnic homogeneity" to the divided nation. I introduce the stories of Yŏnghwa, Sumin, Hiju, Oksŏng, and Minsŏn, five brides who married South Korean farmers under the bride-importing program of the South Korean government to complicate the idealized image of the "model migrant bride" and point us toward a reevaluation of these marriages from the women's own perspectives.

Chapter 2 sketches the evolution of Chosŏnjok-Korean marriages from a government-endorsed social program to a profit-making enterprise run by licensed matchmakers and unlicensed marriage brokers. Accompanying the commodification of these marriages and their proliferation beyond the confines of the countryside is an abrupt shift in the popular perception of Chosŏnjok brides. No longer hailed as saviors of the rural patriarchal family and catalysts for ethnic reunification, Chosŏnjok brides became the subject of intense criticism in the South Korean media for the unbridled materialism and opportunism presumed to motivate their marriages. I extend the discussion of the public debate over the morality of Chosŏnjok brides to a broader consideration of the cultural contradictions that frame the negative perception of Chosŏnjok migrants in South Korea more generally. These contradictory representations ultimately prompt South Koreans and Chosŏnjok migrants alike to question beliefs about the unity and essential sameness of Koreans across the globe, regardless of class or national origins.

Chapter 3 builds on current understandings about the interplay of power and gender in transnational contexts. Contrary to studies that emphasize the exacerbation of gender inequality through transnational migration, I introduce four ethnographic examples that point to Chosŏnjok women's ability to pursue their own goals of upward mobility independent of, and often in opposition to, their husbands and marital families. My main argument is that in marrying into South Korea, Chosŏnjok brides confront powerful and contradictory constructions of gender that variously promote or constrain their freedom of mobility at different points in their quest for a better life in South Korea.

Chapters 4 and 5 in Part II, "Migrant Workers, Counterfeit Kinship, and Split Families," extend the scope of investigation beyond cross-border marriages to examine the geographically dispersed families of already-married migrant workers. In chapter 4, I retrace in step-by-step detail the plots of two Chosŏnjok migrant mothers to enter South Korea with falsified kinship documents. One of my objectives is to evoke the human dimension of these women's experiences as "illegal border crossers." Their stories illustrate the many anxieties that would-be migrants and their families faced as a result of the logistical complexities and emotional and financial costs involved in carrying out counterfeit kinship schemes. Another aim of this chapter is to shed light on the role of fraudulent documents in migration processes and provide vivid examples of the pressures "from below" that challenge the territorial sovereignty of the nation-state (see Sadiq 2009, chapter 4). While disenfranchised migrants the world over deploy similar tactics of "paper citizenship," the cases presented here add a dimension of complexity because Chosŏnjok illegal migrants violated more than the laws of bureaucratic governance. They "denaturalized" the very meaning of family and genealogy, tropes that are used in South Korea to project a sense of enduring solidarity between South Korean citizens and their overseas "kin."

Chapter 5 considers the ways in which gender, conjugal, and parent-child relationships were stretched, sometimes to the breaking point, to accommodate particular patterns of transnational family dispersal. I show how everyday norms of parenting and married life were doubly challenged in the case of the Chosŏnjok, first by the very act of forming "split transnational families," and second by the extraordinary risks that Chosŏnjok migrants were pressured to take with their marriages in order to reap the financial rewards of working in South Korea.

In chapter 6, I examine the impact of the 1997 Asian financial crisis on marriage and migration trends in the region. One year before I started my fieldwork, South Korea plunged into a severe currency and debt crisis, and the government applied for emergency loans from the International Monetary Fund (IMF). As a condition for the bailout funds, the government had to accept measures to open the economy to foreign investment and make the labor market more flexible. The crisis soon became known as the "IMF crisis" (*aiemep'ŭ sat'ae*) or simply "IMF," terms which evoke for South Koreans the sweeping political, economic, and social consequences associated with the economic downfall—soaring rates of unemployment, a perceived loss of national sovereignty, polarized levels of wealth and income, neoliberal restructuring of the economy, and widespread fears of "family breakdown."

The precipitous economic downturn, financial collapse, and subsequent draconian restructuring agreement imposed by the International Monetary Fund (IMF), suggested to the Chosŏnjok the seeming fragility of South Korea's standing in the economic world order. In response, Chosŏnjok migrants have sought what they consider to be more stable parts of the world, such as Japan, to carry out their strategies of transnational marriage and mobility. South Korean men, meanwhile, have turned primarily to Southeast Asia as an alternative source of foreign brides. In thinking about the implications of these geographic shifts and the unprecedented departure from notions of ethnic endogamy and homogeneity they appear to signal, I offer some final thoughts on transnational kinship making (and faking) as an arena in which people confront, contest, reproduce, and rework understandings about national belonging, their kinship and gender relations, and their place in the shifting global order.

Part I

MIGRANT BRIDES AND THE PACT OF GENDER, KINSHIP, NATION

Chosŏnjok Maidens and
Farmer Bachelors

It was nearly dark by the time my research assistant, Chiyŏng, and I reached our destination: the home of Kisŏn, a pineapple farmer in a far-flung region of South Kyŏngsang Province. In March 1991, Kisŏn had been selected by a local government office to participate in one of South Korea's first "marriage tours" to northeastern China. Following a lead from the organization in Seoul that sponsored the tour, Chiyŏng had phoned him the week before to arrange an interview. "Are you the ones who phoned?" growled a voice as we exited the taxi. There was no one in sight but a gaunt, ruddy-faced man straddling a moped, his stern eyes trained on me. When I looked in his direction, his gaze did not soften. I turned to Chiyŏng to guide us through the awkwardness of the moment, but she appeared equally uncomfortable. The three of us stood in silence, the man unrelenting in his cold stare. I summoned the courage to stammer a greeting. Kisŏn expressed relief that I spoke Korean and apologized that he had been caught off guard to see a foreigner's face.

Not yet sure whether I would be welcome in his home, Chiyŏng and I followed as he led the way through the courtyard of his L-shaped house, into the living room where he beckoned us to sit on the floor. His seven-year-old son and six-year-old daughter, wound up by the arrival of unusual houseguests, ran wildly about the room, whooping and giggling and wrestling each other to the ground. When Kisŏn commanded that they leave the room, his daughter curled up like a cat in his lap, while his son clambered on top of them. It was impossible to talk amid the whining and tumbling. Several times Kisŏn picked up a broom and bellowed at his son to leave the room. The boy ran out shrieking, but no sooner did his father put down the broomstick than he would stubbornly reappear. Kisŏn explained apologetically that his kids never listen to him. I took a small pound cake out of my backpack and offered it to the children, thinking this might help them settle down. The boy snatched it up. *"Masi ŏpda!"* (yuck) he exclaimed and pushed it away. My hopes for a productive interview session were rapidly fading. Kisŏn explained that he had had a quarrel with his wife just before our arrival and that we should await her return before attempting a formal interview.

Eventually Kisŏn's wife, Sumin, came home with a big smile on her face, seemingly fully recovered from their domestic dispute. Her long hair was swept back and she wore large gold hoop earrings and red lipstick. Chiyŏng commented on her beautiful appearance, noting that she looked nothing like a "country woman."

Sumin instantly reestablished order in her household. The kids were fed and put to bed, and the general mood shifted to a more cheerful register. The atmosphere grew more festive still when Kisŏn picked up the phone and invited his neighbors to join us, a Chosŏnjok–South Korean couple (one of three living in the village at that time) who had married two years ago and were expecting their first child. We crowded around a small table on which Sumin had placed a plate of sliced fruit, shot glasses for me and the men (the women demurely abstained), and a bottle of *soju*. I placed a small tape recorder in the middle of the group, and each person, at my prompting, spoke of their personal experiences of marrying across borders.

I open with my entry into the home of one particular farm family—one of nine home visits in five different provinces over the course of my first year of fieldwork—to provide a sense of my itinerant research methods. Including week-long stints away from my home base in Seoul, treks from one village to the next by a combination of plane, train, boat, bus, and/or taxi to remote rural locations where I had prearranged interviews, the process itself resembled a kind of "marriage tour." To stretch the metaphor a little further, similar to the "lightning quick" (*pongae sik*) style of court-ship that moved couples from first meeting to marriage proposal to wed-ding in just one week's time, I too was pressured to move from foreign anthropologist to intimate confidante, often in just a matter of hours. With-out fail my hosts rewarded me with the "rural hospitality" they were so proud of—they fed me, offered me a sleeping mat for the night, and, most important, regaled me with the intimate details of their hasty courtships and their experiences of married life in the remote villages they inhabited.

I asked every farmer a blunt, and to them probably naive, question as an entry point to our conversation: "Why did you go all the way to China to find a bride?" And each time I received the same straightforward re-sponse: "No *agashi* [unmarried woman] wants to marry a rural bachelor." Kisŏn elaborated slightly, pointing to age as a factor. "If you're thirty-four [years old], that's it. You're too old. After trying and trying, if a man ab-solutely can't get married, he goes to China." Kisŏn made it seem like a logical progression, part of the natural order of things.

That a man whose local marriage prospects are dim would expand his search overseas is not usual. The mass media in the United States, despite its distortions and sensationalized imagery, has familiarized the American public with what are commonly referred to as "mail-order marriages." In these marriages, men and women from different parts of the world typically meet through the assistance of introduction agencies and agree to marry often after meeting face-to-face for only the first time. Marriages between Korean men and Chosŏnjok women tend to unfold along these lines, but one important aspect that makes them unique is the official sanction they receive from the Korean government. Why would the Korean government back something akin to a "mail-order marriage" program for its unwed farmers? What culturally specific understandings of family and nation in Korea allow transnational marriages to be placed in the realm of public pol-icy? What larger social and political forces made Chosŏnjok women appear to be a logical, and even patriotic choice, for the nation's farmers?

This chapter explores these questions and considers how the issue of Chosŏnjok brides became a political one, with implications not just for the individual farmers but for the nation as a whole. It stretches back before my time in the field to the beginning of the 1990s when diplomatic ties between China and South Korea were first established and unions between Chosŏnjok brides and South Korean farmers were celebrated in discourses of ethnic reunification and rural revival. As I show, uneven regional and global development, political economic changes between mainland China and South Korea, and Korean ethnonationalist sentiment combined to make Chosŏnjok brides the most politically expedient and patriotic choice for the nation's farmers throughout the 1990s.

The second part of this chapter presents the stories of a number of Chosŏnjok women who married Korean farmers through the assistance of the Research Association for the Welfare of Korean Farm and Fishing Villages located in Seoul. When Mr. Na Chongkŭn, the director of the agency, referred me to these couples, he emphasized that these were people who "lived well" (*chal sanŭn saram*) and that the brides had been "innocent and "pure maidens" at the time of their marriages. This image of the "good Chosŏnjok bride" held sway during an already-bygone era, just ten years before the ethnographic present of this book in the late 1990s. It stood in stark contrast to the then-prevailing imagery of the cunning Chosŏnjok woman who opportunistically discarded marital partners, both at home and in South Korea, in the interests of obtaining South Korean citizenship.

In the following chapter, I address the larger social and political context in which this fall from grace took place. My concern here is to introduce a cast of Chosŏnjok wives who, by simple virtue of staying put in their rural marriages, bearing children, and caring for aging in-laws, conform to the family-making expectations imposed by the state and their marital family members. It is my hope, however, that a closer look at the texture of their lives, their disappointments, and their varied outlooks on marriage and mobility will begin to complicate the idealized images that have legitimized, and continue to legitimate, the reliance on foreign women in South Korea to rehabilitate unwed, underprivileged men and, by extension, the patriarchal family as the basis of the nation's social order.

Understanding the Rural Boycott

To appreciate how the search for rural brides came to be viewed as a political issue with ramifications beyond the welfare of individual farmers, we must consider the broader social forces that engendered the "marriage crisis." The rural exodus of young people to the cities can be traced back to the 1960s when the South Korean state first implemented its export-led, labor-intensive strategy of development. As in the case of other rapidly industrializing nations, the South Korean state depended on the relatively inexpensive and flexible labor of unmarried rural women to fill the ranks of its industrial labor force. By neglecting the development of the rural sector and siphoning off its population of unmarried women (and young men, to a slightly lesser extent) to work in urban industries, the state accelerated the pace of rural-urban migration to a devastating degree.[1] By the mid-1980s the Korean government was faced with a bride shortage in the countryside so severe it could no longer be ignored.

While young rural women have been targeted as an inexpensive, easily controlled urban labor force in nations across the global economy, these gendered patterns of labor recruitment do not, in and of themselves, inevitably culminate in a marriage squeeze among rural bachelors. Mills (1999), for example, describes the labor migration experiences of young, rural Thai women who return to their native villages more often than not, to marry and resettle after a stint of factory work in Bangkok. A number of factors account for this pattern of return migration, including perceptions of city men as "unreliable providers," uxorilocal patterns of marriage, and widely held Buddhist beliefs about a daughter's ongoing obligations to obey and materially support her parents after marriage (1999, 76–80).

South Korean women, unlike their Thai counterparts, rarely return to their rural roots. One important factor explaining the ubiquity of the "rural boycott"[2] among young women in South Korea is that, unlike Thai parents, South Korean parents do not discourage their daughters from settling in the city. In fact, rural parents, especially mothers, are said to urge their daughters to find husbands with jobs in the city. A middle-aged female farmer interviewed by Sorensen in the late 1970s captured the disdain with which rural existence was already regarded at that time when she avowed, "I'd even tell a dog not to farm" (1988, 202). At the turn of the millennium, Korean mothers continue to counsel their daughters to forsake the farm and marry men who live in Seoul.

The path that rural Korean sons are expected to take as they approach marriage also differs sharply from the Thai case. Eldest sons in Korea are bound to the countryside by obligations to take care of aging parents and

---

1. Lie (1998) argues that the underdevelopment of the rural sector was a deliberate and necessary component of South Korean state planning in order to ensure a steady supply of cheap labor.

2. I borrow this term from Yoon (1990, 270).

help maintain ancestral farmland acquired over generations. These cultural expectations, combined with patrilocal marriage customs and the near impossibility of securing a good job in the city without skills or education, pressure eldest sons to stay in the village or return there after a stint of migrant labor. Younger sons, while less bound by ties of filial obligation, face the same difficulties succeeding in urban occupations. Women's work in rural areas, by contrast, is considered harder and lower status than even the lowest-paying jobs available to women in the cities. Their best hope, as their mothers often see it, is to remain in the city by marrying into an urban household, a distinctly female option given the customary emphasis placed on hypergamous and patrilocal marriage patterns. A married-out daughter's parents might also benefit (practically and symbolically) from establishing connections with affines in urban locations.

Farmers I met as well as activists advocating on their behalf noted the irony of the situation in which farm families universally send their daughters off to Seoul to marry while simultaneously complaining that they are unable to recruit a daughter-in-law into their rural households. Behind these comments is the implicit notion that rural mothers are in large part to blame for the bride shortage problem. When I asked Kisŏn what measures might be taken to redress the situation, he immediately identified rural mothers as the root of the problem: "Mothers in the countryside tell their daughters not to marry rural bachelors. Meanwhile, their own sons can't find wives. It's very contradictory. That's why there's a problem. We have to change this way of thinking." These comments hint at the ways that gendered patterns of marriage and migration in contemporary South Korea are shaped not only by economic factors and government policies but also by competing constructions of kinship obligations, gender roles, and the widespread devaluation of rural ways of life.

Marriage Makes the Man

Regardless of how the bride shortage crisis is thought to have emerged, the plight of Korea's rural bachelors strikes a sympathetic chord with most Koreans. Plummeting marriage rates and surging divorce rates nationwide[3]

---

3. One third of all marriages ended in divorce in 1997, while one in two marriages ended in divorce in 2002 (Uhn 2005, 19).

have done little to lessen the expectation that marriage is obligatory. Those who cannot marry for reasons beyond their control are viewed as worthy of pity, while those who opt not to marry are treated with suspicion. I witnessed the daily angst of the unmarried, forty-year-old librarian who shared her apartment with me in Seoul. She was haunted by the possibility of a run-in with the disapproving gaze of the elderly neighbor down the hall and resorted to weaving elaborate lies about an imaginary husband and children in an effort to appear "normal" to the classmates in her evening English classes. Lesbians and gays in South Korea engage in much larger-scale and more complicated acts of deception in order to fulfill their filial obligations of being married. Cho (2009) describes the "contract marriages" or marriages of convenience that lesbians and gays contract with one another, which entail enormous effort, emotional volatility, and financial risk, all the while hiding their homosexual partnerships from their family, relatives, and employers.

The pressure to conform to the norms of married life applies to both men and women. However, as John Cho points out, "[M]en, in particular, need to marry in order to fulfill their filial obligations, acquire social status, and get promoted at work" (2009, 406). In the countryside, it is through marriage and by establishing himself as the head of a stable, patriarchal household that a man succeeds in asserting his masculinity and consolidating his social status. The sense of disabled manhood[4] must have seemed unbearable for the some sixty rural bachelors who took their lives in protest in the 1970s (Na 1997a, 9).[5] The slogan that appeared on banners throughout towns and villages at the height of the farmers' agitation—"Farmers are people too! Let's get married!" (*Nongmin do saram ida! Changga chom kaja!*) (Na 1997b)—speaks to the importance of marital status in attaining full social personhood in Korean society.

Body and Soil Are One

The "marriage problem" in the countryside, as it is commonly referred to, threatens more than the masculinity and moral integrity of individual rural bachelors. It also spells the demise of the small farm family as the basic unit

---

4. I am grateful to an anonymous reviewer for pointing out the sense of "disabled manhood" associated with men not being married.

5. I do not have further details of this incident. Kendall makes only passing reference to it and the coverage it received in the popular press in the mid-1980s (1996, 4). Park notes that the farmers committed suicide by ingesting pesticides (1996, 217 fn4).

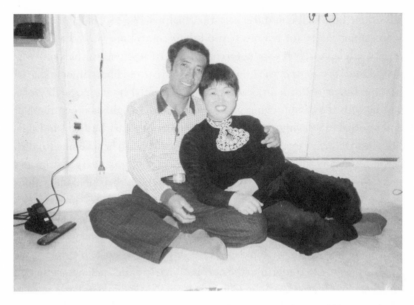

A Chosŏnjok–South Korean couple poses for a picture in their rural home.

of agricultural production and with it the ability of Korea to produce its own staple crops without heavy reliance on foreign imports. Unlike most Americans who purchase agricultural products with little knowledge or awareness of their geographic origin, Koreans place a great deal of importance on where their food comes from. Fruits, vegetables, and grains grown on native soil are thought to have superior taste, quality, and nutritional value. The nationalist trope of *sint'oburi* (the idea that body and soil or place of origin are one and the same) is emblazoned on locally produced sacks of rice and other agricultural goods, reminding Korean citizens that consumption of food produced on native soil constitutes an act of patriotism. As Grinker observes, "Food grown on foreign soil is symbolically contaminated and anti-national, whereas food grown at home is Korean and pure" (2000, 61).

The farmers who produce the food are also believed to embody *sint'oburi*, having invested their "sweat and blood" in the cultivation of the land handed down to them by their ancestors. This imagery is further reinforced by a particular notion of rural Korea as a repository for the "traditional" Korean values of filial piety, simplicity, cooperation, and community, which are widely lamented as disappearing in urban Korean society. While most scholars are quick to describe Korean preferences for locally produced goods, particularly agricultural goods, as a form of economic nationalism, I suspect they may be rooted in deeper, long-standing beliefs about the relationship between people and the land, though they are undoubtedly renewed and reinterpreted through nationalistic sentiments in present-day South Korea.

Bringing the Sound of Crying Babies
Back to the Countryside

Despite the widespread popular belief that farmers and farming play a vital role in sustaining the nation, literally and symbolically, the government has done very little to ensure their welfare.[6] In the absence of any substantial public welfare or government support for indigent farmers, a number of private-sector and self-help organizations (*min'gan tanch'e*) rallied to help rural bachelors find brides. With financial support from the government, a nationwide Marriage Aid Program (Sŏnghon topki p'rok raem) was launched. One of the earliest programs was initiated by the Research Association for the Welfare of Korean Farm and Fishing Villages (RWFFV), a government-subsidized organization. Observing that farm families send their daughters en masse to Seoul to marry, the leaders of the RWFFV reasoned that "we must get daughters-in-law back from Seoul" (Na 1997a, 9). Under the slogan "Bring the sound of crying babies back to the countryside" (*nongch'on esŏ aki urŭm sorika tŭllike*), the RWFFV launched a campaign to match rural bachelors with unmarried women in the cities. In the course of brokering the marriages of six hundred couples between 1978 and 1990, the director of the organization became known as "the only free matchmaker in the country" (1995, Kim Sŏho: *Chŏt mannam sŏ maŭm e tŭl myŏn—ponchi Kim Sŏ-ho Chungguk Simyang kanda* [If he likes her at first meeting— Reporter Kim Sŏho goes to Shenyang, China], unknown newspaper).

Despite its initial successes, the task of recruiting brides from the city became increasingly difficult, and advocates of the Marriage Aid Program

---

6. Lie characterizes the state's attitude toward the rural sector as one of "indifference and neglect, punctuated by periods of intense attention" (1998, 108). These periods of "intense attention" included the Saemaŭl undong (New Village Movement) and the government's protectionist agricultural policies of the 1970s. According to Lie, neither the rural reform movement nor the restriction of agricultural imports succeeded in alleviating the underdeveloped condition of the countryside, the steady exodus of young people to the cities, or the widespread devaluation of rural life.

turned their focus instead to facilitating marriages between rural residents. Beginning in 1986, marriage counseling bureaus (*sŏnghon sangdamsil*) were opened in 182 townships across the country. Their purpose was to offer cross-regional matchmaking services for men and women living in rural areas as well as to supply impoverished farmers with the ritual essentials needed to perform a respectable wedding ceremony, including a *churye,* or master of ceremonies,[7] and wedding hall. Each bureau compiled a database listing the women and men of marriageable age in a particular locality. A system was then set up to circulate this information among the various marriage bureaus throughout the country with hopes to identify suitable matches. To help rural men and women boost their attractiveness to the opposite sex, the Marriage Aid Program also offered village-level classes in etiquette, conversational skills, and general strategies of self-improvement. Farm households with rural bachelors were eligible to receive financial aid to help them clean up their living spaces and create a home environment that would appeal to a prospective bride (Kim 1994, 24–25). These grass-roots matchmaking efforts resulted in 9,905 marriages over a seven-year period, but most of the successes occurred in the early part of this period and enthusiasm for the program, as in the case of the rural-urban match-making campaign, appears to have dwindled steadily over time (see chart, Kim 1994, 25).

As South Korea entered the late 1980s and early 1990s, a number of major diplomatic and economic events converged to both intensify the severity of the rural bride shortage and present new solutions to the problem. Korea's hosting of the 1988 Olympic Games heightened the international awareness of ordinary Koreans and instilled in Korea's leaders the confidence to expand the nation's economic and diplomatic relations abroad. This "sports diplomacy," as Chae-jin Lee calls it (2000, 172), acted as a catalyst for Korea's diplomatic overtures toward the Soviet Union in 1990 and then China in 1992, marking a decisive break from Korea's insular cold war foreign policy. As Korea assertively expanded its network of diplomatic relations, it faced mounting pressure from the United States and other industrialized countries to liberalize its trade relations and financial markets.

---

7. See Kendall for a description of the role of *churye* in Korean wedding ceremonies (1996, 35–41).

In the final phase of the Uruguay Round (UR) negotiations[8] in 1993, South Korea finally capitulated to external pressure to open its agricultural markets to foreign imports, much to the chagrin of the nation's farmers. So emotionally charged were the farmers' protests, which preceded and continued throughout the duration of the negotiations, that the minister of agriculture, forests, and fisheries was forced to hand in his resignation (Lee 2000, 188).

Just prior to the UR negotiations, amidst the farmers' protests of what appeared to be an impending agricultural crisis, the Korean government endorsed a new type of marriage aid made possible by the thawing of diplomatic relations with China. In addition to the agricultural goods and capital that had been given clearance to enter the nation from abroad, the state added Chosŏnjok brides to the list of acceptable foreign imports (though, as I describe below, Chosŏnjok brides were construed not as foreigners but as overseas "Koreans" who were being repatriated). Director No Sŭng-ok of the RWFFV who had spearheaded the movement to match rural men with city women in the early 1980s now focused his efforts on leading four-day matchmaking tours (*massŏn'gil*) to the northeastern region of China where rural bachelors were told they could find the ideal "wife material" (*saeksigam*).

Purity and Patriarchy

In its promotional literature on marriage tours to China, the RWFFV makes moralistic comparisons between Chosŏnjok women who willingly embrace the opportunity to marry the nation's farmers on the one hand, and South Korean women who have "betrayed" their ancestral roots (*kohyangttang*) and deserted their male counterparts on the other. Chosŏnjok

---

8. The Uruguay Round negotiations refers to a series of multilateral trade negotiations, which were launched in 1986 in Punta del Este, Uruguay, under the auspices of the General Agreement on Tariffs and Trade (GATT). After seven and a half years of negotiations among ministers from 123 participating nations on the issue of global trade liberalization, an agreement was finally signed in April 1994 to reduce tariffs, quotas, subsidies and other domestic policies restricting exports to world markets. The Uruguay Round agreement is historic not only as the most ambitious and contentious worldwide trade negotiations ever undertaken but also as the first time that multilateral trade regulations extended to the agricultural sector (see Croome 1995). Under the UR agreement, Korea reluctantly liberalized its import policies for agricultural products, despite the immense economic and political pressure it created for farmers.

women are described as unspoiled by the urban prejudices thought to have provoked South Korean women's wholesale rejection of rural matrimony and therefore imagined to be better adapted to an agrarian lifestyle (Na 1997a, 10). Behind these comparisons are essentializing and primordial notions of the Chosŏnjok as occupying a space and time untouched by modernizing influences, where the slower pace of economic change under communism is believed to have preserved traditional Korean virtues, particularly traditional feminine virtues of chastity, purity (*sunjinhada*), and obedience (*sunjong*).[9] Many men I spoke with reported they had been drawn to China by the expectation that they would find women there who would make better wives than South Korean women, who they viewed as not only spoiled by commodity fetishism and loose sexual mores but also less apt to respectfully serve their in-laws while living under the same roof. While cultural and economic purity are traits that could only be presumed, the sexual purity of potential brides was guaranteed through the administration of virginity tests in China at the behest of the South Korean government (Park 1996, 221).

Theorists of nationalism working in various parts of the world have noted the crucial role that gender plays in symbolically constructing the boundaries of the nation-state. In nationalisms worldwide, women are often viewed both socially and biologically as reproducers of the nation, its "traditional" culture, and its people. Jager (2003) traces the emergence of new gendered subjectivities in South Korea in the context of Korea's nation-building efforts. Jager describes, for example, how the Confucian ideal of the virtuous and loyal wife was called upon by dissident historians writing in the 1980s to strengthen the "essence" of Korean national culture, perceived as weakened by national division and Western imperialism. "As the pliant conduit of paternal regeneration, women unwittingly became both the object of concern over the state of Korea's racial (inner) 'purity' and the subject of active resistance to (outside) foreign 'contamination'" (Jager 2003, 73). This nationalist preoccupation with female virtue and chastity as a signifier of racial/national purity explains why Chosŏnjok brides are considered "Korean" only when they appear loyal to their Korean husbands.

---

9. See Fabian 1983 on the projection of non-Western "others" into a mythologized past by anthropologists; see Grinker 2000 (60–64) on "the suppression of time" with respect to South Korean constructions of North Korea.

As I explore in later chapters, when their actions threaten the stability of the Korean patriarchal household, they are perceived as transgressive outsiders who threaten the integrity of the nation through their insufficient domesticity.[10]

Restoring Ethnic Homogeneity through Marital Diplomacy

The significance of marriages between Korean farmers and Chosŏnjok women for the Korean government and the organizations that promoted them lies not only in the restoration of "traditional" extended-family households to the Korean countryside but also, as stated in the RWFFV literature and quoted throughout the mass media, in their contribution to the sacred goal of "restoring ethnic homogeneity" (*minjok tongjilsŏngdo hoebok halsuida*) to the nation. The concept of "ethnic homogeneity" is part of an idealized vision of the Korean "people," or *minjok,* as a racially and culturally homogeneous entity that extends beyond the boundaries of the nation-state, uniting Koreans throughout the global diaspora on the basis of blood ties. More important than the litany of cultural similarities ("same language," "same traditional customs," and "same diet of rice and *kimch'i* [pickled cabbage])" that Chosŏnjok are professed to share with South Koreans, Chosŏnjok women are believed to share the same blood (*hanp'itchul*). In light of this belief, repatriating them to South Korea through ties of marriage was not simply pragmatic social policy but utterly patriotic.

Though nationalist historians project the concept into Korea's ancient past, the ideology of ethnic homogeneity is a contemporary construction,

---

10. Scholars of Korean society have also noted the potential for the figure of the "traditional woman" to stand not only for the preservation of Korean culture against the vicissitudes of modernity but also paradoxically for the forces that hold the nation back from modernization. As Abelmann observes, when it is politically expedient, Korean women "can be feminized, not as...protectors of the patriarchal household in vulnerable national times, but as antimodern, 'traditional,' anachronistic and unproductive in their femininity" (2003, 202). Amidst the upheaval of the IMF crisis, middle-class housewives were widely critiqued as "keepers of a familistic modernity" that worked against the broader interests of society (Abelmann 2003, 202). Kendall notes that in some circles the IMF crisis itself was blamed on the excessive consumerism and shady real estate dealings of "avaricious housewives" (Kendall 2002, 11; see also Nelson 2000). It seems whatever the social ill, commentators in South Korea are quick to place the blame on women.

first created to resolve the political contradictions that emerged in the colonial period (see Em 1999; Grinker 2000, 21–22). Projecting the concept into Korea's primordial past enables nationalist historians to frame the post–World War II state of national division as a temporary aberration from what is presumed to be a centuries-old norm of ethnic homogeneity. As Grinker notes, "The received view is that national division disrupted Korean cultural and national identity and homogeneity and that unification [between the north and south] will recover them" (2000, ix). If regaining ethnic homogeneity is about unifying the nation, then marriages between Chosŏnjok women and South Korean men were symbolically embraced as giving hope to a future unity, as bringing the Korean people (*minjok*) one step closer to recuperating their idealized homogeneous nation.

Although the most salient use of the word "unification" refers to unifying North and South Korea, South Koreans commonly treat the Chosŏnjok as a proxy for North Koreans, with whom any significant contact or communication is still politically impermissible. Drawing a typical parallel between the Chosŏnjok and North Koreans, social scientist Pak Hyeran introduces her study of the Chosŏnjok as an ethnographic window onto North Korean society:

> Through a firsthand understanding of the lives of Chosŏnjok women, I will indirectly gain an understanding of the lives of North Korean women in the hopes that after unification, the heterogeneity of the North and South Korean people can be restored to one homogeneous people [*minjok*]....China has been a brother to North Korea, and the Chosŏnjok have had free access to North Korea. It thus follows that the people [*minjok*] of the two nations are relatively homogeneous—have the same way of living and same way of thinking. Therefore, we can understand North Koreans indirectly by studying the Chinese. (Pak Hyeran 1994, 11)

Because of South Korea's coterminous geographical location and relatively permeable border with North Korea, many missionaries, social workers, entrepreneurs, and academics I talked with in the South saw northeastern China as a place to hone their strategies of economic expansion, democratization, and Christian proselytizing for eventual application to North Korea. Many seemed to believe that the effects of their work in China would gradually trickle across the border to North Korea, helping lay the ideological and economic groundwork widely perceived by

South Koreans as integral to the unification process. The underlying idea is that North Koreans have not "progressed" as far as South Koreans, that they are in need of both capitalist markets and spiritual salvation, and that these elements will bring them into the fold of "modern civilization." As Grinker observes (2000, 66), South Korean discourses on North Koreans resemble British colonial discourses on Africans insofar as "civilization and progress became synonymous with capitalism and Christianity."

A conversation with a South Korean friend, Kang Chansuk, who volunteers much of her free time, both through her Christian church as well as independently, helping Chosŏnjok migrants in South Korea, illustrates the colonial-like connections many South Koreans make between the Chosŏnjok, North Koreans, and unification. Chansuk explained to me that she had majored in Chinese in college, but after studying abroad in China for one semester, she returned to South Korea disenchanted by what she had seen and experienced there. "After traveling to China, I wanted nothing to do with the Chosŏnjok. But my professor explained to me that we must help the Chosŏnjok because it is the first step toward reunification with North Korea. Since North Korea is off limits, we must begin with the Chinese Chosŏnjok.... The Chosŏnjok are very similar to North Koreans. They speak like North Koreans; their textbooks are produced in North Korea." Chansuk then proceeded to discuss the importance of exporting South Korean textbooks to China. Highly regulated by the Ministry of Education, South Korean textbooks are used by the state to inculcate its own young people with the desire for unification (see Grinker 2000, chapter 6). It is not surprising that Chansuk would see them as a powerful tool for extending South Korean views of nationhood into China and eventually into North Korea. "The best way to change the way North Koreans think," she concluded, is through economic, educational, and religious forms of persuasion.

As Chansuk's commentary suggests, when South Koreans envision unification, it is primarily construed as the absorption or assimilation of North Koreans into South Korea and not a complementary integration of the two national communities. "Restoring homogeneity" thus entails transforming North Koreans into South Koreans. While these discourses of assimilation or conversion hearken back to the ideas of evangelists and colonists (Grinker 2000, 66), they are also suggestive of the patriarchal, Confucian notion of marriage as the complete transfer of a bride from her natal household to her husband's family's household.[11] From this perspective, incorporating a Chosŏnjok bride into a South Korean household enacts in symbolic terms the appropriation of the North by the South. In more concrete terms, Chosŏnjok brides are in many cases expected by their South Korean families to change their style of dress, their manner of speaking, their food preferences, and their way of thinking in an effort to transform themselves from Chosŏnjok into "Koreans" (han'guksaram).

The gendered hierarchical relations underlying this process of absorbing and transforming Chosŏnjok brides are made more palatable to South Koreans by invoking culturally patterned narratives about the power of love to overcome political divisions. Other scholars have noted the ways discourses on unification and division are framed in South Korea within the idiom of marriage, particularly the metaphorical representation of North and South Korea as separated lovers anxiously awaiting their conjugal reunion (Grinker 2000, 122; Jager 2003, chapter 4).[12]

For Mr. Na, who succeeded Mr. No as director of the RWFFV, marriage is the ultimate symbol and most effective means of overcoming the political obstacles that undermine the idealized unity of the Korean "people." Mr. Na is interested in using "marital diplomacy" to begin to dissolve not only the opposition between North and South, but also regional prejudices among the provinces of South Korea, particularly the long-standing political rivalry between Chŏllado and Kyŏngsangdo. He recounted to me with disappointment the government's failure to fund his proposal for eroding interprovincial animosities (chibangsaek) by fostering social interactions between young people from Chŏllado and Kyŏngsangdo, which over time would lead to cross-regional marriages, he argued. Mr. Na has not,

---

11. John R. Shepherd (personal communication) observes that this notion of absorption and transformation also resonates with the Confucian concept of jiaohua (moral transformation) employed by the Qing state in its project to incorporate the so-called barbarians into the Chinese empire.

12. According to Jager, the allegorical relationship between reunified nation and conjugal reunion first emerged as a "new romantic narrative strategy" by dissident historians in the mid-1980s as a way of voicing their opposition to national division and decades of cold war rhetoric that portrayed North Koreans as the "enemy" (2003, 61). In linking conjugal romance and patriotism, Jager also notes that dissident writers drew upon historic themes and symbols (that is, love overcoming separation and political prosperity as a reward for personal suffering) as found in the eighteenth-century Tale of Ch'unhyang (Tale of the faithful wife, Spring Fragrance), Korea's most renowned love story (65–68).

however, given up on his "biggest dream," which, he explained, is to arrange marriages between North Korean women and South Korean men,
uniting them in a symbolic group wedding at Panmunjom. "It would only
have to be five or six couples—a realizable goal," he explained, indicating
the example of the Chinese table tennis player who married a player from
the South Korean team after the 1988 Seoul Olympics, despite strong opposition from both governments. "Love won out in the end," he said, "and
their marriage became a symbol of the possibility of friendship between
the two nations."

Chosŏnjok Brides as Instruments of the State

Feminist commentators like Heh-Rahn Park look with skepticism upon
the rhetoric of ethnic homogeneity that is often applied to these marriages,
arguing that it masks an underlying exploitative relationship between
the state and Chosŏnjok women. Park writes, "[T]he state's promotion of
marriages between Chinese Korean [Chosŏnjok] brides and South Korean
peasant men mobilizes the myth of a homogenous Korean identity to mask
its complicity in the international traffic in women" (1996, 220). Her argument hinges in part on the timing of the plan to supply rural bachelors
with Chosŏnjok brides. Noting that the plan emerged during the period
of intense political protesting by farmers in the months leading up to the
UR negotiations, Park makes a convincing case that the state conveniently
mobilizes Chosŏnjok women as a type of farm subsidy, doling them out
to pacify farmers' heated demands for economic security. Instead of taking the political and economic action necessary to protect the agricultural
sector against the volatility of the global market, she argues, the Korean
government shifts its own responsibility for rural reform onto the backs of
Chosŏnjok brides, whose productive and reproductive labor is expected to
resuscitate the rural economy and repopulate the countryside (1996, 219).

Earlier I referred to the state's planning policies that targeted young rural
South Korean women as a quiescent and inexpensive labor force to fuel the
country's rapid industrialization. In light of this precedent and decades of
state neglect toward farmers, it is quite plausible that Chosŏnjok women
were mobilized on the basis of similar patriarchal and economic assumptions to smooth over the undesirable effects of the state's urban-centered

planning policies. The reference to trafficking above alludes to the money-making marriage brokers that the state has, for the most part, allowed to proliferate, except for a short crackdown between 1996 and 2003 to prevent "fake marriages."

While in the field, I did not seek to investigate the extent or range of government support for these marriages. Scholarship that has since been published suggests that local governments and assemblies were more active than the central government in promoting and financing marriage tours to China throughout the 1990s. By the mid-2000s, however, the issue of migrant brides had unquestionably become an explicit focus of the central government's population planning policies as well as a vast array of research projects and social support services mandated at both the local and national level.[13]

According to anthropologist Hyun Mee Kim, since 2006 central government documents make clear and open reference to the migrant woman as an "object" that can be used to solve Korea's plummeting birth rate and accelerated aging of the population (2007, 106), which is no longer just limited to the countryside. Local governments across the country have stepped up efforts to encourage international marriages by offering generous financial incentives to men working in the agricultural and fishing industries to find brides overseas (Kim 2007, 110). Observing this new frenzy of government-led efforts to recruit and retain overseas brides, Kim echoes critiques aimed at the earlier wave of Chosŏnjok-centered efforts: "Representatives of local governments are rushing rural men off into the international marriage market instead of making long-term policies that would help improve rural areas" (110).

In the new millennium, the government endorses a much wider pool of potential partners for Korean bachelors, looking to Southeast Asia and other continental neighbors[14] for brides who are touted as "cheaper" and

---

13. At least five government ministries, including the Ministry of Education and Human Resources Development, the Ministry of Culture and Tourism, the Ministry of Agriculture and Forestry, and the Ministry of Gender Equality and Family, sponsor multicultural family projects (Kim 2007, 105).

14. The nationalities of marriage migrants (both men and women) living in South Korea in 2009 were as follows, in order of most to least numerous: Han Chinese (68,000), Chosŏnjok (34,000), Vietnamese (29,000), Filipinos (6,200), Japanese (4,900), Cambodians (2,800), Mongolians (2,300), Thais (2,000), Americans (1,500), and Uzbeks (1,400) ("Female Foreign Spouses

"more compliant" than their coethnics in China.[15] By 2007 an astonishing forty percent of all farmers were married to foreign brides;[16] one in six of those foreign brides came from Vietnam.[17] Promoted under the new banner of "multiculturalism," the movement to recruit brides of non-Korean descent may seem like a radical, and even progressive, departure from the ideology of "one blood" used to legitimize marriages to Chosŏnjok women in the last decade. However, the same "rural family welfare" goals remain the heart of the government's interest in importing foreign brides. This is clearly seen in the pro-natal support programs, incentives, and laws the government passed after 2005, which extend rights and privileges only to migrant brides who, in Kim's words, have "fulfilled their purpose in family-making, in other words housekeeping, child-bearing, and child-rearing" (2007, 109).

It is relevant to note that in the same historical moment when Chosŏnjok women were called upon to lift farmers out of their personal and national predicament in the 1990s, middle-class housewives were asked to do the same for their urban, white-collar husbands. June J. H. Lee provides a fascinating account of how the state mobilizes middle-class housewives to "heal" their husbands, popularly perceived to have worked themselves sick in the course of creating South Korea's economic success. Media-spun "illness narratives," which circulated throughout the 1990s and reached a peak during the 1997 financial crisis, sent a message to the public that if middle-class, white-collar men "could only be revitalized by familial care, their enhanced productivity would revive the nation" (2002, 74).

The crisis of the "salary man" parallels the crisis of the "rural bachelor," both emblematic of a host of social ills, not the least of which is the widely perceived breakdown of the "traditional family." Singling out male household heads as victims worthy of social attention and equating

---

Outnumber Males 7 to 1." *Digital Chosunilbo.* August 7, 2009. Available at http://english.chosun. com/site/data/html_dir/2009/08/07/2009080700468.html.)

15. Based on a survey commissioned by the Ministry of Health and Welfare in 2005, "Korean husbands state that the most important reason for choosing Vietnamese and Filipino wives is because they deem them to be more submissive, obedient to their parents, and traditional than other nationalities" (HK Lee 2007, 24–25).

16. "Concerns about Migrant Brides Growing." *Digital Chosunilbo.* March 17, 2009. Available at http://english.chosun.com/site/data/html_dir/2009/03/17/2009031761002.html.

17. "Why Do Vietnamese Women Marry Korean Farmers?" *Digital Chosunilbo.* March 27, 2007. Available at http://english.chosun.com/site/data/html_dir/2007/03/27/2007032761029.html.

their plight with the widespread sense of family breakdown,[18] policymakers have legitimated their use of "family welfare," which Lee defines as the practice of assigning to Korean wives as mothers and daughters-in-law "a *state-defined* responsibility to take care of children, the elderly, the disabled, and other dependents" (Lee 2002, 58; emphasis added).

Feminist critiques of state policies and narrative strategies toward migrant wives are an important part of understanding the larger institutional and ideological context in which Chosŏnjok women in Korea have had and continue to operate. However, individual Chosŏnjok women do not submissively or uniformly comply with state strategies that seek to mobilize them as a form of "family welfare." The issue of Chosŏnjok women's agency, whether migrating to South Korea for marriage, work, or a combination of purposes, is a theme interwoven throughout this book. The following ethnographic vignettes begin to consider Chosŏnjok women's role as active decision makers in the matrimonial process, shifting the focus from state-level strategies to individual agents without losing sight of the broader structures of inequality and gendered nationalist ideologies that frame women's experiences.

Living in Perseverance: Yŏnghwa

Yŏnghwa had refused many introductions to local Chosŏnjok bachelors, pinning her hopes instead on a South Korean husband. For years the women in her village had been marrying to South Korea, and she too yearned for the good life that South Korea was rumored to offer. When her father, after forty years of separation, visited his birthplace in South Korea's rural Kyŏngsang Province, he used his kinship connections there to locate for his daughter an eligible farmer bachelor[19] by the name of Chunho. During our interview, Chunho specified the links in the chain of connections that brought him in contact with his wife:

---

18. See Kim and Finch (2002) and Song (2006) for accounts of how the government, civic groups, and media collectively forged links between "family breakdown" and the IMF crisis.

19. I considered following Garrison Keillor who has familiarized American listeners with the term "bachelor farmer" but opted instead to preserve the Korean word order (*nongch'on chonggak*).

I went into business with the head of our village. His friend is my wife's *sach'on oppa* [first cousin, literally "fourth-degree older brother"]. When my wife's father visited Kyŏngsang Province, he gave a picture of my wife to his nephew—my wife's cousin. The cousin then showed the picture to me when he came to our village.

When Chunho saw the photograph of Yŏnghwa, it was 1995, the year many of my Chosŏnjok interviewees noted as the peak of the "marriage boom" (*kyŏrhon ppum*) in northeastern China. The government-funded RWFFV was recruiting rural bachelors for its eighth marriage tour to China. This time the bachelors would be traveling to Shenyang, which happened to be near Yŏnghwa's hometown. Chunho's father gave him money and urged him to go with the tour to meet Yŏnghwa. At thirty-five years old with elderly parents to care for and a family farm to manage, Chunho complained that finding a bride in Korea was "more difficult than plucking stars from the sky," invoking a common yet poignant cliché.

While bringing home a bride from China presented a potential solution to his dilemma, it also conjured up a host of reservations for Chunho: Would he be able to communicate with a Chosŏnjok bride? Would she be too "strong" (*kanghada*) as a result of living under communism, or worse, evil-hearted? Would she run away after getting Korean citizenship? "I was tempted to take my father's money and spend it in a karaoke bar," Chunho recalls. But when two of his friends signed up for the marriage tour, Chunho cast his doubts aside and joined them.

Yŏnghwa's cousin in South Korea phoned Yŏnghwa's family and told them that the man to whom he had showed Yŏnghwa's photograph would be arriving in Shenyang with the marriage tour and advised them to have Yŏnghwa sign up at the Shenyang office as a participant in the arranged meeting. On the day the seven bachelors arrived in China, Yŏnghwa traveled from her parent's home in the countryside to a hotel in Shenyang, where she was joined by thirteen other Chosŏnjok women, to meet the bachelors.

Though she had great difficulty understanding Chunho's dialect, Yŏnghwa says she trusted her cousin who had helped arrange their meeting. Chunho recalled with a chuckle, "I knew in my heart I would choose my wife, but I wanted to chat and have a good time with the other women first." After lunch in a Chosŏnjok restaurant and a trip to a karaoke bar, the men and women were asked to match up if they had identified some-one they liked. While narrating the events as they unfolded the day of their first meeting, Yŏnghwa showed me a photo album containing pictures of her and Chunho singing cheek-to-cheek in the karaoke bar and posing arm-in-arm together in front of historical landmarks. The pictures struck me as conveying a surprising degree of comfort and intimacy for having just met for the first time.

A newspaper reporter who accompanied Director No on the RWFFV's eleventh marriage tour to China emphasized the swiftness of the progres-sion from meeting for the first time to filing the paperwork for interna-tional marriage the next day. The article depicts a Korean man who, after his experience in the karaoke bar, heads back to his hotel room with the conviction that he has found a bride. The next day he immediately be-gins taking the necessary steps to hasten the marriage proceedings. He and his prospective bride huddle into a photo booth on the street to have snap-shots taken for their marriage certificate. Next, he pays an obligatory visit to the woman's family. The reporter refers to these instantaneous couplings as "matches made in heaven" and remarks that "the clasped hands of the couple may not yet be evidence for ethnic homogeneity [*minjok t'ongjil*] but a giant seed has been planted."

The seven couples in Yŏnghwa and Chunho's group had exactly one week to explore their marital compatibility. They spent much of this time as a group, each Chinese-speaking woman guiding her husband-to-be by the hand on a tour of Shenyang's historic and entertainment attractions. At the week's end, six out of the seven men had secured promises to marry, visited the homes of their prospective brides, and begun the lengthy and politically complicated process of applying for a marriage visa.[20]

Looking back after five years of marriage to Chunho, Yŏnghwa says she did not realize there was something lacking about men who go to China to

---

20. At the time of my research, the Korean government set about making the marriage visa application process more costly and complicated to prevent paper marriages. In some cases, cou-ples reported waiting as long as six months to complete the necessary paperwork. In the time be-tween the first meeting in China and the arrival of the bride in South Korea, men and women developed their relationship through letters, usually reserving costly international telephone calls for practical communication regarding the visa application process. In 2002 the government simplified the marriage visa application process as a way of resolving the "family crisis," which reached new heights in the post-IMF era.

find brides. She enumerates the potential detriments: "Either their jobs are unstable or they are too poor, too short, or too ugly. Why else would they go all the way to China to get a bride?" She laughs when she thinks back to how naive she must have been to believe that "Korea was a paradise." Nearly all the farmers' brides I met expressed their disillusionment with the same declaration: "Had I seen where I would be living, I would never have gotten married!" Many confessed to having entertained the notion of running away, at one time or another, in the initial period of adjustment.

Another Chosŏnjok woman recalled her impressions immediately following marriage to a farmer on a tiny island off the southern coast of South Korea:

> When I first came here, I had to take a boat to this island and then a bus and, *ŏmmaya!* How would I ever live in a house like this? I couldn't imagine. When I was in China, I thought that people lived well in Korea. But here's a mud-thatch house; there's a house made of straw. I thought the houses would all have tiled roofs and that everyone lived well here. When I first came, I really hated it here. I must have said twelve times a day: "How can I live in this place?"

Sumin, the Chosŏnjok bride featured in the opening anecdote of this chapter, echoed similar discontent with the hardscrabble conditions she had married into, emphasizing that it took her seven full days from the time she left her home in China to the day she arrived at the doorstep of her husband's modest dwelling. She recalled feelings of expectancy fading to disappointment as she passed all the "nice villages" along the way. "I thought to myself, is it this one? But it wasn't. We kept going and going." In contrast to the expansive vistas and open fields she remembered in China, she described feeling suffocated in her marital village by mountains that pressed "right up against her back," a situation that might have been tolerable, she said, if the house itself was nice.

But what caused her the greatest consternation was the inaccessibility of public transportation and the inability to indulge in the small pleasures she used to take for granted, such as a trip to a market or a theater. Again she measured life in South Korea against China: "Here in the country, there's only a bus every three hours. If you want to go anywhere it takes an entire day. So there's no way to enjoy 'cultural life' here. In China, there are at least five buses a day, so you can go to the market, the movies, and the theater. You can't do anything like that here." "You can watch television!" her husband interjected. Ignoring his comment, Sumin drove home her point: "It's totally empty here." "It's like living in a prison," her Chosŏnjok neighbor affirmed.

Another common complaint among Chosŏnjok brides was that the work regime in South Korea was longer and more physically demanding than what they were accustomed to in China. Sumin lamented, "I thought it would be a dream to live in Korea, that we could just sit back and relax while the machines cut the grain and tilled the land. But after coming, I realized that you have to work even harder here than in China." To make matters worse, Chosŏnjok women often remarked that they had to work twice as hard as their South Korean counterparts in the village to overcome what they perceived to be condescending attitudes toward them. One woman explained how she disliked being introduced as a "Chinese person" (*Chungguk saram*), "because people look at me funny. They think we don't live well [in China]. I hate to hear this so I have to work very hard to compensate. It's very exhausting."

Neither their upbringing nor their expectations had prepared brides like Yŏnghwa and the others for the hard physical labor of running a farm,[21] the cultural imperative to serve her in-laws and husband, the isolation of living beyond the reach of public transportation, or the stigma of being treated as a "foreigner" in her father's homeland. In light of how much she claims to have suffered in the early years of her marriage, Yŏnghwa says she does not advise other Chosŏnjok women to marry to Korea. "If a [Chosŏnjok] woman is well educated and capable, she won't be able to endure [marriage to a Korean], especially if she sees she is not living as well as other people. Only if the man treats her very well will she be able to resist the temptation of running away."[22]

The story of Yŏnghwa highlights the gap between the fantasies that entice Chosŏnjok brides to South Korea and the constraints of their social and economic realties. The rural-bound brides I interviewed were

---

21. Though large numbers of Chosŏnjok brides hailed from rural parts of China, some were spared having to help their families with the farm work while pursuing a high school education.

22. Chunho wanted me to note during our interview that taking in a Chosŏnjok bride was no easy task for the husband either. He said he had worked hard to help his bride adjust to quotidian novelties of life in a foreign country from the food and language to how to farm and do the shopping.

nothing short of shocked to discover that their marriages had destined them to live in remote villages nestled deep in the mountains where they were expected to serve as dutiful wives and daughters-in-law. Profound disillusionment has driven many Chosŏnjok brides to desert their husbands and, in some cases, their young children. Most farmers' wives that I interviewed, however, were accepting of what they viewed as their marital "fates" (*inyŏn*). While many said they felt that they were no better off by marrying to South Korea—the work being too difficult, the standards of living too low, and the expectations of their husbands (and mothers-in-law) too high—they blamed themselves for their naive expectations and focused their energies on the hard physical labor of farming, household chores, and care of their children.

Filial Daughter: Hiju

Although many do, not all Chosŏnjok brides in South Korea suffer from disappointed expectations. Hiju, a slender, attractive twenty-five-year-old who married a Korean construction worker in rural Kyŏngsang South Province, is one example. When I interviewed her in her home, she had been married for three years and was the proud mother of a three-month-old baby. Hiju's account of her marital experiences and, to some extent, those of her Chosŏnjok friend, Oksŏng, who married into a neighboring fishing village the year before Hiju, differ from most of the others I gathered in that both women claimed to be satisfied with their marital circumstances, despite the modest conditions in which they lived. Chiyŏng and I had first interviewed Oksŏng in her home where she lived with her two-year-old son, her husband, and her mother who had come from northeastern China to help her with the childcare. The next morning, Oksŏng took us to Hiju's house where the four of us spent several hours getting acquainted and sharing our different life trajectories and, at my behest, our perspectives on marriage.

Hiju invited us to sit on the floor of a sparsely furnished room that opened onto the courtyard of her house. She closed the sliding paper doors to keep out the glare of the morning sunlight, and we spoke in hushed tones so as not to wake Hiju's infant daughter who was sleeping in a padded recliner on the floor beside her. We chatted awhile, lavishing praise on the slumbering baby and listening as Hiju described the medical complications that had culminated in a premature delivery and a precarious eight-week stay in a distant hospital for her newborn. When the time seemed right, I asked for permission to start my tape recorder and nudged the conversation in the direction of Hiju's marital experiences.

It was common for Chosŏnjok migrants of all types to downplay the degree of economic hardship they faced in China before coming to South Korea. For some, this stemmed from a defensive pride toward their country of origin, intensified by the attitudes of economic condescension they regularly encountered in South Korea. Others, primarily brides who take up residence in the Korean countryside, are simply unimpressed by their new living standards. In explaining her reasons for marrying a Korean man, however, Hiju highlighted the impoverished circumstances of her natal family in China as the primary motivating factor:

> My family was having a difficult time. My father had been working for a number of years in Siberia. The alcohol there is very strong. When my father returned to China, he continued to drink alcohol everyday. One year later he died of alcohol poisoning. After his death, things became very difficult for my family. If I married to Korea, I would be able to help my family. I have a younger sister and we needed money to send her to school. In China, you can't earn more than 5–6,000 yuan a month. If I married to Korea, my mother would be able to come with me and earn more money.

At the age of twenty-one, Hiju actively sought out the services of an international matchmaker. Though she was turned away for being too young, Hiju was not discouraged. The following year she managed to receive introductions to ten Korean men but ended up dismissing all of them as unsuitable marriage partners. "Looking at the choices, in the end I no longer wanted to come [to Korea]" she said. "The men were not normal. They were not very smart. They all had reasons why they couldn't get married. There was something lacking about all of them. But then at the last minute I had one final arranged meeting and I said to myself, 'If this doesn't work out, I'm giving up.' Fortunately, my husband seemed like he was the smartest one of all."

From Hiju's description of how she met her husband, I gathered that, despite her filial intentions of using marriage to help her natal family in China, she adhered to certain standards in choosing a mate. She had, after all, turned down ten potential partners. I was interested to know what criteria she had used to make her selection. I was struck by the simplicity of her response. "The other men I met were not dressed very well compared to my husband. But my husband was dressed immaculately. So I liked him. As for criteria," she pondered, "how can you really know anything about a person just meeting them a couple of times? When people meet each other for the first time, they want to see if they are connected by fate [*inyŏn*]."

Repeatedly, Chosŏnjok brides (and their husbands) spoke of *inyŏn,* an indefinable force that brings people together in marriage, friendship, and other types of partnerships and can be sensed intuitively upon first meeting, as the basis of their decision to marry. While feelings of romantic love might be hoped to be discovered or cultivated later, they play no role in the initial decision-making process in these cross-border marriages. Given the fact that most Chosŏnjok couples who marry locally in China today have the advantage of an extended courtship period prior to marriage in order to explore their marital compatibility, I found it difficult to believe that basing one's marital decision on nothing more than an inkling of *inyŏn* was not an unsettling experience for the brides. But both Hiju and Oksŏng insisted that it was quite expected and not at all frightening to marry a man they hardly knew. "Everyone who comes to Korea marries like that," Hiju stated matter-of-factly. "Usually you would date for a while, get the approval of the parents, etc. But this is an *international* marriage. It can't be helped. You can't keep buying plane tickets. They're too expensive." Though admittedly unaware of the specific challenges they would face in marrying a man they hardly knew in a country they had never been to, Hiju and Oksŏng believed the risks involved were unavoidable in this type of marriage. In choosing to marry into a foreign country, they consciously opted to negotiate whatever obstacles they would encounter.

In the course of my research, I had collected many stories of marriages that ended in disappointment or deception. Yet even when cautionary tales of marriages gone awry travel back to China, potential migrants prefer to ignore them in favor of preserving their fantasies of a better life in South Korea. "There were rumors and bad stories," Hiju admitted, "but I just listened to the good ones. I just heard that there were many women coming to Korea to marry." Oksŏng interrupted, "You were naive." Then, turning to me, she said, "She was twenty-two years old. What does a twenty-two-year-old know about anything? She was coming no matter what with the intention of making money."

Oksŏng, who had married at the age of twenty-six, had given a similar account the day before of being somewhat blindly swept away by the tide of popular desire to travel to Korea. If not motivated by specific monetary goals like Hiju, many of the migrant brides I interviewed were propelled into the marriage market by a vague but nevertheless enticing sense of the wealth and material comfort that could be enjoyed in South Korea. "At the time [1995], absolutely everyone was going to Korea," Oksŏng explained. "So I wanted to see what kind of place Korea was too. I wanted to experience it myself. Everyone else was going, so why couldn't I? I decided I would go through marriage or some other way to see what it was like." Oksŏng's opportunity arose when her friend Yŏnghwa and her newly acquired Korean husband-to-be, Chunho (whose story is recounted above), offered to introduce her to a Korean man—the only man on Chunho's "team" (*t'im*) who had not found a bride.

With just three days remaining before the bachelors would have to return to Korea, Oksŏng agreed to meet him. The couple made an instant decision to marry and hastily completed the paperwork needed to register their marriage on the Chinese side. Though Oksŏng's mother said she regretted sending her youngest daughter to a country where she and Oksŏng's father "could not travel freely," she refrained from interfering and instead organized a last-minute wedding banquet at a restaurant to celebrate her daughter's marriage.[23] Three months later, a marriage visa was issued and Oksŏng flew to Korea to join her husband.

Though they had both been drawn to Korea by dreams of economic advancement, neither Hiju nor Oksŏng reported feelings of disappointment or disillusionment with their material circumstances. To the contrary, both women seemed grateful for even the smallest conveniences that life in Korea afforded them. Pointing to the padded recliner that cradled her sleeping baby, Hiju said, "We can't buy things like this in China." "One

---

23. Most Chosŏnjok families followed this practice of sending their daughters off with a celebratory feast, complete with a table stacked high with traditional Korean wedding cakes, fruit, and other symbols of wealth and fertility. A more formal wedding ceremony was generally held in Korea after the bride arrived. In Oksŏng's case, it was attended by her mother's brother who was working as a migrant laborer in Korea as well as her father's South Korean cousins who lived outside Seoul and whom they had not seen for forty years.

month's salary in China wouldn't buy that," Oksŏng chimed in. "Even if you could buy it with one month's salary, there would be no money left to live on!" Hiju exclaimed. Oksŏng added that it was a relief not to have to heat the house with a wood-burning stove or have to live in a straw-thatch house, as many do in the Chinese countryside.

Perhaps most important, Oksŏng was grateful for the chance to earn a living and make a decent wage. Cultivating oysters—the primary industry aside from fishing in the village—is difficult work. Hiju said that she tried but found she lacked the upper-body strength needed for the job. Oksŏng, who is small but solidly built, took me to the docks to see the machinery she operates to lower and raise large tangles of oyster shells strung together on wire cables. Oksŏng tends to the oysters year round, from the time the seeds are first cultivated and planted in the shells to the time they are lowered into the water in the spring, until they are finally ready to be shelled, processed, and packaged for export to the United States and Japan. Despite the physical demands of the labor and the low level of her wages by Korean standards, Oksŏng feels she is well compensated for her hard work. "In China," she says, "no matter how hard you work, your labor has no value." Even Sumin, who was fond of enumerating the ways life in China surpassed life in South Korea, acknowledged that the possibilities for capital accumulation were infinitely greater in South Korea. "That's what's good about Korea," she said. "You get a salary and can buy a television, a refrigerator, or whatever. In China, a year's salary can't buy these things. Here if two people work, one person's wages can go toward living expenses and the other person's wages can buy these things." Oksŏng's earnings enable her to send a small allowance each month to her brother in China. Her ultimate goal is to save enough money to buy the equipment she and her husband need to raise their own oysters. Hiju put it simply, "Life is better here than in China." Oksŏng agreed.

Even though Oksŏng and Hiju perceived themselves as having "married up," their relationships with their husbands, in-laws, and members of the wider Korean community in which they lived were not completely free from tension. Both reported almost daily arguments with their husbands during the first couple of years of marriage but disagreed when I suggested that the discord might have stemmed from the challenges of bridging the social and economic differences inherent in a cross-border marriage. Instead, they insisted their fights were over trivial matters and that a certain

A Korean mother-in-law sends her granddaughter off to school in rural Kangwŏn Province.

amount of bickering was inevitable in the early stages of any marriage, local or transnational. Hiju explained that her relationship with her husband was strained by her unwillingness to live with and serve her in-laws. Her husband, as the youngest son, lives with his parents not because of filial obligation but because he cannot afford to purchase his own house. Hiju said that over time she has come to accept the constraints of their financial situation and says she is treated well by her in-laws.

Oksŏng also had few complaints about her marriage, saying that her husband used to drink heavily when they first got married but has shown much restraint since the birth of their son, now two years old. "He still drinks and smokes a little bit, but he's not a bad person. He doesn't curse at me or hit me. We live harmoniously [*hwamokhada*]." Oksŏng said this in such a cheerful manner that that I was taken aback by just how low her expectations of marriage seemed. Later in the interview, Oksŏng's mother added further insight into her son-in-law's character:

> Our son-in-law doesn't talk. Even when he drinks, he doesn't talk when he comes home. He just talks to his son. Some people drink and then come home and complain [*chansorihada*] about the food, etc. They make life

unbearable for the wife. But our son-in-law, when he comes home after drinking, he just goes to sleep. This is really good about our son-in-law, so my heart is at ease now and I can return to China with peace of mind [knowing that my daughter is living well with her husband].

When Oksŏng heard the sounds of her husband entering the house that evening at nine o'clock after having put off serving dinner until his arrival, she announced that there would now be an opportunity for me to interview "the baby's father." But true to his mother-in-law's depiction, we only caught a brief glimpse of his red face and disheveled hair as he nodded in greeting before making his way into the bedroom to sleep without eating dinner. "He doesn't talk much," Oksŏng said, clearly a bit disappointed, "and probably wouldn't have made a good interviewee anyway."

Working for a Dream: Minsŏn

I introduce Minsŏn's story because it stands in striking contrast to Yŏnghwa's and Sumin's account of downward mobility and disappointment on the one hand and Hiju's and Oksŏng's understated expectations for married life on the other. Minsŏn was neither disillusioned with her rural surroundings nor complacent about remaining a farmer's wife. She aspired toward something better for herself and her two sons, ages one and six, and she was determined not to rest until she had achieved her goal. Minsŏn's marriage to a farmer from Chejudo, an island off the southernmost coast of South Korea where I was told the women are renowned for their exceptional work ethic, seemed to provide the proper setting for Minsŏn to pursue her ambitions. Her husband, a short, stout, jovial-looking farmer whose suntanned face was complemented by the local garb he was wearing when I first met him—a deep salmon-colored, traditional-style *kamot* or persimmon-wear, so named because its rich, distinctive color comes from a dye made from persimmon skins—wished to clarify the conventional wisdom about Cheju Island and its women. "Chejudo is known for its three abundances: rocks, wind, and women," he said. "Chejudo might have rocks and wind, but it is a myth that there are lots of women here. The women are just more visible because they are always outside working in the fields."

His words struck me at first as the lamentations of a once brideless farmer bachelor. But soon it became apparent that I would have to follow Minsŏn into the fields if I were to get a word in edgewise with her. At my request, Minsŏn outfitted me with a large button-down shirt, a towel to drape over my head for protection from the sun, a pair of work gloves, and a bucket. Our task was to clear a field—about the size of two soccer fields—of rotting potatoes in preparation for the next season's crop of beans. We headed off in separate directions with buckets under our arms, stooped over in silence, only periodically coming together to savor bottles of melting ice before returning to the glare of the afternoon summer sun in an open field.

When we had covered every inch of the field, we headed back to the house, exchanged our buckets for shovels, and set off to shovel garlic, drying out in rows on the pavement, into plastic bins. Minsŏn's husband had been working that afternoon in a nearby fruit orchard. He returned home to eat a quick dinner with the family before he and Minsŏn rushed out the door to make productive use of the final hours before sunset. As the hour grew late, the possibility of conducting a formal interview with the couple seemed very remote.

While I waited for them to return, I sat on the front porch talking with Minsŏn's mother who had been living with Minsŏn for the past year, helping her with the childcare, cooking, and housework. In what appears to be a common arrangement between Chosŏnjok brides and their mothers, Minsŏn paid her mother five million won a year (approximately U.S. $5,000), which the mother in turn remitted to Minsŏn's father in China to cover the costs of caring for the two youngest of the six siblings in her family. A plump, dark-skinned woman, with long, grey hair rolled in coils at the nape of her neck, Minsŏn's mother joked about how the relentless work regime on Chejudo had helped her to lose weight. Originally from a village in Jilin Province, most of her married life had been spent moving from city to city with her husband and six children in order to evade the stiff penalties levied against families in China that exceeded the birth limit. While I imagined the everyday life of an "excess birth guerrilla," as they are called in China for their itinerant tactics of resisting the state's population policies (see Greenhalgh 2003), to be physically and emotionally challenging, Minsŏn's mother maintained that her life in Shenyang, where she had eventually settled with her large family, had been relatively sedentary compared with the demands of her new responsibilities in South Korea. Back home, she told me, she had been "very fat and lazy." "My daughter works from early in the morning until the sky gets black in the evening, every day of the week, only taking a rest when it rains. No one works like this in China. In China everyone stops work at five p.m.," she complained. Yet Minsŏn's mother said she approved of her daughter's marriage, praising Minsŏn's husband for his active involvement in village affairs. "He is well respected in the village. He is number one!" she boasted, holding up her index finger.

That evening, my efforts to cultivate rapport with Minsŏn in the potato field were rewarded when Minsŏn asked her husband for permission to spend the night with me in a nearby guest house. He agreed, and we promptly made a trip to a general store to buy shrimp crackers and a bottle of *makkŏlli* (rice liquor). Nibbling on our midnight snack after repeated rounds of toasting each other with shot glasses of *makkŏlli*, Minsŏn spoke of her dream, as she called it. "My *mengxiang* [dream]," she said, "is to build a large addition to our house. Eventually I will become a housewife and stay at home in our big house and take care of the housework and children. I also hope to have time to pursue my studies."

When I asked what she was interested in studying, I was startled by her answer. "I want to study computers and Chinese," she declared definitively. "Why Chinese?" I probed, curious to know why a fluent speaker of Mandarin would need to study it and of what use it would be to her on Cheju Island. Minsŏn explained that her greatest ambition was to become an interpreter for the large number of Chinese tourists who had recently begun vacationing in Chejudo's tropical climate.[24] These Chinese tourists will need interpreters, she shrewdly calculated. While Minsŏn could speak Chinese, she was less skilled at reading and writing. In order to pass the exam for her interpreter's license, Minsŏn would need to improve her literacy. "But this is just my *mengxiang*," she said modestly. "I will probably never be able to realize it."

Minsŏn aspired to take full advantage of the skills that many Chosŏnjok inherently possess by virtue of their social and geographic positioning

---

24. The influx of Chinese was due to the special "no-visa program" that the South Korean government had extended to Chinese travelers to Chejudo in an attempt to boost tourism, the main industry on the island. Chejudo's tropical climate and unique volcanic topography have also made it the number one destination for honeymooners in South Korea.

between two languages and cultures. While some scholars have focused on the marginalization and disadvantaged positioning of Chosŏnjok subjects with respect to dominant Han and South Korean social processes, I want to draw attention to the way in which Chosŏnjok endeavor to capitalize on their "neither-here-nor-there" status by acting as brokers or middle-men figures, mediating social and economic relations between the two countries. As I argue throughout this book, marriage itself can be seen as an example of this kind of strategic maneuvering across the symbolic and political boundaries between China and South Korea. In Minsŏn's case, as well as that of many other Chosŏnjok brides in similar circumstances, marriage to a Korean man has, on the one hand, enabled her to advance the economic interests of her natal family in China, by employing her mother as the caretaker of her children. On the other hand, the unique situation in Chejudo as a destination for Chinese tourists provides Minsŏn with an opportunity to take further advantage of her betwixt-and-between positioning. As I explore in chapters 2 and 3, more opportunities for this kind of cross-cultural maneuvering exist in urban areas of South Korea where Chosŏnjok brides can utilize their bilingual and bicultural capabilities to pursue careers in the fields of international trade, tourism, entrepreneurship, and international matchmaking.

Given her career ambitions, I was puzzled by Minsŏn's description of her ideal lifestyle as "staying at home in our big house and taking care of the housework." A brief exchange I had earlier in the day with Minsŏn's husband in which he complained about her lack of enthusiasm for housework made this seeming contradiction even more perplexing. When I had a moment alone with Minsŏn's husband, I had asked him, somewhat naively, how marriage to a Chosŏnjok woman differed from marriage to a Korean woman. He responded at first by saying, "How should I know? I never married a Korean woman!" But upon further reflection, he declared, "The biggest difference is that Chinese women are not willing to do housework. In the beginning my wife and I fought nonstop over this. I thought to myself, I would have been better off if I had not married at all. Now things are better, but we have not adjusted completely." When I raised the subject later with Minsŏn in the privacy of our hotel room, she admitted that housework had been a source of contention at first. But she explained, "If I didn't have to work in the fields all day, then I would gladly do the housework. It doesn't make sense [*meiyou daoli*] that I should have to do both, does it?"

Korean gender norms that dictate that a woman should single-handedly manage household affairs, whether this involved housework, relations with husband's kin, or supervision of the children's studies, were deemed unfair and unreasonable by nearly all the Chosŏnjok women I spoke with, in the countryside as well as in the cities. My interview with Kisŏn and Sumin, the reader may recall, was delayed due to a marital dispute they had had shortly before my arrival. After eight years of marriage, Sumin still had frequent arguments with her husband over household chores. "Korean men are all egotists," she fumed. "They expect women to all the housework. We are a double income family [*matbuli*]. I have to go out to earn money every day shucking oysters. So when can I do the housework?" In China, Sumin argued, household labor is not a distinctively female domain but rather subject to practical considerations of skill and time. "If you see something that needs to be done, you do it. That's how they do things there [in China]...Korean men think only about themselves. That's why we fight a lot," she said. Feeling sympathetic toward Kisŏn and the neighbor who did not say a word in their own defense, I nudged Sumin to qualify her dramatic assertions. "Here the men really do *nothing*?" I asked with incredulity. "Absolutely nothing!" the Chosŏnjok neighbor snapped.

Though most Chosŏnjok women I met wished to participate in the paid workforce, they were not necessarily opposed to identifying themselves primarily as the caretakers of their marital families. I interpret Minsŏn's desire to become a "housewife" as a longing to acquire certain freedoms she associates with a middle-class, and perhaps urban, lifestyle: the freedom not to labor in the fields and the freedom to develop the skills necessary to pursue a more lucrative, less labor-intensive career. The attitudes of Chosŏnjok women toward the gendered and spatial division of labor in the family differ in a subtle but important way from some of the Filipina and Chinese women in Nicole Constable's study of correspondence courtship who are motivated to marry middle-class American men by visions of modernity and marriage in which the husband is the sole breadwinner and the wife is his domestic partner, "free" from working outside the home (2003a, 66). Most of the Chosŏnjok women I met recognized the power in working for a wage and were motivated as much by a sense of novelty as financial gain in trying out their earning capacity in a capitalist system. The idea of staying at home and not putting their labor power to good use was as impractical an arrangement as being asked to shoulder the full burden of housework by themselves. As I examine in chapter 3, Chosŏnjok women living in the city did not willingly take up the role of "housewife" when it categorically inhibited them from engaging in outside labor.

Complexities of Agency and Mobility

This chapter has sought to make sense of the South Korean government's role in facilitating marriages between Chosŏnjok women and South Korean farmer bachelors. The South Korean government's neglectful attitude and policies toward the rural sector point to the state's culpability in creating the extreme iniquities that culminated in the bride shortage in the countryside. Critical feminist analyses draw our attention to the state's reluctance to take responsibility for the human costs of rapid economic development and its reliance on the bodies of Chosŏnjok brides, and more recently on brides of different nationalities, to mitigate the crisis in Korean agriculture. Building on the insights of existing feminist scholarship, I have argued that the state elides the more fundamental sources of the farmers' discontent by relying on a foreign supply of women as a form of "family welfare." In promoting a national campaign to find wives for farmers, the state extends its "familialist ideology" (Lee 2002) to Chosŏnjok and other foreign wives who, alongside the South Korean wives of middle-class urbanites, are discursively and politically constructed as responsible for restoring the health, fertility, and productivity of the nation's male citizens in an era of enormous social and demographic upheaval. Narratives that celebrate these marriages in nationalistic metaphors attach additional significance to Chosŏnjok women, representing them as not merely restoring productivity to the countryside but returning "ethnic homogeneity" to the Korean people.

Despite attempts to channel the unwaged (and waged) labor of foreign brides to benefit nation-building goals, I argue that Chosŏnjok women are not simply instruments of the state's familialist policies. The ethnographic examples in this chapter demonstrate that Chosŏnjok brides choose to marry South Korean farmers based on their own personal goals and motivations. Though Chosŏnjok women may feel pressured to find a Korean husband by a range of factors, most notably the impoverished circumstances of their natal families and the desire to be a filial daughter (as seen in the case of Hiju), the marriage decisions of the Chosŏnjok women I met were never coerced. As Minsŏn's story in this chapter begins to suggest and as the vignettes illustrate in increasingly bolder terms over the next several chapters, Chosŏnjok women who marry South Korean men tend in many instances to be a self-selected group of extraordinarily independent, courageous, and strong-willed women with aspirations that defy both the state's attempts to regulate their mobility and the conservative gender ideals of their husbands.

Hiju and Oksŏng are examples of women who view their marriages to South Korean farmers as having advanced their socioeconomic positions. Oksŏng not only notes an improvement in her material living standards but appreciates the opportunity to earn what she perceives to be a decent wage. She does not see her labor, productive or reproductive, as being appropriated by her marital family. Nor does Oksŏng view her labor as commodified by the Korean government. Instead, she sees her labor as justly compensated by a wage, which she uses to help her natal family in China as well as to contribute to the economic well-being of her marital family.

Juxtaposed to Oksŏng and Hiju, Minsŏn's story highlights the subjective nature of social mobility, its openness to the interpretation and imagined possibilities of the people who experience it. One might imagine that economic stability and amenities of life in South Korea are a welcome change from the extreme poverty she experienced growing up in China, as the oldest of six siblings in a family of "excess birth guerrillas." However, Minsŏn, along with Yŏnghwa, Sumin, and other Chosŏnjok wives living in rural settings, experience profound dissatisfaction with their living standards, with the rigors and long hours of farm labor, and with the rigid gendered assignment of household labor. But Minsŏn's story does not end with a declaration of downward mobility. Her spirits buoyed by the potential earning power conferred by her betwixt-and-between positioning as a Chinese-speaking Chosŏnjok living on Cheju Island, Minsŏn intends to muster all the resources at her disposal to change the course of her own and her marital family's fate.

At the same time, it is hard to deny that in many ways, while the brides featured here do not identify themselves as performing the work of the state nor as helpless or oppressed in any way, they do, in many ways, fulfill the states' expectations for them. Whether they willingly devote themselves to the role of wife and mother as in the case of Hiju and Oksŏng, whether they chafe at the forms of gender subordination they encounter like Yŏnghwa and Sumin, or whether they aspire to achieve in the realm beyond the domestic like Minsŏn, all of them are actively rearing children, laboring alongside their husbands, serving their in-laws, and charting their futures (at least for the time being) within the confines of the patriarchal extended family. They are what the South Korea government would consider and reward as "model migrant brides."

How can we reconcile the view of Chosŏnjok brides as strong and determined women who *choose* to pursue cross-border relationships and negotiate the risks involved with the view of them as domesticated and dominated within the rural patriarchal household? We might ask: in "bringing the sound of crying babies back to the countryside," healing rural bachelors of their faltering masculinity, and propping up the waning patriarchal social order, do migrant brides operate as subjects or objects of power? The productive and reproductive positions that rural Chosŏnjok brides assume within their families are unavoidably ambivalent and complicated. Abelmann offers a flexible reading of the apparent ambiguities of gender and power in South Korea based on her analysis of three Golden Age melodramas: "[women] are…posed to operate both as masculinized enablers of male refuge…and simultaneously as feminized cultural workers in the reproduction of patriarchy" (2003, 202).[25] The following chapters continue to explore the complexities of women's agency and examine what happens when the actions of Chosŏnjok brides appear to threaten, rather than uphold, the stability of the patriarchal household.

---

25. I am grateful to an anonymous reviewer for directing my attention to Abelmann's words and for suggesting a more nuanced reading of the workings of gender and power.

2

BRIDES AND BROKERS UNDER SUSPICION

I first made the acquaintance of Mr. Na, director of the Research Association for the Welfare of Korean Farm and Fishing Villages, during an interview in his office in the fall of 1998. A series of identical-looking photographs hung on the wall next to his desk. In each of them, a long row of serious South Korean men in black suits stood behind their Chosŏnjok brides who wore equally grave expressions and were uniformly clad in wedding white. These photographs commemorated the chain of mass wedding ceremonies Mr. Na's office had helped bring to fruition. Displayed in such a collection, they suggested the sense of accomplishment Director Na, and Director No who preceded him, must have felt in helping initiate so many farmer bachelors into full social personhood as married men. Over the years, Mr. Na has sought to publicize the successes of the government-funded matchmaking program, writing numerous editorials and speaking publicly about the benefits Chosŏnjok brides bring to South Korea's farmers and to the nation as a whole.

Yet during our first of what was to be a series of periodic meetings, Mr. Na expressed profound cynicism about the future outlook for his matchmaking efforts in China. Disheartened by the daily onslaught of telephone calls from farmers whose Chosŏnjok wives had reportedly deserted them, Mr. Na spoke of his increasing reluctance to send farmers to China, vowing to look elsewhere for solutions to the rural bride shortage problem. (High on his list was North Korea.) While he readily put me in contact with farming couples he deemed to be "living well" (*chalsanŭn saram*) in far-flung places scattered throughout the peninsula, he cautioned me, "If you want to report the whole truth, you need to address the issue of fraudulent marriages [*wijang kyŏrhon*]—the women who come here to make money and take advantage of innocent farmer bachelors."

Mr. Na's loss of enthusiasm for Chosŏnjok brides, I quickly discovered, was indicative of a widespread about-face in the public's attitude toward Chosŏnjok brides in particular and, as I explore, Chosŏnjok migrants in general. In countless casual conversations with South Koreans of all walks of life that I chanced to meet in the course of my fieldwork, I was repeatedly told that the bottom line with respect to Chosŏnjok women's motivations is "money, money" (*ton, ton*), often said twice for dramatic effect while curling thumb and forefinger into a coin-shaped symbol. Kang Chansuk, the South Korean woman we met in the previous chapter who volunteers her time helping Chosŏnjok migrants, challenged me to introduce her to one harmoniously united couple from my pool of interviewees, stating that she would have to see the man and woman with her own eyes in order to believe that a well-matched pair existed. Echoing a similarly pessimistic view, a South Korean immigration official, who spoke with me in a coffee shop in exchange for the opportunity to practice his English conversation skills, estimated that between seventy and ninety percent of all marriages to Chosŏnjok women were fraudulent (*wijang*). With a hint of weariness in his voice, he explained: "Everyday Korean men come to my office asking for my help in finding their wives who have run away." Then he added a commonly heard refrain. "These wives run away and take all of the men's money with them."

The public disillusionment with Chosŏnjok brides in South Korea, like the nationalistic embrace with which they were initially received, to a large extent has been shaped by the mass media, which has popularized the familiar image of the "runaway bride" who abandons her Korean husband after obtaining citizenship. The prototypical story of a so-called illegitimate marriage (*wijang kyŏrhon*), which has appeared over and over again in various permutations in print and television media throughout South Korea, features an ingenuous South Korean man (*sunbakhan*), often a farmer bachelor, who invests a small fortune in matchmaking fees, travel to China, and betrothal gifts in order to bring home a bride who then disappears without a trace immediately after receiving her residence permit. If the farmer bachelor had been a tragic figure in the popular imagination, the broken-hearted farmer deserted by his Chosŏnjok bride struck an even more poignant chord in the hearts of most Koreans. Indeed, the public perception when I arrived in Korea in the fall of 1998 was that the overwhelming majority of these marriages were "illegitimate" (*wijang kyŏrhon*)—in the sense that they were believed to have been founded on the bride's desire for Korean citizenship rather than a sincere conjugal commitment.

Alongside the "runaway bride," the legion of matchmaking bureaus and unlicensed brokers, which appeared in the mid-1990s, also aroused public suspicion. One licensed matchmaker I spoke with in South Korea in 1998 estimated that there were over thirty such agencies involved in the business of arranging marriages with Chinese Chosŏnjok brides in Seoul alone. A matchmaker I interviewed in China offered a slightly higher number for Seoul that same year, venturing that there were approximately forty bureaus in Seoul that ran marriage tours to China, another forty in the southern port city of Pusan, and six agencies in Yanji, the capital of the Korean Autonomous Prefecture in the PRC. Today there are over 1,250 officially registered international marriage agencies operating in South Korea and an unknown number of unregistered brokers. They are involved in brokering as many as one-third of all rural marriages in South Korea.

Unlike the government-sponsored matchmaking programs that were founded upon and guided by the specific goal of placing "Chosŏnjok maidens" (*chosŏnjok chŏnyŏ*) in the homes of "farmer bachelors" without any designs of profit making, commercial matchmakers charged steep fees for their services. Among the small sample of licensed matchmakers that I interviewed, most reported charging between five and six million won, or approximately U.S. $4,200–$5,000 for a five-day marriage tour to China, half or more of which was taken home as profit by the matchmaker. The remainder was used to cover the brokerage fee for the Chinese matchmaker (generally 500,000 won), the costs of filing for an international marriage, round-trip airfare to China, and room and board in a Chinese hotel. As Mr. Na of the Research Association for the Welfare of Korean Farm and Fishing Villages noted, there were additional expenses above and beyond the matchmaking fee which were commonly deemed to be the responsibility of the groom, including: gifts to the bride's parents; the costs of transporting the bride, accompanied in many cases by her parents, to South Korea; an engagement banquet in China; and a wedding ceremony in South Korea. When all these expenses were taken into account, the total cost of procuring a bride from China could easily amount to roughly ten million won.

The proliferation of money-making matchmakers in South Korea with connections to China enabled farmers and nonfarmers alike from extreme ends of the class spectrum, including men who were widowed or divorced, to bring home a bride from China. Rather than targeting farmer bachelors exclusively, these agencies and brokers extended their services to anyone who could afford them. This is not to imply that they were entirely undiscriminating when it came to recruiting clients. Most required a South Korean man seeking a Chosŏnjok bride to meet the minimal criteria of being steadily employed and able to furnish housing. One licensed matchmaker reported that she required both the bride and the groom to have completed a high school education. This was unusual, however. The matchmakers I spoke with seemed concerned that grooms have a reliable source of income above all else.

The proprietors in the matchmaking bureaus I visited all noted that while the overwhelming majority of their male clients seeking brides from China were of humble origins, either living in the bride-depleted countryside or eking out a living in the city as manual or technical laborers, a small percentage were white-collar professionals with college degrees. One matchmaker ventured that "one hundred percent" of these upper-crust candidates were either widowers or divorcees in search of *sunjonghanŭn yŏja* (obedient women). Another matchmaker observed that educated businessmen might be interested in Chosŏnjok brides to help them negotiate the ins and outs of doing business in China.

Matchmakers working on the Chinese side (or shuttling across national borders) also culled Chosŏnjok brides from a diverse population that defied generalization, from the residents of remote villages to those living in urban centers, from middle-school to college graduates, from never-been-married young women to middle-aged divorcees and widows. The money that changed hands opened matchmakers up to charges of profiteering, and the expansion of these marriages beyond the confines of the country-side was accompanied by a pervasive sense of unease among South Korean residents.

This chapter is concerned with making sense of the rising public critique that enveloped Chosŏnjok–South Korean marriages at the turn of the millennium, casting doubt on the morality of the marriage facilitators, the Chosŏnjok brides, and, on occasion, the South Korean grooms. My aim is to provide a spectrum of personal narratives from each of these three perspectives, adding depth and complexity to a cast of characters who might otherwise be viewed as stock villains: the avaricious matchmaker, the bluntly opportunistic Chosŏnjok bride, and the deceitful husband. The second part of this chapter leads us to a more general consideration of the contradictions at the core of South Koreans' attitude of mistrust toward the Chosŏnjok migrants in their midst, namely, the tensions between territorial nationalism and de-territorialized ideals of ethnic solidarity.

I turn first to the matchmakers, both amateur and professional, licensed and unlicensed, who have acted as a conduit for expanding the demographic origins and marital destinations of Chosŏnjok brides in South Korea. Drawing on my discussions with matchmakers of various backgrounds, qualifications, and motivations, I hope to evoke a sense of the range of services they offer, the procedures they employ, the challenges they face, and the factors propelling their involvement in the business of cross-border marriages. It is my hope that the matchmakers' personal reflections on their trade will problematize the widespread view in South Korea that morality unequivocally and universally takes a backseat to money making in the business of international marriage brokering.

Commercial Matchmaking Bureaus

Despite their wider range of clientele and their profit-driven ambitions, commercial matchmaking bureaus that offer marriage tours to China appear to operate in much the same way as the government-funded matchmaking programs. The groom is first presented with an array of photographs of eligible Chosŏnjok women and asked to select five or six that he is most interested in meeting. Unlike the glossy, commodified images of women that are used to market Asian brides to Western male consumers through "mail order bride" catalogs and websites, the snapshots of Chosŏnjok women in the matchmaking bureaus I visited had a distinctly noncommercialized quality, displayed between the pages of ordinary family photo albums. In one bureau I visited in Seoul, the backs of the pictures were marked with a list of biographical data intended to aid the man in his selection. Height was listed first, widely regarded in Korean as well as Chinese society as an important criterion to consider, for both men and women, in the selection of a spouse. (Beneath the woman's height, there appeared the woman's name, followed by her birth date, education level [*munhwa chŏngdo,* literally cultural level], number of members in her family, age, and occupation.) The practice of exchanging pictures and the priority given to height suggests the importance placed on attributes of physical appearance when choosing a spouse at the initial stage of transnational matchmaking. A Chosŏnjok marriage broker I chanced to meet on a train described a hierarchy of marital destinations for Chosŏnjok women based on physical beauty. Of the Chosŏnjok women marrying out of the northeastern region, he explained, "the prettiest go to Korea, the second prettiest marry to Beijing, and the ugliest stay [in northeastern China]."

When a requisite number of Korean men present themselves to the matchmaker—most licensed matchmakers I spoke with said they required a minimum of six men to make the trip profitable—the matchmaker personally escorts the group to northeastern China. There, in coordination with a matchmaker on the Chinese side, the Korean matchmaker orchestrates face-to-face meetings between the Korean men and the Chosŏnjok women whose photographs have been previously selected. As in the case of the government-supported marriage tours to China, there is pressure for the grooms to choose their mates as quickly as possible, since in the course of one week there are many tasks to accomplish. The men spend the first day or two meeting the candidates, deciding upon a partner, and participating in a series of organized activities intended to offer an abbreviated experience of group "dating," as one matchmaker called it. Next on the agenda is a visit to the woman's parents to ask for their consent and discuss the matter of gift exchange. Before the groom's departure, a banquet is customarily held in honor of the couple's engagement, which is often paid for out of the betrothal money the groom gives the bride's parents.

The groom then returns to South Korea to file the paperwork for an international marriage. In the meantime, the comparatively greater challenge of registering the marriage falls to the bride who must expend an extraordinary amount of time, energy, and expense to ferry documents of all sorts for official notarization at each level of the Chinese bureaucracy, from the local government agency to the distant Korean embassy in Beijing. The opening of the Korean consulate in the city of Shenyang later shortened the final pilgrimage in the visa application process, but the political gauntlet involved was no less complicated. As it was described to me by the matchmakers I interviewed on the Chinese side, the Chosŏnjok bride must first obtain permission to marry at the local level before proceeding to the city government and the Korean embassy or consulate in China. The groom must then submit the documents to the Chinese embassy in Seoul before making a second trip to China to obtain an official marriage certificate (*kyŏrhon pojŭng*) from the Korean embassy there. The process by most accounts took roughly eight months to complete.

Of the five matchmaking bureaus I visited,[1] all except one were located in well-furnished high-rise offices that appeared at first glance no different from any other type of professional consulting firm. The exception was a dark, dingy crawl space under a stairwell that one entered by ducking through a door that looked too small to lead to anything other than a closet. The sixty-seven-year-old man who sat behind the desk inside this dank and unadorned space was a retired construction worker who was looking for an alternative to manual labor and claimed that arranging marriages was something he had "wanted to do for a long time." New to the matchmaking business, he was in the midst of arranging his first marriage between a Korean man and Chosŏnjok woman he had located through the assistance of a matchmaking bureau in Heilongjiang Province. The matchmaker showed the Korean man a photograph of his prospective bride, collected five million won, and sent the man on a solitary mission to Mudanjiang in Heilongjiang Province to meet his bride-to-be.

---

1. I visited two matchmaking bureaus in Seoul, two in Ch'ŏngju (the provincial capital of Ch'ungch'ŏng North Province), and one in Yŏngju in North Kyŏngsang Province.

For the most part, however, the professional matchmakers I encountered in South Korea[2] were relatively experienced in leading group "marriage tours" to China. One matchmaker, who introduced himself as the "Chairman of the Korean Association of Matchmakers," boasted twenty years' experience in the business of arranging marriages, starting out as a domestic matchmaker before expanding the scope of his operations to include international marriages. In addition to supplying local men with Chosŏnjok brides, "the Chairman" also satisfied a growing demand among Japanese men and overseas Korean men, particularly in the United States, for South Korean brides. Another matchmaker I interviewed, Mr. Pak, advertised his practice as catering specifically to "Chinese compatriot marriages" (*Chungguk kyop'o kyŏrhon*). Having married a Chosŏnjok himself in the early 1990s, Mr. Pak has capitalized on his wife's Chinese language skills and social networks in China to develop his own specialized niche in the international matchmaking business. In the first year alone, he claimed to have arranged forty marriages between Chosŏnjok women and South Korean men.

The Ubiquitous Broker

Working alongside and sometimes in direct coordination with commercial matchmaking bureaus in Korea, a multitude of unlicensed, itinerant matchmakers engage in a culturally legitimate but unlawful form of arranging marriages for pay.[3] Matchmaking as a paid profession (*maep'a*) has a long history in South Korea, going back to the "itinerant female peddlers" of the preindustrial past (see Kendall 1996). The unlicensed "broker" in this study, whose existence was a direct product of the newly

---

2. As noted in the introduction, I located matchmaking bureaus through advertisements in the phone book for "international marriage bureaus" (*kukche kyŏrhon sangdamso*) and requested interviews by phone.

3. While the Korean government began licensing matchmaking bureaus in 1973 (Kendall 1996, 143), unlicensed matchmakers were not officially banned under the Family Ritual Code until 1980 (133 fn10). The major crackdown against unlicensed professionals that ensued targeted the practices of each matchmaker who "for an extortionate fee and sometimes with the threat of blackmail, schemes the matches of the rich and powerful" (133). The unlicensed marriage brokers in my study, by contrast, typically arrange transnational marriages for the poorest sectors of society.

emerging opportunities for travel and trade between China and South Korea, is probably most comparable to the underground traveling cotton merchants (*miyongbae changsa*) of the Japanese colonial period (1910–45). These petty traders arranged marriages between the daughters of poor farming families in South Chŏlla Province and the sons of wealthier families in Kyongki Province while peddling cotton along the same trade route (see Yoon 1989, 95). Today Chosŏnjok merchants of various kinds, including the employees of large and small trading companies, independent entrepreneurs, and itinerant peddlers (*pottali changsa*), travel back and forth between China and South Korea by boat or by plane, all of whom are strategically positioned to act as go-betweens in the marriages of Chosŏnjok women and South Korean men.

The merchant-cum-matchmaker figure, however, accounts for only one variety in a vast range of individuals who do matchmaking "on the side" while moving back and forth between South Korea and northeastern China. To distinguish the licensed from the unlicensed professional, South Koreans commonly invoke the English-derived term "broker" (*pŭrokkŏ*) to refer to anyone who arranges marriages between Chosŏnjok women and Korean men for money without an official license to do so. My sense is that the term "broker" implies some degree of expertise, while also carrying with it a slightly shady connotation. The term "broker" (comparable to the English term "snakehead") is also widely used in northeastern China to refer to Chosŏnjok who offer a full range of services to help prospective migrants of all types enter South Korea, including the forging of fictive identities and paper marriages (see chapter 4). The licensed matchmaker I call "the Chairman" described the marriage broker as a crook who arranges fraudulent marriages and charges exorbitant fees. "In essence," he said, "these people are making money by helping Chosŏnjok women cheat Korean men."

Brokers have honed their matchmaking skills, connections, and knowledge of how to comply with—and often how to circumvent—the ever-changing immigration laws that selectively admit Chosŏnjok migrants to South Korea. However, the overwhelming majority of unlicensed matchmakers are amateurs whose matchmaking ambitions are relatively modest, sporadic, and unpracticed. Chosŏnjok migrants who come to South Korea as workers or brides, or simply to visit relatives, may broker marriages on a casual basis, particularly when relatives or acquaintances in

China call upon them to use their overseas connections to scout out good groom material (*silanggam*).

Mrs. Ko, a retired government official from Jilin City who was sent to Korea on a one-year business visa as a representative of the Chinese trading company she works for, was drawn into the business of matchmaking out of a combination of economic opportunism and personal obligation. "I travel back and forth [between China and South Korea] for my work, so it occurred to me to make some money [arranging marriages] on the side," she explained. The main stimulus for her fledgling matchmaking operation, however, was the more than twenty requests she received from people she knew in her hometown, most of them "friends of friends," to supply them with South Korean husbands. Overwhelmed by the demand and lacking the extensive connections needed for matchmaking on the South Korean side, Mrs. Ko enlisted the assistance of a licensed matchmaker in South Korea to recommend suitable spouses for her long list of female candidates back home in China.

Chosŏnjok brides who marry to South Korea are similarly perceived as occupying a privileged position from which to match Chosŏnjok women from their hometowns with South Korean men in their marital villages. Once a Chosŏnjok bride joins her husband in South Korea, she might encounter a second round of requests from neighbors and in-laws, who, inspired by the bride's good example, decide that they too would like a daughter-in-law from China. One transnationally married couple I interviewed in a small town in South Korea related how the owner of a nearby matchmaking bureau had knocked on their door to solicit their help in finding Chosŏnjok brides for his South Korean clients. Indeed, all Chosŏnjok brides in South Korea are looked upon by people in their natal as well as affinal communities as potential marriage brokers.

Chosŏnjok brides who dabble in matchmaking do not always expect money for their efforts. One bride I interviewed claimed that she regularly took four farmer bachelors with her each time she visited her natal village, with the expectation of no reward beyond the gratification she felt in "helping the poor farmers" find brides. More commonly, however, an "introduction fee" (*sogaebi*) is not only customary but a potential source of conflict. Hiju, whose story I presented in chapter 1, recounted how a neighbor's failure to pay the full introduction fee resulted in a dispute. "She only paid 300,000 won," Hiju explained, implying that a larger sum had been expected. "My mother-in-law became very angry. They argued, and now my mother-in-law is still not on good terms with the *halmŏni* [grandmother] next door." In Hiju's opinion, the neighbor's unwillingness to pay the finder's fee stemmed from her dissatisfaction with the bride. Hiju explained, "She thinks that she got an idiot [*pabo*] for a daughter-in-law when she had asked for a brilliant wife like me." Concerned perhaps that I might misinterpret her facetious remark, Hiju continued in a more empathetic vein to explain the challenges the bride faced in adapting to her marital circumstances: "She grew up in a Han Chinese neighborhood, so she can't speak Korean well or understand very well. And she stammers when she speaks. She's suffering a lot too. Her mother-in-law does not treat her very well. Every day she yells at her."

The matchmaker risks his or her reputation when one or another of the parties is dissatisfied with the match, particularly when the exchange of money is involved. Mrs. Ko emphasized the difficulties of balancing her desire for material compensation with the need to preserve her ongoing social relationships with her clients in China. Since she was arranging marriages for people who are linked to her by some degree of acquaintance, Mrs. Ko felt she had to be "extremely careful" when recommending a match. As Mrs. Ko explained, people would view her as "greedy and opportunistic" if she were to arrange marriages with no regard as to how they would work out. "How would it look if I pocketed the money and the marriage ended in failure?"

Mrs. Ko's cautious attitude led her to reject all the potential candidates she had met thus far in South Korea, except one. "Recently, I met a man who seems like he has potential," she said and described a thirty-three-year-old elevator repairman who, although short (at 150 centimeters tall, he was considered disappointingly short) made 700,000 won a month. After making a home visit to verify the man's standard of living, Mrs. Ko decided to overlook his small stature and take the man with her to China at the end of the month when she had planned to return home for the Lunar New Year. When I asked her how much she charges as an introduction fee, Mrs. Ko responded that the going rate (among unlicensed brokers) was three million won to take a man to China for a period of three to seven days. "Originally I thought I could make a little bit of money on the side, but it turns out I am operating at a loss," lamented Mrs. Ko with apparent sincerity. Obligation to find good husbands for her friends in China has prompted her to discount her services. In the case of the elevator repairman, Mrs. Ko intended to charge a "mere" 900,000 won, a relative bargain when compared to the price of a marriage tour arranged by a licensed professional.

Mrs. Yi, another unlicensed matchmaker, also emphasized the hassles she faced in leading marriage tours to China. She spoke of the stresses involved in maintaining good relationships with her clients while mediating logistically complicated cross-border marriages. As a native of South Korea, Mrs. Yi fell under the scrutiny of the groom's side of the family. "Psychologically speaking, I have many troubles [*chŏngsin chŏkŭro kosaeng manda*]," she said. Mrs. Yi complained that in the long interim period between arranging a match with a Chosŏnjok bride and completing the necessary paperwork to bring her to South Korea, she receives a flood of phone calls from parents of the grooms who are impatient to receive their daughters-in-law and concerned that Mrs. Yi may have absconded with their money. Though Mrs. Yi charges a steep five million won for joining one of her marriage tours to Liaoning Province, she downplayed the profits she has almost certainly derived in the course of seven years of brokering. Instead she emphasized the humanitarian aspects of her profession, stating that "our men are helping the poor Chosŏnjok women and their families." "The women are like daughters to me," she effused. "I like to see them happily married. But my work is difficult. I have to go to China myself, back and forth with the men. So, there's really no profit in this for me. It's more like volunteer work [*pongsa*]."

Choosing a Matchmaker

Given the range of different matchmaking services available to those in the market for a transnational relationship, how does one decide whether to go to a commercial marriage bureau, an unlicensed broker, or a transnationally connected neighbor or family member for assistance? As in the case of "matchmade" marriages (*chungmae kyorhŏn*)[4] in South Korea in general,

---

4. Marriages arranged through the assistance of a matchmaker are distinguished from so-called love marriages (*yŏnae kyŏrhon*) in which the couple weds without the aid of someone from

a well-intentioned neighbor or family member is often considered a more reliable matchmaker than a professional, whose pursuit of profit casts him or her in a suspicious light. Kendall enumerates the perceived advantages of the amateur in South Korea:

> An intimate acquaintance can represent the circumstances of both families fairly and accurately, and she understands the personalities of the man and woman whom she suggests as life partners.... And because the relationship with an amateur matchmaker preceded and will continue after the match-making...the amateur is trusted over the professional who works for cold cash. (1996, 141–42)

Even when a professional (licensed or unlicensed) is hired, family members are called upon whenever possible to help at various stages of the matchmaking process. Chosŏnjok brides in particular felt that having a close friend or relative involved in the marital negotiations was beneficial since he or she could vouch for the reliability of the groom. The brides I spoke with resented the one-sided immigration laws that enabled South Korean grooms to visit the homes of their prospective brides in China while denying Chosŏnjok women a reciprocal opportunity to view the conditions in which they would live out the consequences of their marital decisions. A member of the bride's family, either a South Korean relative or a Chosŏnjok relative sojourning in South Korea, might be called upon to investigate the circumstances of the groom. One man recounted how, before he had even laid eyes upon his Chosŏnjok wife, the bride's parents, who were working illegally in South Korea at the time, stayed at his house for three days to assess his marriage potential for their daughter. It was only after he passed muster with his future parents-in-law that he scheduled a flight to meet his prospective bride in China.

Though many women I spoke with felt more confident using an intimate acquaintance as a go-between, others, both men and women, recognized certain advantages in hiring a professional marriage bureau. As one

---

the parent's generation, whether a professional matchmaker or relative or friend of the parents. See Lett 1998 (189–91) for a discussion of the different practices and social valuations with respect to love versus matchmade marriages.

Chosŏnjok bride married to a farmer put it, "You run the risk of being cheated if you use an unlicensed broker. Marriage bureaus assume professional responsibility. It's much safer that way even though it costs more money." Mr. Pak, the owner of one of the commercial marriage bureaus specializing in China marriage tours described above, distinguished himself from the unaffiliated or "individual" broker [*kaein*] who he claims is not held accountable for the consequences of the match. "Most of the fraudulent marriages are arranged by individuals [*kaein*]," he said. "They do not take responsibility for the welfare of the couple.... At our marriage bureau we take one hundred percent responsibility. We guarantee the satisfaction of the bride and groom." Mr. Pak stated frankly that about half of the marriages he arranges "work out well" (do not end in divorce), implying that this was a respectable track record. "If the couple has trouble adjusting, we offer counseling. If that fails, I help them get a divorce. If the marriage turns out to be fraudulent [meaning that the bride has married for a Korean passport], we will refund the groom's money."

Mr. Pak offered several examples of his conflict resolution skills, including one in which he arranged for a groom to "trade in" one Chosŏnjok bride for another:

> There is one case in which the woman wanted to work, but the husband refused, so they ended up getting a divorce. The woman was a teacher, and she had married a farmer. The man came back here to the marriage bureau and asked me to find him a woman who could work with him in the fields. I matched him with a heavy-set woman who had grown up in the countryside. She had never left the countryside, had never even been to Jilin City. This woman could carry many sacks of rice on her shoulder. She was a more suitable match for the farmer.

Compared with the other licensed matchmakers I spoke with, Mr. Pak was willing to go to unusual lengths to orchestrate a satisfactory outcome for his customers. Most offered neither counseling services nor exchanges for mismatched couples. They all insisted, however, that in choosing a matchmaking bureau over an unlicensed broker, a man could avoid the perils of a fraudulent marriage, the widespread fear of which had severely tainted the public perception of marriages to Chosŏnjok women in South Korea by the time I arrived in 1998 to begin my fieldwork.

Runaway Brides

Tales of runaway Chosŏnjok brides abounded in the media and circulated through channels of gossip, yet I had a difficult time finding even a single South Korean man who was willing to put aside the stigma of his wife's desertion and relate his personal drama to a foreign observer—that is, until Chansuk persuaded four forlorn men from among the congregants of her Christian church in Seoul to come forward with their testimonies as data for my research. The men claimed to have suffered irreparable emotional damage and financial ruin when their Chosŏnjok wives unexpectedly deserted them, leaving behind, in three out of the four cases, a young child. Two of the men surprised me with their eagerness to talk. Chansuk coaxed the other two with misleading assurances that my research would aid the South Korean government in its crackdown on "illegitimate marriages." One of the more talkative men, Yunsik, agreed and pointed to the then-new nationality law of 1998, which had extended the waiting period for a foreign bride's naturalization from six months to two years, as an example of the type of protective legislation that could be passed if South Korean men were more willing to speak publicly about their exploitation at the hands of Chosŏnjok brides. After attending the morning church service and eating lunch with the predominantly Chosŏnjok congregation,[5] I followed Chansuk into a small room off the kitchen, which I was told served as the sleeping quarters for female Chosŏnjok church members until they got their feet on the ground in Seoul. The four South Korean husbands were waiting for me there, seated on the floor around a square table. The church minister and a twenty-one-year-old Han Chinese migrant worker who received room and board at the church were also in attendance, drawn by curiosity to hear the four men's stories of abandonment and betrayal. Each man spoke more or less in turn about the sequence of events leading up to the dissolution of his marriage, with Chansuk intervening at points to chide the men for not having listened to her cautionary advice. I

---

5. According to Chansuk, the church minister made regular trips to the airport and the port of Inchon to survey the arriving passengers. If he spotted someone who looked as if he or she had arrived from China, he would offer a flier promising a free meal, a place to sleep, and assistance of any kind. Most of the church congregants, the majority of whom are Chosŏnjok, were recruited in this manner.

relied on my tape recorder, stationed in the center of the table, to capture the intricacies of their narratives and on the other listeners to help steer the conversation. Mansu, a forty-three-year-old construction worker whose five-year-old son was roaming the perimeter of the room, volunteered to go first with details of how his eight-year marriage to the boy's mother had ended one year ago with her flight to Japan.

Mansu repeatedly described his wife's departure to Japan as a sudden and unexpected development after eight good years of marriage. Yet, in reconstructing the events leading up to his wife's desertion, he mentioned two prior occasions on which his wife had furtively withdrawn money from his bank account and disappeared to China for months at a time. After the second incident, he reported his wife to the South Korean authorities and asked that her residence permit be revoked, wielding the ultimate weapon in a Korean man's arsenal to punish or persuade an errant foreign bride. When his wife phoned to ask him to return her residence permit, Mansu implored her to come home: "I told her I would forgive her if she came back. I told her I knew that living in her in-laws' home caused her great hardship. I still think she's a good person at heart." Of the four men, Mansu had the most forgiving attitude toward his wife, noting with genuine empathy the double kinship burden she bore as the eldest daughter in her natal family in China and the wife of an eldest son in South Korea.

Chansuk cautioned him not to "make excuses" for his wife's behavior. "Chosŏnjok women are just *like* that," one of the other Korean husbands commented, suggesting the futility of seeking rational explanations for the collapse of his marriage beyond the intrinsic untrustworthiness of Chosŏnjok women. Mansu countered that he had thoroughly investigated his wife's family background while living in his wife's hometown for a full year immediately following their marriage. He claimed to have chosen his wife from among one hundred prospective Chosŏnjok brides based on careful, firsthand observations of his wife's "attitude, actions, and upbringing." His first marriage to a Korean woman had ended in divorce and, as Mansu explained, he was determined "to do it right" the second time around.

Struggling for a way to reconcile his belief in his wife's basic goodness with the reality of his abandonment, he pointed to various external factors beyond his wife's control. "She was really trying to live sincerely, but then she got a job at an insurance company and started socializing with other Chosŏnjok, and that's when the problems began," he reasoned at one point, echoing common fears among South Korean husbands that contact with less marriage-minded Chosŏnjok migrants could lead their otherwise devoted wives down the path to desertion. At another point in the interview, Mansu unwittingly contradicted this theory by pointing to the role of blood type in shaping his wife's aberrant behavior: "She has type O blood. She does what she wants to do and doesn't listen to anyone. Not even her parents." At another point, he mentioned family discord, particularly the animosity that festered between his wife and the wife of his younger brother, as a determining factor. The national economic downturn, widely linked in the popular imagination to discourses of family breakdown (see Kim and Finch 2002), also surfaced in his ruminations: "Maybe if there had been no IMF [referring to the IMF bailout during the 1997 Asian financial crisis], she wouldn't have left. I did not make money after IMF, and things were rough. Maybe that's why this kind of thing happened." His thoughts emerged, not as an orderly analysis of the complex range of factors that can potentially come to bear on the success or failure of an international marriage but rather as a frenzied attempt at each turn in the narrative to rescue his wife and his marriage from charges of fraudulence.

Mansu also sought to absolve himself of any wrongdoing in the dissolution of his marriage. His only shortcoming, as he saw it, was that he had been excessively dutiful as a husband and son-in-law:

> I earned money diligently. I never had an affair. I was devoted to my family.... What I did wrong maybe was that I got up at 4 a.m. and came home at 8 p.m., earned money, and gave it to my wife. That's all I did. I earned 4,000,000 won each month at my construction job, took money out for cigarettes, transportation, and socializing with friends, and handed over the rest to my wife. If I ever marry again, I'd do it the exact same way.

He also enumerated the gifts and favors he bestowed on his wife's family in China—a cow, a new house, copious amounts of spending money, an introduction to a South Korean groom for his wife's sister, visitor's visas to South Korea for his wife's mother, father, and younger sister. Mansu had devoted himself entirely to provisioning his wife and in-laws, making his wife's departure seem, from his point of view, all the more perplexing. Chansuk agreed, saying "She'll never be able to find another as good as you."

The next man to speak was Yunsik, a man in his fifties with thinning hair and protruding eyes. He introduced himself as the first person in South Korea to marry a Chosŏnjok woman in 1989, a distinction the others challenged as unverifiable. Yunsik was eager to tell his tale, which, similar to Mansu's, involved a lengthy marriage (in his case, ten years), the birth of a child, and repeated incidents of his wife disappearing and resurfacing. By his calculation, ten years of marriage in actuality amounted to only five, since his wife consistently ran away two times each year. Like Mansu, Yunsik took a wait-and-see attitude toward his wife's episodic departures. "The first time she ran away," he said, "I didn't react. I just waited patiently. She called and I said, 'The door is always open. Come back when you're ready.'" In striking contrast to Mansu's insistence on his wife's initial sincerity and basic soundness of character, however, Yunsik fumed over his wife's disloyalty and channeled the bitterness he felt toward her as an individual into a dislike of all Chosŏnjok. "Because I was betrayed, I do not have good feelings toward the Chosŏnjok," he stated bluntly. "On the surface they are polite, but I really don't like them."

Whereas Mansu saw his wife's desire to help her family members in China as an inevitable, and even admirable, burden that she was heir to as a firstborn child, Yunsik interpreted his wife's filial devotion toward her natal family as evidence of her individual selfishness and the general failure of Chosŏnjok brides to fulfill the duty-bound role of a South Korean daughter-in-law. Yunsik vented:

> Our Korean women willingly give [spending money] to their parents-in-law, even if they hate them. It's their duty.... The way that Chosŏnjok women reject their in-laws, you can't even imagine! They are selfish, yet they do anything to help their own family members. My wife didn't just help her relatives, but all her neighbors and friends who came here from China. When they came, [my wife] asked me to sleep somewhere else. If anyone came, my wife would take them to our house and she would serve them food five times a day. I treated them so well, and she did absolutely nothing for her marital family.

"They are all the same. I warned you," Chansuk chided. Yunsik retorted that such audacities had to be experienced firsthand in order to believe them truly possible.

Complaints about the seemingly constant flow of visiting Chosŏnjok relatives and friends, the expense of international phone calls, or a wife's remittances to family in China were very common, even among South Korean husbands like Mansu who empathized with their wives' desire to assist natal kin. One father-in-law of a Chosŏnjok bride, for example, pointed to the "line/thread" (*ch'ul*) that connects a Chosŏnjok daughter-in-law to the rest of her family members in China as the most burden-some (*pudansŏlopta*) aspect of an international marriage. When this "line" is perceived to supplant a wife's obligations to her marital family, it can be construed as not merely a burden but a breach of Korean kinship norms, as Yunsik's quote above suggests. It is not difficult to imagine how weighty familial responsibilities on both sides and clashing ideologies of kinship and gender can create volatile tensions for Chosŏnjok women and South Korean men, a topic I explore in greater depth in the following chapter.

As discussed in the previous chapter, many South Korean men who traveled to China in search of a bride were motivated by the desire to find a compliant wife who would live under the same roof with and "serve" (*mosihada*) their parents. South Koreans widely use the verb "to serve" to describe the traditional caretaking role of a daughter-in-law in her marital household, a term that overtly indexes the hierarchies of age and gender at the heart of Confucian concepts of kin and kin work. Chihan, the third husband at the table to offer his testimony, began by voicing his dashed hopes of supplying his aging mother with a servile daughter-in-law. "My objective was to find someone to serve my mother," he stated matter-of-factly. "I went to a poor country because I wanted to find an obedient woman [*sunjonghanŭn yŏja*]. I went to China, but it turned out to be the complete opposite [of what I expected]."

With each man's story, the sincerity of the bride's intentions at the time of marriage appeared increasingly suspect. Mansu was at great pains to convince the others that intervening circumstances or actors had arrived on the scene to sully his wife's once honest aims to be a good wife and mother. Yunsik speculated, but could not say for sure, that his wife, despite ten years of sporadic co-residence, harbored ulterior motives to use mar-riage as means of making money from the start. There seemed to be no doubt in anyone's mind, however, that Chihan's case constituted a clear-cut case of marriage fraud (*wijang kyŏrhon*).

Chihan took stock of the clues that might have tipped him off early on to the fact that something was amiss. There was the marriage broker's attempt to dissuade him from visiting the home of his wife in China on the grounds that his wife's allegedly paralyzed mother was too ashamed by her appearance to receive guests. There was also his wife's "shocking" announcement just ten days after her arrival in South Korea that she was "bored" with her domestic existence in South Korea and wished to seek employment outside the home. "So! She married me to make money!" Chihan exclaimed with the air of a detective who had just solved a case. He also recalled what he saw as his wife's preposterous request that he pay her 2,000,000 won in compensation for her travel expenses to Korea. Frequent phone calls by Chihan's wife to Yunsik's wife (the two wives were longtime friends in China) also aroused suspicion, since, as mentioned earlier, many South Korean husbands feared that socializing with other Chosŏnjok compatriots might lead their wives astray.

Chihan did not dwell on any of these details until Yunsik divulged some unsettling information regarding the situation of Chihan's wife in China. Intercepting a letter from China intended for his wife, Yunsik learned that Chihan's wife had a Chosŏnjok husband and two children living in China. The letter further revealed that Chihan's wife had purchased the identity papers of the author of the letter, a calculated first step in her plan to pose as a never-been-married "maiden" (*chŏnyŏ*) and land an unsuspecting South Korean husband. Upon hearing this news, Chihan called his wife on the phone and asked her to report immediately to his workplace. He described the confrontation in which his desperation to retain a daughter-in-law for his mother neutralized his anger in having been deceived:

> You're hiding something from me, aren't you? She said, no, I'm not hiding anything. I pressed her and she continued to deny it. Finally, she admitted it. I forgave her, since I'd married a compatriot [*kyopo*] and divorce is shameful. I knew she had kids in China and that she had come here to make money for them. I told her to use the money she earns in Korea on her kids in China, and just be nice to her mother-in-law. Later when I came home from work, I found her packing her bags. She said she was leaving. I said, "I'm forgiving you!" I don't understand why she did that. I said to her, "Honestly, I forgive you."

A discussion ensued about the authenticity of Chihan's wife. Everyone present was fully convinced that she had never had intentions to live married life in South Korea and that she had most likely plotted with her husband, and possibly Mansu's wife, in a conspiracy to use marriage as an entrée into the Korean labor market. Mansu commented on how the increasingly widespread practice of Chosŏnjok women arranging paper marriages constituted an ironic reversal: "When international marriages with China first began, the men thought they were helping Chosŏnjok women. Now it's the opposite. We're being used by the women. At first, Chosŏnjok women had true intentions to marry. Now they contract 'fake marriages' [*wijang kyŏrhon*]."

When and in what sense are marriages between Chosŏnjok women and South Korean men considered "fake" or "sham?" The Korean term *wijang kyŏrhon* and the Chinese term *jia jiehun* refer to the illegalities and false pretenses involved in arranging a so-called fake marriage. Though the marriage and sometimes divorce paperwork entailed are filed in accordance with the law, the illicitness lies in the fact that these marriages are being used by women *solely* as a vehicle to cross the border into South Korea. They are not based on affective ties nor are they meant to endure, two of the features presumed to characterize a "real" marriage in South Korea. A "fake" marriage might be said to turn "real" if the participants (unexpectedly) develop emotional attachment to one another and abandon their original intentions of nullifying the marriage (such unexpected reversals are discussed in chapter 5).

Neither the Korean term *wijang kyŏrhon* nor the Chinese term *jia jiehun* specifies the complicity of either party in contracting a marriage. Similarly, the English terms I use interchangeably throughout the book, including "paper," "fraudulent," "sham," "counterfeit," and "fake" do not indicate whether the marriages arise from a mutual agreement between the bride and groom to exchange citizenship papers for money or whether the marriage is predicated on some form of deception. At first I thought to designate a term or invent a distinction that would allow me to make clear whether the "fiction" of the marriage was known to the groom from the outset, but upon reconsideration I decided this was not central to my analysis or discussion. I do, however, deliberately avoid using the term "fictive marriage" or "fictive kinship" to describe these relationships since these are loaded terms in the anthropological literature.

"Fictive kinship" has traditionally been used by anthropologists to connote relationships that have no basis in blood yet are couched in an idiom of blood ties (which in Western folk understandings of kinship generally subsumes references to both sexual reproduction and biological ancestry), as seen for example in adoptive ties, gay kinship, and family-like friend- ships. Kath Weston's (1991) description of gay American kinship and Ju- dith Modell's (1994) study of American adoption challenge the traditional anthropological ascription of biological ties or ties derived from sexual procreation as "real" kinship by showing that families formed by choice can be just as enduring and emotionally fulfilling, if not more so, than families based on blood. Rather than connoting family ties that are "not real" or "untrue" (that is, not based on blood), Modell redefines "fictive kinship" to mean relationships that are purposefully "created" through sustained work and attention (1994, 226). In this sense of the term, a fic- tive kinship tie can be as strong as a blood tie and not simply an inferior, metaphorical approximation of it. Of course, making a distinction between family ties that are crafted and those that are given obscures the fact that biological ties too require care and effort to sustain them. It also belies the fact that people can, and often do, choose not to recognize their biological family members. For this reason, the terms "fictive kinship" and "families we choose" (Weston 1991) are less useful as cross-cultural analytical terms than as the culturally particular categories that inform U.S. folk ideologies of kinship.

While the symbolism of blood also dominates Korean understandings of kin relations, it is not necessarily categorically distinct from relations of adoption. Historically, Korean adoptions occurred almost exclusively within the agnatic group, with eldest sons being given to elder brothers and youngest sons to younger brothers, for example (Janelli and Janelli 1982, 187). Thus, even an adoptive tie might be considered a blood tie in terms of biological ancestry, though removed to a certain degree from the procreative tie between parent and child. The more pertinent distinction in Korean kinship sets paternally related kin apart from maternally related kin. Interestingly, the Korean word for paternal relative, *ch'injok,* literally means "real relations," while maternally related kin or *oejok* translates as "outside relatives."[6] But as far as the Korean laws governing family reuni-

---

6. *Ch'injok* encompasses those who are born into as well as adopted into the patriline, though in practice Janelli and Janelli show the fragility of adoptive ties by pointing to cases where indi- viduals chose to perform ancestor worship to honor their biological rather than their adoptive an- cestors (1982, 57).

fication are concerned, both *ch'injok* and *oejok* count as "real" as long as they can be genealogically verified within the eighth degree (more is said about the legal parameters of the agnatic kin group when I examine the fabrication of genealogical ties to cross the border in chapter 4).

The mere existence of a blood tie (*hyŏlchok*) to a South Korean citizen, however, does not guarantee a Chosŏnjok person's entry into the country. The Korean relative must actively acknowledge the blood tie and agree to sponsor his or her Chosŏnjok relative for the duration of the visit, revealing, in much the same way that Modell and Weston do, the element of choice involved in biological families.

It was not until I had traveled to northeastern China that I realized the extent to which paper marriages and other forms of counterfeit kinship had become normalized as an expedient means of circumventing South Korea's restrictive categories of immigration. A South Korean minister and retired university professor who had spent six years living in Yanbian Korean Autonomous Prefecture in China's Jilin Province described his astonishment when four Chosŏnjok women who had enacted paper divorces with their Chosŏnjok husbands in order to contract paper marriages with South Korean men approached him for help. The women had obtained South Korean citizenship and were experiencing difficulty restoring their legal identities as the wives of their original Chosŏnjok husbands. The professor/minister expressed "shock" that these Chosŏnjok women would talk so unabashedly about their "crimes" to a minister and even go so far as to enlist his help. When he turned them away, threatening to report them to the police, the women registered equal shock, since they regarded themselves as having done nothing wrong.

The South Korean professor/minister used this anecdote to impress upon me the degree to which Chosŏnjok women's pursuit of money had eclipsed their ability to discriminate between right and wrong. When one places the phenomenon of counterfeit kinship in the larger context of South Korea's ambivalent treatment and increasingly restrictive policies toward its "brethren" in China, these acts of faking kinship in order to cross the border begin to appear much less shocking, if not utterly commonsensical. In the final section I show how South Korea's exceedingly narrow labor migration policies leave few legal options outside marriage for Chosŏnjok migrant women to work in South Korea. Given the conflict between their moral and legal claims to belonging, it hardly seems surprising that Chosŏnjok would feel justified in implementing extra-legal measures to circumvent the laws that stand in their way of achieving the belonging that South Korean ethnonationalist ideology dangles before them. The professor/minister's comments are suggestive of the general inability or unwillingness of many South Koreans at the time to recognize the inherent conflict in the situation of the Chosŏnjok.

To render these counterfeit kinship practices understandable, however, is not to deny the tumultuous effects these practices have on family lives and relationships on both sides of the border. A 1996 article in the *Heilongjiang News*[7] reported on the phenomenon of paper marriages from the perspective of the Chosŏnjok husbands and children who stay behind in China. It tells the story of a Chosŏnjok woman who deceives a Korean man by marrying him and hiding the fact that she has a Chosŏnjok husband and ten-year-old son. On the day of the woman's departure to South Korea, the son asks the father in the airport, "Is that the airplane *ŏmma* [mommy] took?" The father says nothing, just smooths the boy's hair. The article concludes by stating, "In pursuing one thing, our women lose so much more. They are losing out on life for the sake of money." The second half of this book takes an inside look at the often unbearable strains that the practice of arranging paper marriages places on Chosŏnjok families in northeastern China.

Statistically, it is impossible to determine what percentage of Chosŏnjok women enter their marriages without disclosing their intentions to divorce after they obtain citizenship. We have seen how difficult it can be for even South Korean husbands like Mansu and Yunsik to speak with certainty about whether their wives harbored plans to leave them from the start. At the extreme end of the spectrum, the experiences of Sanggi, the fourth man at the table, was by far the most bluntly cruel-hearted case I encountered in the field. When it was the thirty-seven-year-old's turn to give his testimony, he sullenly pushed a pile of photos in front of me, saying "These pictures tell it all." The photographs were close-ups of the injuries he had suffered in an attack on his life. In an effort to erase any possible doubt that he was the victim in the photos, Sanggi pulled down his shirt collar to reveal five-inch-long scars on his neck and throat and raised his shirt

---

7. *Chosŏnjok yŏsŏngdŭli ŏnnŭn kŏt kwa inŭn kŏt* [The gains and losses of Chosŏnjok women]. *Heilongjiang News*. August 17, 1996.

to show me more scars on his side and back. Chansuk explained that the incident took place in a karaoke bar in Yanji, China, where Sanggi and his Chosŏnjok wife were peddling merchandise (*pottali changsa*) they had brought over from Korea. Media reports uphold Sanggi's assertion that his wife had conspired with her Chosŏnjok lover in China to murder him and collect the insurance money. An SBS television news broadcast in South Korea ran the story with the headline: "a human face with the heart of an animal" (*inmyŏn susim pullyun*).

Sanggi's traumatic experience represents the kind of worst-case scenario for which the South Korean media and by extension the public imagination had a strong appetite at the time of my field research. As such, it deserves attention but should not be considered in any way representative of the majority or even a significant number of Chosŏnjok migrant brides in South Korea. Instead, in the overwhelming majority of cases I encountered, desertion is best understood as a strategic response to the tensions and cultural disjunctures Chosŏnjok brides encountered in their marital households.

Between the black-and-white tales of marriage fraud, there is a grey area of stories rarely explored in the South Korean mass media at the turn of the millennium. A bride who made a sincere effort to adjust to marital life in South Korea could have been pushed to leave her marriage by a combination of possible factors, including disappointed material expectations, feelings of isolation from the larger society, and incompatibilities with her husband and in-laws. But these contingencies would have been incongruent with the then-dominant view that Chosŏnjok brides are "women obsessed with material wealth who are willing to transgress all moral principles and threaten the very basis of Korean identity" (Park 1996, 222). In the next chapter, I present a fine-grained, ethnographic analysis of the "grey area" in an effort to problematize such stereotypes of the ruthlessly opportunistic Chosŏnjok bride who will stop at nothing in pursuit of money.

Deceitful Grooms

While public opinion in Korea, fueled by the media, tended to focus on sensationalist acts of deception committed by wives like Chihan's and Sanggi's, less publicized accounts depicted Korean men as either physically abusive of their Chosŏnjok wives or guilty of misrepresenting their socioeconomic circumstances to their brides-to-be. In these cases, so-called runaway brides were seen as giving the grooms their just deserts. Tales of mercenary grooms who lured their brides with false promises of wealth and social status circulated widely among Chosŏnjok brides and migrant workers in South Korea. Hyunsuk, a sociable, stylishly dressed woman in her late twenties, was the only Chosŏnjok woman I met who was willing to share the details of her own brush with marital deception. She described a painful experience that was still fresh at the time of the telling:

My father-in-law was interested in getting a Chinese daughter-in-law to help him with a business venture he planned to pursue in China.... My mother's friend had met my father-in-law while she was in Korea on business. She told me that the man's family was very rich—that they had two cars, that the man was a college graduate, and that they lived in a very big house. I was told that in the future they planned to have one house in Shenyang, another in Mudanjiang, one in Japan, and one in the United States. The family said they weren't sure where they would live in the future. Maybe they would settle in Japan, maybe in the United States....

I got married in 1995. We had a big wedding in China. The next month I came to Korea. Just twenty days later we had another wedding ceremony. I thought that since my father-in-law was supposed to be so rich and famous that the mayor would be attending our wedding. I expected to see reporters there and television cameras. But everything turned out to be a lie. Their living conditions were so poor. The house was not even as nice as the one in which we live in China.... When I first met my husband, I thought that he was just a man of few words [*hua shao*], but later I found out that he's not smart at all. He's probably not even a high school graduate, let alone a college graduate.... As soon as I arrived I got the feeling that the entire family were swindlers [*pianzi*]....

I lived one month in his family's house. My husband was never at home anyway, so one day when everyone was out of the house, I just packed my bags and left.... I'm not someone who cheats a Korean man in order to marry him and get citizenship. I honestly had intentions to live with my husband, but my husband really has no "life ability" [*shenghuo li*]. Besides, isn't it clear my family wouldn't have given me such a grand wedding in China if my sole purpose in coming was to make money? My family spent so much money while his family spent nothing....

I have no face now [*meiyou mianzi*]. My personality has become so intro-verted since coming here. I don't like to go out and see people these days. I was never like this before. Just look at the black circles under my eyes...I don't know what I'll do now. I can never return to live in China. I have too much pride to return. How could I go back with no face? I have no choice but to struggle on with my life in Korea [*fendou shenghuo xiaqu*]. I'll just have to depend on myself.

As she contemplated the struggles that lay ahead, Hyunsuk's eyes welled up with tears, and I suddenly felt a twinge of remorse for having provoked her to recall the details of her unhappy circumstances. Hyunsuk's account of leaving a marriage built on deception captures the sense of isolation, anxiety, and humiliation that Chosŏnjok women in situations similar to Hyunsuk's potentially face when they make the decision to leave their marriages. Their story was rarely featured in the South Korean media. The lengths to which Hyunsuk goes to distinguish herself from the stock villain of the Chosŏnjok bride who arrives in Korea with a preconceived plan to abandon her husband also brings into greater relief the widespread, biased presumption in South Korea that all Chosŏnjok women who run from their marriages must have wed under false pretenses and that dishon-esty is the province of the Chosŏnjok bride and rarely, if ever, the groom.

When I relayed the story of Hyunsuk's misfortune to Juju, a Chosŏnjok marriage migrant I had befriended in Seoul, I discovered that feelings of distrust also pervaded Chosŏnjok migrants' perceptions of one another. Juju agonized daily over whether to leave her Korean husband who, by her own account, was similarly lacking in "life ability" and social skills. I thought the two women might derive solace from meeting and talk-ing with one another, but before I could make this suggestion, Juju inter-rupted me, saying I should not believe a word of what Hyunsuk had told me. "I know Chinese compatriots [*tongbao*] too well," she said. "Achh, I can't really talk to you about this on the phone, but believe me, these women don't really come here to marry. They have ulterior motives. They all come here to make money, and the easiest way to do that is to get mar-ried. Oh, I know about this too well." I explained that Hyunsuk struck me as very sincere and described how she had been on the verge of tears dur-ing our interview. "Tears!" Juju snorted. "Oh, you really don't understand Chinese *tongbao* at all."

My phone conversation with Juju left me with a profoundly unsettled feeling. I recalled the words of Yunsik at the conclusion of my interview with the four deserted Korean husbands. He leaned in close and asked, "When you speak with Chosŏnjok women, how much do you believe?" I explained that my research objectives were not so much a matter of determining the truth as presenting different perspectives on the issue. He seemed not to understand my point. He looked at me hard and said, "When talking to Chosŏnjok women, believe no more than fifty percent."

Was I naive to believe Hyunsuk's tale of deception? Why would she have agreed to share the personal details of her marital history with a foreign anthropologist if not to set the record straight and vindicate herself from the public misperception that she was the one who had behaved cruelly and unethically? Besides, was Juju herself not contemplating leaving her own marriage for similar reasons? Juju confessed that, like all Chosŏnjok women, she had come with the intentions of making money but had developed genuine feelings for her husband, which made her feel remorseful and hesitant to walk out the door. Hyunsuk, Juju seemed to be implying, had acted solely in her own self-interest, with little regard for the repercussions of her actions on her Korean husband and family members.

I decided in the end to discount Juju's allegations against Hyunsuk and trust my own instincts that Hyunsuk had not shed crocodile tears. Juju's judgmental attitude toward Chinese *tongbao* who had come through marriage to South Korea may have been an indication of just how infectious the climate of suspicion toward Chosŏnjok brides had become. It had reached a point at which at least some Chosŏnjok brides felt pressured to dissociate themselves from their compatriots to establish their own integrity. Or perhaps by claiming the universality of fake marriages, Juju sought to legitimize her own admittedly utilitarian motives in marrying across borders—motives that interestingly, in her own mind, did not preclude the possibility of developing a full-fledged conjugal relationship with her South Korean husband. In the following sections I explore how economic calculation has become a major element, not only in Chosŏnjok brides' choice of marital destination but in the way the South Korean government has defined and legislated its relationship with its diasporic neighbors in China.

Tensions in the Diaspora

The sensationalized images of "runaway brides" featured in the South Korean mass media and circulating through informal channels of gossip, I argue, say as much about the wider tensions that have arisen in the course of increasing contact between the Chosŏnjok and South Koreans as they do about the immorality of individual Chosŏnjok women. Placing public concern about Chosŏnjok women and the purity of their motives in the broader socioeconomic context in which it occurs allows us to see how the particular expressions of ambivalence toward Chosŏnjok brides are symptomatic of a broader uneasiness among South Koreans regarding their place in a world of rapid historical change, transnational travel, and global economic opportunism. As South Koreans forge ties in this milieu with not only Chosŏnjok brides but Chosŏnjok migrants (and foreigners) of all types, they struggle to resolve a fundamental tension between "globalization and nationalism" (see Kim 2000; Moon 2000; Abelmann and Kim 2005, 107–8). As noted by other scholars, the political economic imperative of globalization (*segyehwa*) and its attendant ideological vision of a transnational pan-Korean solidarity conflicts with the equally powerful nationalist rhetoric that frames the Korean people or *minjok* as a racially and culturally homogenized, politically unified entity, bounded within the borders of the present-day South Korean nation (*han'guk*) (and projected to one day subsume the territory to the north).[8]

While other nations with diasporic populations living outside the perceived "homeland" face similar dilemmas about how to reconcile the apparent contradictions between notions of "territorial nation" and "transnational network" (Ong 1999, 57), the politics of Korean national belonging are complicated both by its "divided" status and by its geopolitical positioning in the region. As Moon notes:

> To welcome diasporic Koreans from China with open arms is to establish a precedent for other would-be entrants of Korean descent, namely, those from North Korea. The South Korean government is extremely nervous

---

8. Ong highlights a similar contradiction in the PRC between "two competing discursive systems that variously deploy Chineseness as a territorially bounded moral entity and as a deterritorialized moral economic force" (1999, 55–56).

about the possible influx of millions of refugees either through the collapse of the Pyongyang regime or through reunification, and knows that northeastern China (the ethnic Korean region) serves as a gateway. (2000, 158)[9]

South Korea's stance against full inclusion of the Chosŏnjok is also motivated in part by a desire to placate anxieties on the Chinese side that increasing contact with South Korea might ignite separatist sentiments. While benefiting from the foreign currency flowing back across its border, the PRC has taken a punitive stance against the Chosŏnjok for developing close ties to South Korea, demoting them, as Park put it, "from their high status as model minority with a glorious past to one of three recalcitrant minority groups that threaten the unity of the Chinese nation" (2004, 27). The three "dangerous ethnic groups" the Chosŏnjok join are the Mongols, Uighurs, and Tibetans.

South Korea faces counterpressures from the broader international community and its own global "cosmopolitan" ideals to make its society more "immigrant friendly." The South Korean government appears acutely concerned that its image and international reputation might suffer if it were to mistreat its foreign workers. As Lim writes, "Time and again, government officials, scholars, and the media have tied the rights of foreign workers to the requirements of living in an increasingly global civil society, where human and labor rights have begun to take center stage" (2005, 15). Ever-mindful that the global community of nations is monitoring its treatment of foreign residents, the South Korean government may be more inclined to find more equitable ways of dealing with the influx of Chosŏnjok migrants. In sum, the challenge facing the South Korean government is how to design and implement immigration laws and policies that are consistent with its rhetoric of pan-Korean unity and global civil society while at the same time strategically preserving the geopolitical, diplomatic, and economic interests of the territorially bounded South Korean nation.

---

9. Moon states that an estimated 150,000 "food migrants" from North Korea, driven by hunger, have slipped across the border into China (2000, 158). According to a 1999 article in a major South Korean newspaper, Moon's estimate falls precisely in the middle of a wide range of figures bounded on one end by the South Korean government's conservative estimate of 10,000–30,000 and at the opposite extreme the estimate by civic groups of 300,000 refugees (Adelman 1999). A U.S. congressional report written in 2007 (available at http://www.fas.org/sgp/crs/row/RL34189.pdf) still gives the same upper and lower estimates for the number of North Korean migrants living in China. The lack of publicly available data in China and the tendency for North Koreans to move back and forth across the China–North Korean border account for the extraordinary and unchanging vagueness of these figures.

An examination of South Korea's immigration policies toward the Chosŏnjok shows that the nation's economic goals and strategic calculations often supersede the blood ties South Koreans hold to be so sacred. In the next section, I trace the South Korean state's oscillating immigration policies from an open-door policy in the name of family reunification to a highly selective admittance of Chosŏnjok migrants, tailored to redress two particular deficits in its population—the shortage of wives for the nation's farmers and workers for its factories. Among the unintended consequences of these two recruitment programs was the creation of a large population of illegal migrant workers that proliferated beyond the state's control. Just as the motives of Chosŏnjok brides came under public scrutiny when they could no longer be confined to the countryside (and when they refused to stay in their marriages), Chosŏnjok migrants categorically became "illegal migrant workers" when they exceeded the boundaries of the state's industrial trainee program. I end with a discussion of the intertwined politics of global capitalism and ethnic identity, considering how revisions to South Korea's citizenship laws in recent years signal a swinging of the pendulum in the direction of excluding Chosŏnjok from a vision of the South Korean nation.

From Long-lost Kin to Illegal Migrant Workers

The South Korean state's ambivalence toward Chosŏnjok migrants is reflected in the capriciousness of its policies governing the Chosŏnjok's access to South Korea, their rights once they take up residence there, and the linked fluctuations in the cultural imagery surrounding them. Before the normalization of relations with the PRC, South Koreans had little access to information on the Chosŏnjok. Prohibited from traveling to China in the early 1980s, South Korean journalists relied heavily upon eyewitness accounts from Japanese and Korean American scholars (Park 1996, 185). These reports emphasized the strong ethnic consciousness of the Chosŏnjok and triumphantly proclaimed the resilience of Korean ethnic homogeneity behind the "bamboo curtain."[10] Park writes that between 1985 and 1988, South Korean newspapers "exploded" with reports

---

10. Characterizing the U.S. media's stance toward the Chosŏnjok, Park writes, "The isolated tribe persistently eating dog meat, *kimchi* [*sic*], and cold noodles had survived the Han Chi-

of "Korea Fever," the widespread desire among the Chosŏnjok to travel to South Korea (1996, 196). Fearing that the Chosŏnjok would affiliate more closely with North Korea, South Koreans were relieved to learn that Chosŏnjok held the South Korean people and their nation's achievements in great esteem. In accord with the prevailing national sentiment in 1988, the South Korean government simplified the entry procedures for Chosŏnjok visitors and urged them to reunite with their separated family members (*isan kajok*).[11]

Just four years later, upon the establishment of formal diplomatic relations with the PRC, the South Korean government reversed its open-door policy. By making the entry procedures more difficult, the South Korean government effectively curtailed the steady increases in Chosŏnjok migration that it had promoted in the previous period. This was partly a response to the Chinese government's concern for the sanctity of its own borders and the containment of the Chosŏnjok, as one of its fifty-five ethnic minorities, inside them. However, the increasingly stringent entry regulations imposed by the Korean government also coincided, as Moon perceptively points out, with the "first presence of foreigners in the workplaces and streets of Seoul" (2000, 222).

The South Korean government had initially turned a blind eye to the illegal economic activities of the Chosŏnjok—most conspicuous being the increasingly large-scale and organized street peddling of Chinese medicines—viewing them as necessary to help the Chosŏnjok pay for their family visits (Park 1996, 200). As early as 1990, however, the first clash occurred between the South Korean government and the migrant Chosŏnjok community when the media released an official report condemning the medicines sold by Chosŏnjok vendors as fake (*jia yao*), that is, not containing the purported ingredients listed on the label (Park 1996, 198).[12] Professor Kim, a visiting scholar from Yanbian University whom I met and

---

nese Communists' acculturation and gloriously preserved their traditions—men first and elders first" (1996, 191).

11. Park describes the televised portrayals of the first visits by Chosŏnjok to South Korea as a "veritable national 'theater' in which every Korean family was reminded of its unbearable suffering from an anguished history of shared *han* (pain) due to the separation of families during the Korean War" (1996, 193).

12. Interestingly, the Chosŏnjok brides who would later enter the country were also criticized in the same language of "fakery" as the perpetrators of "fake marriages."

befriended in Seoul, explained that South Koreans, given their enthusiasm for health-enhancing products, had been willing to pay very high prices for medicinal herbs believed to exist only in China. According to Professor Kim, after Chosŏnjok medicine peddlers "began substituting fake medicine for the real thing, South Koreans caught on and stopped buying it." While Park does not address the issue of whether the charges of counterfeiting levied against Chosŏnjok vendors were justified, she and Professor Kim both point to the incident, which culminated in an official government crackdown on the medicine peddlers, as a critical watershed in South Korean–Chosŏnjok relations. As Park writes, "mutual interest suddenly turned to accusation and humiliation when the South Korean government barred Korean Chinese from importing and selling Chinese medicines" (1996, 201).

Given the stringent entry regulations subsequently imposed by the South Korean government, Chosŏnjok migrants were faced with a limited range of options for legally crossing the border into South Korea. Visitor visas of varying duration were being granted to academics, venture capitalists, political leaders, and, on a more limited scale than before, to separated family members. The gatekeepers of the South Korean border looked upon Chosŏnjok migrants with a new and growing sense of suspicion, with the exception of two groups of migrants that were in short supply in South Korea: rural-bound brides and unskilled laborers.

As in the case of the government-subsidized program to attract Chosŏnjok women to the bride-depleted countryside, the government backed an organized effort to recruit Chosŏnjok workers for its labor-depleted industries. Initially implemented by the Korean government in 1992 to provide skill training for foreign workers already employed by Korean businesses overseas, the government broadened its "industrial trainee" (*yŏnsusaeng*) program, in response to the demands of domestic employers, to include the recruitment of unskilled overseas workers in South Korea's so-called 3D industries (dirty, difficult, and dangerous).[13] Under this initiative, overseas guest workers, among whom Chosŏnjok men and women accounted for the vast majority, received no actual training. They

---

13. Textiles, footwear, rubber, plastics, dyeing, and other low-wage manufacturing industries were among those businesses suffering from a shortage of unskilled workers at the time.

were simply thrust into low-skilled, low-paying, menial jobs without the most basic protections or workers' rights.

Unsurprisingly, in the end, both the rural bride recruitment and worker recruitment programs spiraled out of government control, unleashing a multitude of Chosŏnjok workers and brides who refused to stay within the boundaries of their officially designated destinations. As discussed earlier in this chapter, the government's program to recruit "Chosŏnjok maidens" had opened the door for Chosŏnjok brides of all ages and sundry backgrounds to settle in every corner of the Korean peninsula. With the aid of commercial matchmakers and unlicensed brokers, Chosŏnjok brides were no longer confined exclusively to rural matrimony. What is more, brides who were dissatisfied with married life often voted with their feet and left their affinal households in search of better economic and/or marital opportunities in South Korea and beyond.

Similarly, Chosŏnjok workers, dissatisfied with excessive work hours, inadequate pay, dangerous conditions, lack of employee benefits, and discriminatory treatment, more often than not left their officially assigned jobs for higher-paying ones in the burgeoning underground labor market.[14] Given the government's steady expansion of the industrial trainee system in the face of the large number of "runaway workers," political scientist Timothy Lim argues that the unbridled growth in the number of illegal migrant workers should be viewed not as an unintended consequence of the state's foreign labor program but rather as a planned government objective. The criminalization of migrant labor, Lim perceptively notes, makes it all too easy to exploit foreign workers, deny them basic rights, employ them for substandard wages, and force them to leave when needed (2002, 17). The widespread tendency for Chosŏnjok visiting relatives in South Korea to overstay their three-month family visitation visas also contributed to the rapid climb in the number of undocumented workers.[15] A Chosŏnjok friend writing to me

---

14. Chosŏnjok women were able to find ready employment as domestics, waitresses, cooks, tour guides, interpreters, trading company employees, retailers, and bathhouse workers, while Chosŏnjok men were forced to choose from a narrower range of options, including construction workers, maritime workers, watchmen (*kyŏngbi ajŏssi*), and bathhouse scrubbers (*ttae millinŭn saram*).

15. According to statistics issued by the Ministry of Justice in 1999, Chosŏnjok undocumented workers number 64,232 or fifty-one percent of the total number of illegal migrant workers in South Korea (Sim Jae-yun, *Korea Times,* September 27, 1999).

in October 2003 estimated that she was one of 230,000 Chosŏnjok migrants residing illegally in South Korea. Indeed, when I arrived in Seoul in 1998 to begin my fieldwork, the term "Chosŏnjok" had become virtually synonymous with "illegal migrant worker" in the minds of most South Koreans.

The Crackdown on Brides and Workers

The South Korean government has taken a number of steps to attempt to regain control over the growing population of Chosŏnjok migrants. In the case of illegal migrant workers, the government implemented a series of ever-changing and increasingly stringent policies designed to discourage them from entering while giving those already in South Korea incentive to leave.[16] Illegal migrants were forced to pay steep monetary fines (100,000 won for each month overstayed beyond the expiration of their visas) (Kim 1999) upon leaving the country and additionally faced deportation if apprehended while working.

With the Asian financial crisis of 1997, the situation for Chosŏnjok migrants turned from bad to worse. The Ministry of Justice in South Korea, targeting migrant workers "as an economic burden rather than a boon" to the struggling economy, imposed a deadline of December 27, 1997, for all illegal overseas workers to leave the country (Moon 2000, 165). As incentive for migrants to leave voluntarily, the government began designating one month a year when illegal foreign workers could exit the country without having to pay a penalty. A Chosŏnjok migrant bride informed me by e-mail in 2003 that the South Korean government had again stepped up its efforts that year to rid the country of illegal workers, requiring all Chosŏnjok migrants who had overstayed their visas for five years or more to return home by a deadline of March 31 or face deportation. The ultimatum resulted in the gradual evacuation of Seoul's residentially segregated "Chosŏnjok towns" (in Karibong-dong, Kuro-dong, Taerim-dong, and Kasan-dong districts) and induced at least nine Chosŏnjok workers to end their lives by jumping in front of subway cars and trains (Park 2004, 16).

---

16. It is important to note that at the same time, the Korean government, acting out of concern for its international reputation, has taken steps to improve the treatment and benefits of its legal foreign workers (see Moon 2000, 162–63).

Since the 2003 crackdown, however, the South Korean government has moved in the direction of granting basic rights and protections to both documented and undocumented foreign workers. Bowing to the demands of foreign workers and civic groups that took up their cause, the government enacted the Employment of Foreign Workers Act (EFWA) in 2004 (the law was passed in 2003) which extended to foreign workers the rights to severance pay, worker's compensation, and the right to sue for physical abuse by an employer (see Lim 2005). The new law also guarantees up to three years of employment to illegal migrant workers who overstay their visas for less than four years on the condition that they register with the Ministry of Labor. In 2007, the South Korean state created the Visit and Employment Program (Pangmun Ch'wiŏp Chedo), enabling overseas ethnic Koreans to work up to three years in any South Korean company and granting freedom of entry and departure for a five-year period (Seol and Skrentny 2009, 154). Ameliorating some of the most exploitative aspects of the industrial trainee system[17] and creating new opportunities for short-term, legal employment, the new legislation outlined above might welcome Chosŏnjok migrants to labor more securely and humanely for the South Korean nation, but it still denies them claims to full national membership.

In response to rising concerns of Chosŏnjok marriage fraud, the government has also complicated the procedures and bureaucratic red tape for international marriage, subjecting both the bride and groom to close scrutiny as they carry out the final steps of registering their marriage. In 1997, the Korean government took further measures to discourage fraudulent marriages by enacting a new naturalization law under which a foreign bride must wait two years to receive citizenship rather than six months as stipulated under the old law.[18]

---

17. I do not wish to underestimate the significance of these gains for foreign workers in South Korea. As Lim explains, "The end result is a system that, at least on paper, confers more protection and rights on foreign labor than any other system in Asia, and more than most countries in the world" (2005, 18).

18. It is interesting to note that while the revised naturalization law makes it harder for foreign-born wives to become citizens, it makes it easier for foreign-born husbands to naturalize. In the past, foreign husbands were not automatically eligible for citizenship in the same way that foreign wives were. The new law establishes gender equity in citizenship requirements by enabling foreign spouses, regardless of sex, to qualify for Korean citizenship after two years of residence in South Korea. Abelmann and Kim note, "Implicit in this history is that non-Korean

Finally, the government has also targeted commercial matchmakers and brokers by placing heavy restrictions on group-marriage tours to China. While many matchmakers I spoke with complained that the government's measures (combined with the economic crisis of 1997) had ruined their businesses, the crackdown on marriage tours has spawned a new type of business, what I refer to as "marriage facilitators." These companies, conveniently located near the Chinese embassy in Seoul, assist with the complicated paperwork involved in contracting an international marriage, including the translation of documents and booking of plane tickets to China—all the services a commercial matchmaker offers *except* the actual making of matches. As we took a walk down the narrow alley leading to the Chinese embassy in Seoul, a two-block stretch of tightly clustered China-related businesses that exists in dramatic juxtaposition to the surrounding upscale Myŏngdong shopping district, Chiyŏng and I counted no fewer than eighteen prominent signs amid the Chinese restaurants, bookstores, and tea shops with the words "Chinese Marriage Paperwork" (*Chungguk kyŏrhon susok*). As one marriage facilitator explained, she used to offer generic translation services but after the procedures for international marriage became more complicated, she was bombarded with requests from couples asking for help with their marriage forms. She and seventeen others in the area decided to make it their specialization.

Between Kinship and Capital

Chosŏnjok migrant workers and brides I met in South Korea were angered by the apparent incongruities between the South Korean government's rhetoric of blood, kinship, and homecoming on the one hand and the realities of its exclusionary immigration policies and harsh crackdown on migrant labor on the other. As Timothy Lim describes the conflict, "on the one hand, they [South Koreans] sought to welcome Chinese-Koreans as equals, while, on the other hand, they not only expected them to do the jobs that most South Koreans utterly disdained, but for less pay and

---

women have been assimilable into South Korean families, while non-Korean men have been understood to produce non-Korean households" (2005, 108).

under worse conditions (that is without the benefit of basic legal protection or labor rights)" (2002, 19). Add to the list of expectations the hope
that Chosŏnjok would also marry the men that few South Korean women
are interested in marrying. If the government's mixed messages had
stirred feelings of disillusionment among the Chosŏnjok, the unequivocal prejudice that was built into the 1999 Act on Immigration and Legal
Status of Overseas Koreans (Overseas Korean Act or OKA) incited many
Chosŏnjok to public demonstrations. Drafted by the Ministry of Justice,
the law entitled ethnic Koreans with foreign citizenship to a host of new
privileges, including the right to stay in Korea for up to two years regardless of the purpose of their visit, the right to purchase or sell land, and
the right to work or engage in business activities. Overseas Koreans who
reside in South Korea for more than ninety days were additionally granted
medical insurance benefits as well as the right to vote (Shin 1998). What
was under dispute was the legal definition of "overseas Korean" (*chaewoe
t'ongpo*). By defining overseas Koreans as those who at one time had South
Korean citizenship and their lineal descendants, the bill virtually excluded
ethnic Koreans in China, Russia, and Japan, most of whom were displaced
during or before the Japanese colonial period, prior to the establishment of
the Republic of Korea (*Taehanmin'guk*) in 1948.

South Koreans who view the Chosŏnjok as the descendants of the "independence fighters" who fled colonial Japan or were forcibly displaced
to China have joined Chosŏnjok migrants in voicing their protest of the
new law. A 1999 Korean editorial criticized the law for violating the prin-
ciple of one bloodline, one people (*minjok*) by upholding an ideology of
"past citizenship" (*kwagŏ gukchŏk chuŭi*) rather than *jus sanguinis* (*hyŏlt'ong
chuŭi*).[19] One migrant Chosŏnjok worker expressed the sense of injustice
many Chosŏnjok feel when he told a Korean reporter: "[South Koreans]
treat us, ethnic Chinese Koreans, worse than they treat foreigners. How
can the government talk about unification when they divide Koreans
based on economic power? This bill should be called something else, and
not have 'Koreans' in the title" (Kim 1999).

Under vocal pressure from Chosŏnjok migrant workers and the non-
governmental organizations (NGOs) representing their interests, the

---

19. 1999. Chaewoe tongp'o bŏp'an daet'ongnyong kŏbukwŏn haengsa yoku [President calls
for veto of law on overseas Koreans]. *Han'gyore*. August 15.

Ministry of Justice passed a revised Overseas Korean Act in 2004 that eliminated the criteria of past nationality and established instead the family register (*hojŏk*) as the defining criterion for the category of "overseas Korean." The new criterion of family registration, though meant to appear more inclusive and appease the Chosŏnjok, is in practice just as restrictive as the older definition. Since the system of family registration did not come into existence until the Japanese colonial regime implemented it in 1922, those who migrated before 1922, as well as those who migrated after 1922 but did not have the proper documentation, are still excluded. To add insult to injury, as Park observes (2005, 235–36), the use of the family register as a criterion of membership is reminiscent of past acts of injustice suffered by the Chosŏnjok living under Japanese colonial rule in Manchuria. At that time, family registration was the determining criterion for Korean nationality and, by extension the right to own private property. This posed a problem, as it does now, for Koreans who migrated prior to 1922.

Despite repeated attempts by South Korean immigration officials and lawmakers to block the entry of Chosŏnjok migrants, and despite the anger and resentment with which the Chosŏnjok community has responded, the force of Korea Wind—the widespread desire to migrate by any means possible to from China to South Korea—showed no signs of abating. In fact, Chosŏnjok appeared more determined than ever to circumvent the immigration restrictions they deemed unfair and discriminatory. In chapter 4, I explore the lengths to which the Chosŏnjok have gone to subvert South Korea's entry regulations by bending the government's definitions of kinship and patriotism to their own advantage.

As the above discussion has illustrated, Chosŏnjok migrants, as migrants elsewhere, do not operate in free-flowing circumstances but in environments that are controlled and shaped by the interests of nation-states in the context of globalizing capital and labor markets. As the South Korean government equivocates in its immigration policies over pan-Korean kinship and solidarity on the one hand and its economic and territorial interests on the other, it has created the social categories and conditions for the overall stigmatization of the Chosŏnjok in South Korea. It is clear from the episodic history of South Korea's opening and closing its borders to the Chosŏnjok—of welcoming them as long-lost kin to later criminalizing them as "fake medicine peddlers," of portraying Chosŏnjok women as saviors of the countryside and emissaries of ethnic homogeneity to later demonizing them as "runaway brides," of inviting them to labor for the nation and then condemning them as "illegal migrant workers"—that the South Korean government's immigration policies and representations, in conjunction with the mass media, have helped create the larger climate of fear and suspicion in which all Chosŏnjok migrants must operate.

Fears of deception at the hands of a dishonest matchmaker, Chosŏnjok bride, or South Korean groom were not entirely unfounded. The interviews and personal dramas contained in this chapter make it impossible to deny that some Chosŏnjok women do in fact contract marriages of convenience without the knowledge and consent of the groom, just as some South Korean grooms have little interest in a Chosŏnjok bride beyond acquiring a filial daughter-in-law for aging parents. Yet the comments of "runaway" brides, deserted grooms, and matchmakers of diverse types also point to the ambiguities involved in the realm of international marriage and matchmaking, making it difficult for an intimate insider—let alone an outside observer—to pronounce with any degree of certainty where the distinction lies between real and fraudulent marriage. As the case studies contained in the following chapter illustrate, it is within this context of mutual suspicion and moral ambiguity that Chosŏnjok brides must negotiate their relationships with their husbands and marital families. I show how these tensions shape the strategies Chosŏnjok brides devise to cope with their new marital situations.

3

GENDER LOGICS IN CONFLICT

While living at my rural host mother's house in China's Heilongjiang Province during the still-frigid springtime of 2000, I found the monotony of village life indoors eased by the regular, unannounced visits from a coterie of neighbors and relatives. I began to recognize names and faces after only a day or two in Creek Road Village. These spontaneous drop-in visits would occur at all hours of the day and evening, bringing a continuous stream of ethnographic encounters to my doorstep. Uninvited guests would slip wordlessly through the door and settle onto the *kang* (fire-heated platform) in our one-room house, with no intended purpose other than to sit and chat (*laoke*)—a local passion facilitated by the long winter.

Among this small cast of characters was thirty-eight-year-old Yunŏk, who had returned from Seoul to her natal village to file the paperwork for a marriage visa to South Korea. Yunŏk's daily visits brought us updates on the status of her visa application and complaints about bureaucratic red tape and corruption which had drawn out the process to nearly one year. One afternoon as my host mother was dishing out cold noodles for lunch, Yunŏk stumbled through the door, clutching her stomach, complaining in characteristic fashion of feeling ill after having waited in line for hours at the Public Security Bureau. She regaled us by reenacting the playful exchange that took place with the Chinese official who tended to her case:

Official: Are you divorced?
Yunŏk: ŭng. [Indicating an affirmative response]
Official: You're marrying to South Korea?
Yunŏk: ŭng.
Official: A fake marriage?
Yunŏk: ŭng.

My host mother and Kyuyŏng, the neighbor's daughter, burst out laughing after the third and final affirmative grunt, while I struggled to pinpoint the source of the humor. Yunŏk had always spoken of her intentions to marry as nothing less than sincere. I quickly realized that the Chinese official's allusion to marriage fraud had been made in jest, and Yunŏk in turn had played along with him. Yunŏk ended her story by recounting how the official had lamented, "We've lost another woman to South Korea. What are all the bachelors in China going to do?" "Farm and take care of the children," had been Yunŏk's nonchalant reply. Again the others erupted in laughter. As he was about to stamp Yunŏk's documents with his seal, the official paused to ask, "Are you absolutely sure you're not going to regret this? You know your husband in South Korea will abuse you, lock you up, and never let you leave the house!"

This vignette reveals several points about the sometimes unexpected ways in which the flows of women through transnational marriage intersect with and disrupt power imbalances of gender, nationality/ethnicity, and geography. First, the humor surrounding the Chinese official's insinuation that Yunŏk is marrying to South Korea under false pretenses reflects the inversions of gender and national hierarchies that have accompanied Chosŏnjok women's newfound transnational mobility. Rather than respond defensively or angrily to the insinuation that Chosŏnjok women marry exclusively for their own material gain, Yunŏk and her friends in the village appear to delight in the somewhat ironic prospect that Chosŏnjok women, despite their otherwise marginalized social and geoeconomic positioning, might actually be capable of exploiting men in South Korea.

Second, the official's observation that the exodus of Chosŏnjok women to South Korea is creating a marriage squeeze among Chosŏnjok bachelors is in fact a pressing concern in the rural areas of northeastern China.[1] I emphasize that the opportunities for mobility open to Chosŏnjok women in some ways exceed not only those of the South Korean men they marry but those of the Chosŏnjok men they leave behind. When I prodded Yunŏk and the others to reflect more seriously on the plight of China's Chosŏnjok bachelors, Kyuyŏng responded matter-of-factly that since "Chosŏnjok men are not as capable as the women, there simply is nothing for them to do but farm and do the housework." Images of "feminized" Chosŏnjok men left behind to mind the domestic sphere point to the fact that gendered patterns of global mobility have potentially transformative effects on the balance of power between men and women not simply in the host country but in the home country as well.

Finally, the official's warning about the excesses of Korean patriarchy cautions us not to romanticize transnational marriage as a vehicle for geographic mobility and gender empowerment. If Chosŏnjok women are at least partially motivated to marry into South Korea out of a desire for upward and outward mobility, as the case studies in this chapter show, their dreams are often fettered upon arrival in South Korea by kinship norms that bind them physically to the house and morally to the demands of their husbands and in-laws. Rumors of South Korean husbands who restrict the freedom of their Chosŏnjok wives traveled back to Creek Road Village and frequently emerged in the course of casual conversation. "Chinese gender equality" versus "Korean patriarchy" combined to give Chosŏnjok women a shared discourse in which to articulate the cultural conflicts they experienced as they adjusted to married life in South Korea. These essentializing discourses on gender, kinship, and nationality traveled back and forth between China and South Korea. They influenced how potential marriage migrants assessed the quality of their own transnational marriages as well as those of friends and family members. But, most important, they armed

---

1. Many Chosŏnjok as well as Han Chinese bachelors in northeastern China turn to the growing population of North Korea female defectors in their midst as a potential source of brides.

Chosŏnjok brides with a set of ideals that enabled them to aspire toward more gender egalitarian marriages.

While the process of negotiating differences is part and parcel of any marriage, the competing understandings of the domestic and public spheres complicate Chosŏnjok women's adjustment to conjugal life. I first examine these divergent cultural constructions and then return to the story of Yunŏk and introduce three other Chosŏnjok brides. Some analysts emphasize the intensification of male privilege and gender inequality through transnational mobility, but the experience of Yunŏk and the other three women show us how Chosŏnjok women can resist and, to some degree, overcome the gendered inequalities they encounter within their marital families.

A Preponderance of Male Privilege

Are transnational processes conducive to reconfiguring the assumptions and practices associated with gender? The cases reported in the anthropological literature, for the most part, are not very optimistic. In her study of rural Salvadoran women with migrant husbands overseas, for example, Sara Mahler (2001) shows how transnational migration exacerbates preexisting inequalities between men and women. While the women in Mahler's study are located in isolated, rural communities, their husbands are depicted as the exclusive beneficiaries of transnational travel and communication. Other analysts present a more complicated view of women's agency and call attention to the resourcefulness and creativity exercised by individual women in transnational contexts (see Fouron and Glick Schiller 2001; Brennan 2001). However, the overall picture still seems rather pessimistic. Brennan's study of sex workers in the Dominican town of Sosua, for example, shows that despite the women's creative strategies, the power imbalance between female sex workers and male sex tourists remains virtually unchanged. As Mahler observes, "though people negotiate gender across transnational space, the articles in this volume show that transnational space does *not* appear to be a place where the hierarchy of gender relations is reconfigured" (2001, 611).

Aihwa Ong's study of "flexible citizenship" among overseas Chinese capitalists also emphasizes the reproduction of gendered inequalities across transnational space. Ong links the transnational business practices of Hong Kong emigrants with what she calls "familial regimes of dispersal and localization" (1999, 128). In these families, men are "in charge of mobility while women and children are the disciplinable subjects" (20). Moreover, Ong also describes young migrant women working in Shenzhen and other cities along the eastern seaboard of China, who aspire to marry the overseas Chinese businessmen in their midst, as victims, not just of men but of their own fantasies. As Ong concludes, "This particular conjunction of working women's middle class dreams and mobile men has reinforced conditions ripe for the masculinist thrust and scope of sexual and class exploitation throughout Asia" (156).

Gilmartin and Tan examine the long-distance marriage migration patterns of Chinese women inside the People's Republic of China. Crossing provincial instead of national borders, increasingly large numbers of young women have been marrying out of poor rural areas of the southwest and into richer agricultural regions along the eastern seaboard. As their title "Fleeing Poverty" suggests, the authors emphasize the economic instrumentality involved as these women decide to marry. Female marriage migrants, Gilmartin and Tan argue, treat "the selection of a husband as a type of market activity in which they are using demographic advantage to maximize their economic benefits." The benefits are offset, however, by the male-dominated family regimes with which these women have to contend upon arrival in their marital homes. Gilmartin and Tan conclude that "by relying on their roles as wives and mothers to effect this shift from the poorer to the richer regions of China, they are in fact tending to reinforce male power within marriage relationships" (2002, 215).

As this brief ethnographic survey suggests, husbands are often portrayed as the beneficiaries of transnational (and translocal) mobility, whether or not it is men who are actually doing the moving. Wives, by contrast, are depicted as controlled or constrained by patriarchal family regimes and broader structural inequalities that either limit their options after migration or preclude their movement altogether. One notable exception is Constable's study of correspondence relationships between Filipina and Chinese women and U.S. men. Against the prevailing imagery of men "in charge" of mobility and women "on the receiving end,"[2] Constable

---

2. Massey makes a distinction between those "in charge" and those "on the receiving-end" of transnational movements of various kinds but does not specifically address the role that gender plays in differentiating these two groups (1994, 149). Clark (2001) builds on this notion to suggest

emphasizes the privileges and possibilities—not just the restrictions—
that patrilocal kinship practices afford women in a transnational context.
Constable writes, "[Chinese women] gain mobility by virtue of gendered
familial roles and expectations, and they contemplate relationships with
western men as a means to fulfill personal dreams of marriage and mobility" (2003a, 174). Constable focuses primarily on the process of correspondence and courtship leading up to the decision to marry (or not to marry)
across transnational space. In this book, by contrast, I am interested in
the gendered dynamics between spouses *after* migrant brides arrive at
their marital destinations in order to assess the extent to which Chosŏnjok
women succeed in fulfilling their dreams.

Like wives represented in the several studies noted above, Chosŏnjok
women encountered gendered inequalities within their marital families
regarding kinship roles and expectations, the division of labor, and household authority. Many Chosŏnjok brides I spoke with complained that their
personal ambitions and visions of marital life were at odds with those of
their marital family members. However, Chosŏnjok women's frustrations
are not the final word on the subject. That migrant brides faced challenges
and obstacles does not tell us how these women responded to them. Some
women I met vowed to persevere and continue living (*chamgo salta*) despite
familial tensions; others, like Yunŏk, contested kinship conventions and
destabilized gender hierarchies within their marital relationships in order
to accommodate their own personal agendas.

Men Are the Heavens and Women Are the Earth

What are the dominant assumptions that Chosŏnjok women hold about
"wifely" roles in China versus South Korea? Such images shape their expectations as well as the ways they respond to conflicts that arise within
their marital families. South Korea is a patrilocal, patrilineal society where
women are expected to adjust to the kinship practices and expectations of
their husband's families, and South Korean women and Chosŏnjok women
face the same sorts of challenges in their marriages to South Korean men.

---

that Asian men in search of foreign brides have more control over their mobility than Chinese
women in search of foreign husbands (105, cited in Constable 2003a, 174).

But while Chosŏnjok women's complaints may not be unique, the women tend to view marital discord as resulting from a clash of Chinese and Korean kinship regimes. Their understanding is informed by a distinctly "Chosŏnjok" cultural logic. Socialization within the PRC, where gender equality (*nannu pingdeng*) prevails as an ideology if not a lived reality, creates a shared discourse among Chosŏnjok brides which influences them, in some cases, to pursue visions of kinship and conjugality that depart from those projected by their marital families.

Filipinas and other transnational marriage migrants have been described in the literature as motivated to marry overseas by the imagined prospect of "more egalitarian family life" abroad (that is, in a Western country) (Constable 2003b, 167). Chosŏnjok women, by contrast, generally had a less sanguine vision of gender relations in South Korea, both before emigrating and after living there. For Chosŏnjok women, marriage to a Korean man did not hold forth the promise of conjugal equality. Quite the opposite: most Chosŏnjok women I spoke with imagined themselves moving from a system of relative gender equality in China to one of gender oppression in South Korea (*nuren bei yapo de*).

It was not uncommon for parents to object to a daughter's prospective marriage to South Korea out of concern she would be burdened by her wifely responsibilities in the Korean family system. One young Chosŏnjok woman I interviewed spoke of concealing her decision to marry a South Korean man until the last possible moment. "My parents objected strongly when I joked with them years ago about marrying a Korean man," she recalled. "They told me in South Korea 'men are the heavens, women are the earth' [*namja hanŭl igo yŏja ddangida*]. They didn't want me to suffer." By way of explanation, she offered, "While things are difficult in China in terms of material and economic standards of living, Chinese men help with the housework, so it's more convenient [*pyŏnhada*] to live in China."

The opposite scenario—daughters who turned down their parents' suggestions that they marry to South Korea—was also common. One Chosŏnjok mother in Creek Road Village angled to have one of her two daughters marry to South Korea so that she herself might obtain an entrée into the South Korean labor market. But fearing a life of enforced domesticity, her daughters staunchly opposed the idea. "They refuse to marry a Korean man," the mother lamented. "My daughters say they will only marry to Korea if they are too poor to buy wood or coal to light the stove."

The mother attributed her daughters' refusal to marry a South Korean man to the lack of freedom for wives in South Korea, a situation she contrasted with the relative equality perceived to govern married life in China. "In China, both the husband and wife are income earners. Both are free to lead active lives," the mother explained. "But in Korea, women must serve their in-laws. The husband calls home in the afternoons to make sure the wife has not left the house. Women are essentially imprisoned, forced to stay home all day like caged birds."[3]

After experiencing married life in South Korea firsthand, many Chosŏnjok brides voiced their dissatisfaction with what they perceived to be excessively rigid gender roles in their marital households. In particular, Chosŏnjok brides objected to limits placed on their ability to earn a living, their restricted access to spending money, the gendered assignment of household labor, obligations to live in the same house and serve their in-laws, and, in extreme cases, physical abuse. Chosŏnjok women generally considered these practices to be rooted in conventional and long-standing South Korean norms, though some believed their foreign status as Chosŏnjok was an exacerbating factor. The following statements made by Chosŏnjok brides in South Korea convey not only their sense of indignation but also their tendency to contrast the hierarchical nature of Korean kinship practices with what they claimed to exist in China:

A: [This woman had temporarily moved out of her husband's house because of his opposition to her desire to seek outside employment.] In China, a woman earns her own money, has her own job, decides what to do with her own money, whether to buy clothes or something to eat.... My husband expects me to do everything around the house as if it is my duty, my obligation. For example, when my husband is sick, he expects me to prepare his medicine and set it in front of him. Shouldn't it be the sick person's responsibility

---

3. South Korean men were thought to make good partners based on their perceived employability, their work ethic, and their ability to be good economic providers. Chosŏnjok women also praised South Korean husbands for their devotion to family. While the perceived ubiquity of extramarital relationships (*param piuda*) amidst South Korea's expansive drinking and sex industry was a common cause for concern, Chosŏnjok women (and South Korean women too) commonly drew solace from the popular observation that South Korean men typically maintain their first loyalty to their wives and children and, unlike Chinese men, tend not to allow their extramarital affairs to impinge on the integrity of their family life. Some Chosŏnjok women asserted that South Korean men were on the whole more "romantic" and "chivalrous" than their counterparts in China based on images they said they had gleaned from Korean television dramas.

to take his own medicine? In China, you wouldn't ask your wife to give you medicine. You'd just take it yourself. It would be one thing if he asked politely, but he demands that I do it as if it were my duty.

B: [when asked how married life in Korea compares to China] Chinese men treat their wives much better. When they get home, they do the housework and cooking. There is no distinction between men's work and women's work. In Korea, men expect women to take care of all the housework.

C: Look at the way I live now. Would a Korean woman be able to live like this? I doubt it. Women are the ones who do the housework. Women are the ones who make the plans [for the family].... In all honesty, my husband doesn't treat me like a wife. I'm more like a domestic [*pach'ulbu*]. If he tells me to work, I work. If he sends me into the fields, I go. If he tells me to clean the house, I clean the house.

D: I heard that there are Korean women who live like we [Chosŏnjok women] do. We have no economic power. Our husbands give us just enough to exist on. I saw on the news once a woman whose husband gave her so little money that she filed for divorce. The court ruled that this was valid grounds for divorce, and the court ordered that the man give the woman a certain amount of money each month. So you see there are cases like that in Korea, it's not just like this for Chinese women like us.

E: Since I've lived here, I've seen young [Korean] men go into the kitchen on TV, but I've never seen it with my own eyes.

Women's experiences differ according to age, lifestyle, income level, generation, and geographic region, as well as idiosyncrasies of personality and preference. Not all men, for example, objected to their wives' desire to work outside the home, just as not all women objected to having to perform the lion's share of domestic duties. However, despite such variations, nearly all the women I interviewed interpreted instances of marital discord as reflecting the differences between "South Korean" and "Chinese" practices. These essentialized views did not simply grow out of individual experiences of transnational marriage in South Korea. They were informed by standard Chosŏnjok narratives—both academic and popular—about gender and national/ethnic identity, which circulated widely through everyday encounters in public and private life.

Private conversations with Professor Lee, a Chosŏnjok feminist scholar I befriended in Seoul, revealed the ways in which representations of Chinese "gender equality" and South Korean "gender oppression" create a framework for Chosŏnjok criticism. Professor Lee had been invited to

spend one year at a university in Seoul as part of a scholarly exchange program with her home institution in northeastern China. She welcomed me
on several occasions as a guest in her home in Seoul and later in Yanbian
where she candidly offered her personal views on transnational marriage.
At our first meeting, she surprised me with her unequivocal opposition.
"If you ask me," she said, "I'd say these marriages are futile. In fact, I don't
approve of them [*buzancheng*]." She spoke of turning down a large sum of
money several years ago to broker a marriage for a Korean man, explaining that she "couldn't have done it in good conscience." In Professor Lee's
view, the majority of marriages between Chosŏnjok women and South
Korean men ended in failure, an outcome she attributed to "cultural differences" (*wenhua chayi*), particularly as reflected in the realm of gender
relations in the family.

She then spelled out, without any of the subtleties or contingencies
one might expect from a social scientist, the differences as she saw them
between gender constructs, categories, roles, and behavior in China and
South Korea. "Women and men in Yanbian are equal," she stated matter-
of-factly. When two people interact in Yanbian,

> they do not regard one another as man and woman but as colleague or class-
> mate, for example. They make no distinction between men and women.
> In Korea, by contrast, people are judged first and foremost by their gen-
> der. Women have very little decision-making power in the family. Women
> in Korea are oppressed [*beiyapo de*], especially by their mothers-in-law. Fa-
> thers-in-law are also oppressive. You simply don't see this kind of thing hap-
> pening in Yanbian.

She continued with an example: "In Yanbian, when a daughter-in-
law plays a game of cards with her father-in-law, the atmosphere is very
carefree, relaxed. In Korea, even when playing a game of cards, relations
are tense." According to Lee, Chosŏnjok brides who run away from their
marital households should be understood as fleeing an oppressive gender
regime that not only subordinates wives to their husbands but also places
them under the authoritative control of their in-laws.

Mr. Na, director of the Research Association for the Welfare of Korean Farm and Fishing Villages (RWFFV), agreed that Chosŏnjok and
South Koreans adhere to radically different gender and kinship norms,

but, like other South Korean men I spoke with, he saw the differences not in terms of more or less gender equality but rather more or less respect for "traditional" sources of authority and "proper" intergenerational relations. While Professor Lee advocated a more relaxed style of interaction between parents and children, Mr. Na pointed to the fact that "in China it's okay to smoke in front of your father" as evidence of the breakdown of proper filial relations. "In China, the mother-in-law gets up early in the morning to cook rice while the daughter-in-law sleeps in. The daughter-in-law speaks to her mother-in-law as if she were an equal," he stated with barely concealed disapproval. "In Korea we must serve our parents," he said. In terms of gender relations, Mr. Na painted the situation in China as a world turned upside down: "In China, they think men and women are the same. The husband watches the children at home while the wife goes out to work."

Several weeks later I attended a talk given by Professor Lee at her host university in Seoul entitled "Chungguk yŏsŏng ŭi kibon sanghwang" (The fundamental situation of Chinese women). Before a large audience of mostly Korean students and faculty, Lee painted in sweeping strokes the history of communist liberation as having elevated and empowered women in Chinese society. As she had done in our private conversations, Lee treated "Chinese women" as a single basic category, without regard to ethnic, class, generational, or geographical differences, to make a case for the overall equal distribution of power between men and women in postrevolutionary China.

Lee enumerated the ways the lives of Chinese women are easier than their South Korean counterparts. She contrasted the prevalence of the "mother-in-law problem" in South Korean families with its absence in Chinese families. She compared the elaborate rituals of ancestor worship and the enormous burden they pose to South Korean wives with the simplified rituals adopted in China and the relative ease with which Chinese wives carry them out. She also weighed what she described as compulsory domesticity imposed on South Korean wives against the shared division of inside and outside work presumed to govern the lives of Chinese couples. I was surprised that Lee would use South Korea as a foil to project such a rosy picture of gender relations in China instead of seeking to establish points of connection between her status as a Chosŏnjok and her Korean listeners. Without any apparent skepticism about Lee's essentialized pronouncements, the members of the audience sighed in amazement and nodded their heads in awe and understanding.

One week earlier I had attended a talk by the former dean of Women's Studies at Ewha Women's University in Seoul, one of the most prominent women's universities in Korea. Her objective was to give a historical overview of Korean women's history as part of a women studies lecture series organized for English-speaking expatriates living in Seoul. This talk in many ways paralleled Professor Lee's lecture. Both were attempts by feminist scholars to give a comprehensive account of women's history from their own national standpoints to a foreign audience. While Professor Lee began with the Communist Liberation (*jiefang*) as her pivotal reference point and recounted a story of women's emancipation, the former dean spoke of the continuous and systematic domination of men over women throughout 5,000 years of Korean history. The South Korean scholar structured her historical narrative around a distinction between the "traditional" period, which she traced back 4000 years to the Tang'un origin myth, and the "modern" period, signaled by the imposition of Japanese colonial rule. During the "traditional" period, women were said to be entirely dependent and subjugated to men in accordance with Confucian principles of patriarchal social organization.[4] Although I had to leave the lecture just as the "modern era" was dawning, with the arrival of Western naval ships in Korea's ports in the 1880s, the overall message was clear. Though much was said to have changed in the modern era, women were decidedly still dominated by men. Interestingly, the dean did not call attention to the active role of men in controlling women so much as she criticized women's passive enslavement to "tradition." Even more surprising, she invoked Freud to explain why the subjugation of women is etched so deeply in the psyches of Korean women.

I point out these grand, simplistic narratives of gender emancipation in China versus gender oppression in South Korea not because I think they

---

4. By drawing upon Confucian philosophy to explain the subordination of women in the "traditional" period, the speaker elides thousands of years of history before the adoption of Confucian reforms, which did not occur until the Yi dynasty (1392–1910). In the preceding Koryŏ Dynasty (935–1392), husbands often resided uxorilocally and daughters were entitled to an equal share of their father's inheritance (see Deuchler 1992). Locating the roots of present-day gender asymmetry in Confucian "tradition" also overlooks important changes that have occurred in familial arrangements over the course of the twentieth century.

directly influence the gendered outlook of the brides I met. Popular culture's representations of gender in the form of television soap operas, talk shows, feature films, and the Internet are far more likely than academic lectures to have a powerful and immediate impact on the popular imagination. Rather, my interest in scholarly narratives is to provide evidence of the unmistakable parallels between the "language of gender" deployed by intellectuals and by ordinary Chosŏnjok. Such resonances prompt us to consider the larger ideological regimes of meaning within which both popular and elite constructions are situated. I suggest that Chosŏnjok women contemplate their lives at the crossroads of two competing national discourses on the ideal woman or wife—the communist ideal of the publicly engaged "model wife," which held sway in Mao-era China, and the Confucian-inspired gender discourses of South Korea, which extolled the virtues of women who remained in the home.

At a macro-structural level, South Korea and China appear to have undergone similar changes in family relations and family composition, including a decline in power of the parental generation, an increase in importance of the conjugal relationship, and an increasing preference for nuclear family households rather than extended ones (see Yan 2003). In both China and South Korea, these shifts have created opportunities for new conceptualizations of women's roles and status. However, these reconfigurations have played out differently in the two countries. The contrasts are particularly salient with respect to how women's relationship to home and work has been ideologically defined.

Scholars working in both China and South Korea have described the ongoing reconfigurations of gender constructs in response to rapidly changing times, as well as the coexistence of multiple visions and experiences of gender. No single model of the ideal husband-wife relationship dominates the social landscape in either South Korea or China. Indeed, married women in both countries can avail themselves of a variety of positions, though individual women differ greatly in their ability to realize these idealized visions.

Attempts to understand gender constructs among the Chosŏnjok are further complicated by their minority status in the PRC and the tendency for both the Chosŏnjok and the Han to deploy gender discourses as markers of ethnic difference. Chosŏnjok women viewed female domesticity in South Korea as symptomatic of patriarchal privilege and power, but many married Chosŏnjok women in northeastern China, by contrast, spoke of their domestic roles as an honorable cultural trait that distinguished them from their Han Chinese counterparts. In the words of my fifty-something host mother in Harbin, "Hanzu men do everything, and the women are all fat and lazy." My host mother reacted in disgust when I told her that the Han Chinese professor who had invited me to his home for lunch had prepared the meal himself while his wife chatted with me in the living room.[5] "All Hanzu men are like that," she said disapprovingly. "I can just picture it," she continued. "The man with his apron in the kitchen and his wife entertaining the guest. It's totally backward." According to Chosŏnjok custom, she explained, a man should entertain the guests while the woman prepares the meal and serves it. "Men are *nanzi han* [manly, in the sense of a he-man]," she explained. "You have to give them face when there are guests."

Interestingly, she felt compelled to tell me that her husband was quite capable of preparing a meal if circumstances called for it. She was also fond of reminiscing about the "old days" when they had to burn coal to heat the water for cooking. Her husband would fetch the coal, start the fire, and heat the water before she would do the cooking. Like other Chosŏnjok men and women I talked to who had years of marital and childrearing experience to reflect upon, she defined men's work around the house as "heavy" labor (*hen lei de huo*), whereas women performed the "lighter" (*bu lei de huo*) tasks such as cooking. These clearly demarcated roles were defended as not only egalitarian and complementary but the basis of harmonious marital relations.

These conservative gender assumptions might be expected from a woman of my host mother's generation. I was caught off guard, as were the Han Chinese male professors in the room, however, when their female colleague at the university—a woman in her late thirties—described an ideal Chosŏnjok wife as one who takes full responsibility for the domestic realm. She proclaimed, to my astonishment, that she quite happily takes care of all the cooking, housework, and childcare. "To a Chosŏnjok, it seems strange

---

5. The Han Chinese professor, incidentally, was equally critical of Chosŏnjok men on the same grounds, stating that "Chaoxianzu women are very capable [nenggan] while the men are lazy [lan]." When I asked what he meant by this, he replied that "Chaoxianzu women do all the housework, and the men do nothing."

to see a man cooking or a man in the kitchen," she explained. When her children were younger, she recalled feeling tired, but now she claimed to view her domestic responsibilities as simply "a little extra work." Like my host mother, this highly educated, comparatively young woman seemed to fully embrace a wife's naturalized association with domestic labor, reasoning that women were perhaps better able to accept an inferior status than men. "To assume a low status is a great blow to a man's self-respect. It's not the case for a woman," she stated. Drawing on comparisons with her Han Chinese neighbors, she also noted with some measure of pride that Chosŏnjok marriages were far less vulnerable to disputes over housework given the clear gendered assignment of household labor.[6] Perhaps it should not have come as a surprise to discover the persistence of conservative gender ideals among a younger generation of mothers and wives. In her study of mothers and daughters in urban China, Evans emphasizes the connections and divergences between the two cohorts, complicating any attempt to make neat generational distinctions in terms of gender expectations and practices (2008, 30–31).

The apparent contradiction of rendering Korean female domesticity as a sign of gender oppression and Chosŏnjok female domesticity as a sign of propriety underscores the complexity of gender constructions. Not surprisingly, many Han Chinese women I met imagined Chosŏnjok women to be "traditional," "unliberated," and "subservient" (*hen tinghua*). The malleability of gender symbolism and the way it is implicated in "otherizing" processes is further illustrated by the case of North Korean settlers in South Korea. Hae Yeon Choo describes how popular discourses in South Korea construct North Korean women as victims of patriarchal oppression and sex trafficking while casting South Korean women as the mirror opposite—as beneficiaries of South Korea's progressive gender ideals and practices. North Korean women who have settled in South Korea respond to these discourses of victimization by framing themselves as virtuous wives in contrast to aggressive and promiscuous South Korean women (2006, 599). Abelmann's observations regarding South Korean "gender

---

6. I am not certain whether younger, unmarried women shared these conservative gender assumptions. It was more common for young Chosŏnjok women I met to speak about their conservatism (*baoshou*) regarding premarital sex and cohabitation as opposed to the loose (*suibian*) sexual mores they perceived to reign among young people in South Korea.

sign systems" are thus relevant within the Korean diaspora: "There is a tendency for women to locate the extremes of desirable and undesirable femininity in other women: the extremes of womanhood are always located elsewhere or in another" (2003, 202). These examples show how these moral discourses on femininity also tend to operate in highly context-dependent and sometimes contradictory ways as markers of (intra)ethnic difference and stratification.

Though the gendered narratives that women tell about themselves and others are often contradictory and in flux, women in both South Korea and China have had to negotiate highly politicized, state-drawn notions of feminine identity, in the past as well as the present. Whether these politically motivated and historically contingent constructs are accepted or challenged in the course of everyday life, they are influential in delineating the contours of women's self-perceptions and ambitions, producing stereotypes to strive for or to avoid. In marrying across the Sino-Korean border, Chosŏnjok women must confront competing definitions of what it means to be a woman and a wife. In the next section, I examine official discourses on gender as they developed in conjunction with the divergent political agendas of South Korea and China in the latter part of the twentieth century.

Definitions of Woman, Wife, and Worker in South Korea and China

The anthropologist Cho Haejoang sketches the evolution of the middle-class ideals of womanhood that have come to dominate South Korean social life today. Cho (2002) describes how, throughout the social dislocation and widespread poverty of the postcolonial and Korean War eras, women were primarily defined as "mothers" enmeshed in extended family households. Over the course of Korea's remarkable transition to a predominantly urban, industrial society, the once-cherished image of the industrious mother whose productivity formed the backbone of a collective family enterprise gave way to a new ideal—that of the modern housewife whose primary role was to manage a nucleated domestic sphere that was symbolically detached from the world of productive labor. Cho describes how South Korea's rapid industrialization, which began in the 1960s, created the social conditions necessary for the "housewifization" of large segments of the population, giving more and more families the financial means to keep their wives out of the workforce. In this changed economic and discursive context where domesticity and work were ideologically and spatially distinct, wives were assigned the auxiliary role of tending to "family matters" while their husbands performed legally and emotionally privileged work out in "society."

Cho traces the ideological precedents for this division between gendered spheres of work and home to the "wise mother, good wife" (*hyŏnmo yangch'o*)[7] ideal of Meiji Japan, first imported by modernist reformers in the 1930s (2002, 172). As in Japan, the Korean model of the "wise mother, virtuous wife" was constructed through explicit national policies and directives that paid tribute to women who remained in the home, singularly devoted to their husbands and children. Men, by contrast, were exhorted to build the nation through their hard work in the formal economy (173).

The gendering of public and domestic space—men as the heroes of industrialization, women as their helpmates in the home—continues to structure state-family relations in South Korea. In chapter 1, I discussed how the absence of a comprehensive welfare system in present-day South Korea stems in part from the state's expectation that women, as wives and mothers, assume responsibility for nurturing the nation. The state-facilitated program to recruit Chosŏnjok brides as a resuscitating force for the nation's beleaguered farmers is yet another instance of the state casting wives as the enablers of men's socially important and patriotic work (in this case farming) and the protectors of the patriarchal family in troubled times (in this case the perceived disappearance of the "traditional" extended, agricultural household). In keeping with this masculinist vision of patriotism, family, and the public sphere, fathers were called upon to save the nation from economic decline when the nation's economy hit hard times in 1997. In 1998, I arrived in Seoul to do my fieldwork at the height of the Asian financial crisis to see the city festooned with banners bearing the

---

7. In Japan, where this womanly ideal originated, "good wife" precedes "wise mother." Citing Pae's work (2007, 169), Hyun-Key Kim Hogarth provides an explanation for why Koreans reversed the word order when they adopted this phrase from Japan: "The reason...is that traditionally to the Korean woman being a mother is more important than being a wife, which testifies to the strong presence of matrifocality in Korean society" (104).

slogan "Fathers Fight On!" (*abŏji hwait'ing*).[8] The banners were meant to cheer on the nation's fathers, for they had been vested with the important patriotic duty of revitalizing the economy by dint of their hard work.

Since the maturation of South Korea's domestic consumer market in the 1980s, visions of feminine identity have become increasingly inter-twined with consumer-oriented ideas and practices. Daughters coming of age at this time, surrounded not only by the new consumerism but the progressive ideals emanating from Korea's broad-based feminist and de-mocracy movements, aspired to define themselves outside the confines of their familial relationships, in opposition to the ideals of motherly self-sacrifice embodied by the previous generation (Cho 2002, 179). However, as Cho argues, structural and familial impediments pressured educated young women to look outside the public sphere for ways to express their desires for "self-realization" (*chaa shilyŏn*), the new buzz word. Inundated with a barrage of commoditized and sexualized images in the mass media instructing women on the importance of being sexy, attractive, and com-pliant, many young women in their twenties and thirties have come to express their sense of individuality by cultivating an ultrafeminine physical appearance, what Cho calls "the Missy syndrome" (2002, 186). The no-tion of "Missy" (*misijŏk*) housewives, a term first coined by the advertising industry in the mid-1990s, has been widely adopted to signify a married woman who succeeds in maintaining a sexy, youthful appearance. "Missy" housewives are intensely interested in their physical appearance and in material comfort. They spend money on the latest fashions, make-up, ac-cessories, and brand-name household appliances, turning their bodies and homes into sites for self-realization (see Nelson 2000).

Many Chosŏnjok women I interviewed, particularly young women who lived in urban areas of South Korea, consciously styled themselves after

---

8. In recent years, a derisive critique of women's domesticity as impeding, rather than protect-ing, the well being of the nation has complicated what it means to be a housewife in South Korea. While Korean men were called upon to save the nation from economic decline, Korean women were categorically blamed for undermining the nation's economic well being (see Kendall 2002, 11). Nelson (2000) examines how mass-media-influenced public perceptions have turned middle-class housewives into scapegoats for a wide range of contemporary social ills, including real estate speculation, excessive consumerism, the inequities of extracurricular education, and "the vulgari-ties of modernization" in general. Underlying this public critique is a notion of the home as a place organized according to the selfish, materialistic ambitions of women, defined not simply in contrast to, but pitted against the interests of the public sphere, a realm governed by the selfless, patriotic deeds of men (see Nelson 2000, chapter 5).

the latest "young miss" (*agassi*) fashions, including their choice of clothing, make-up, hairstyles, jewelry, cell phones, and other accessories. To the dismay of South Korean husbands who may have imagined their Chosŏnjok brides to be free of consumer-oriented desires, many Chosŏnjok women looked forward to exchanging their Chinese-style wardrobes for South Korean fashions and acquiring what they perceived to be "modern" conveniences and household appliances. During an interview with a couple living in Seoul, I heard the husband complaining about his Chosŏnjok wife's "demands" when she first arrived to "buy this and buy that." In her defense, she explained, "I did not bring a lot of clothing with me here, because the styles are different and I needed to wear Korean-style clothing." Yunŏk, the Chosŏnjok woman who opened this chapter, dramatically transformed her physical appearance upon returning to Seoul from her natal village in China. I nearly failed to recognize her at our agreed meeting place outside the Midopa Department Store near her marital home. The woman in her thirties who I remembered as staggering into our mud-thatch house nearly every evening in Creek Road Village, looking somewhat disheveled and complaining of indigestion, was now standing before me in tight-fitting white jeans, a sporty striped T-shirt, and a pink baseball cap, her face radiant and her make-up carefully applied.

If Chosŏnjok women were interested in fashioning themselves after the image of the Korean-style "young miss," they were less inclined to act like a "missy housewife." Chosŏnjok women of all ages and backgrounds were highly critical of the spatial and symbolic split between male productivity and female domesticity that they perceived as governing South Korean family life. This resistance to the rigid gendering of home and work must be understood in light of the radical redefinition of women's roles in post-1949 China. Though most of the Chosŏnjok brides I met in South Korea were socialized in the political and ideological context of the reform period (post-1979), they are the inheritors of a Maoist ideological history that championed "male-female equality" (*nannü pingdeng*). Below I map out the shifts in the Communist Party's approach to gender relations, highlighting the ways it diverges and overlaps with the dominant ideology in South Korea at particular historic junctures. This is the background against which we can make sense of the clash of gender norms that Chosŏnjok brides experienced in their marital homes.

At a time when the South Korean government was extolling the virtues of women remaining inside the home and outside the formal economy, official discourse in Maoist China pressured women to do precisely the opposite: to shift their loyalties away from the domestic sphere and fully participate in the world of public affairs.[9] The "wise mother, virtuous wife" (*xiangqi liangmu; hyŏnmo yangch'o*) ideal, which South Korean leaders had enthusiastically embraced, was denounced during the Mao era as promoting the narrow interests of the home over the collective interests of state and society (Evans 2002, 337). Evans describes the ideal of "socialist conjugality" that dominated the public discourse in China from the 1950s to the 1970s: "Ideally, a 'revolutionary couple' were 'social activists,' and a revolutionary husband had no right to demand that his wife stay at home all day looking after his own comforts, any more than a woman should desire to spend her time servicing her husband" (337). "Model wives" aspired to be "model workers" who participated alongside men in the workforce and were judged according to "masculine" standards of achievement.

From the perspective of Ying, an urban, educated, twenty-four-year-old Han Chinese woman married to a South Korean resident of Seoul eighteen years her senior, the "housewifization" of South Korea is not a progressive phenomenon but rather a sign that the patriarchal patterns of the past have yet to be challenged. "What angers me the most is the way Korean women are expected to act in Korea. I don't think there is any country in the world where there are so many housewives," she told me during an interview. "Korea is like China was before 1949. I could never be just a housewife. A woman is not really a person unless she works."

Though the socialist ideal of the "working wife" radically departs from the ideal of the South Korean "housewife," there are some underlying similarities. In the official rhetoric of both countries between the 1950s and 1970s, women's work, whether divided between work and home as in China or focused exclusively on the matrifocal family as in South Korea, was constructed as contributing to the well-being of the country—for the good of the industrializing economy in South Korea, for the good of the socialist collective in the PRC. Both countries demanded selfless

---

9. While many working-class wives in South Korea may be forced by economic necessity to work in the public sphere, such work has never been promoted by the South Korean government as a cultural ideal. To the contrary, as discussed above, except during the politically charged and short-lived decade of the 1980s, married Korean women have been discouraged from defining themselves through their work outside the domestic sphere.

commitment and self-sacrificing hard work from wives in the name of the public good, and in both countries these nationalist injunctions were reinforced by images of arrestingly powerful women. Images of women steelworkers and militia women in postrevolutionary China share something of the strong character and spirit of self-sacrifice embodied in the figure of the assertive managerial wife or mother in South Korea who postpones her personal enjoyment to ensure the economic vitality of her family and, by extension, the nation.[10] Finally, while gender asymmetry in women's and men's prescribed roles is more overtly supported in the official rhetoric of South Korea, Evans perceptively points out that in China a woman's obligation to serve her husband, manage the domestic sphere, and uphold the stability of the marital relationship persisted despite the radical redefinition of gender norms that took place during the Mao era (2002, 338–40). The underlying linkage between women and the domestic sphere becomes particularly pronounced in times of economic duress, as evidenced by the fact that Chinese women are encouraged to leave their jobs and stay at home when unemployment becomes a problem for men. This was the case in the 1950s and again in state enterprises in the late 1990s (339).

After opening its doors to the global marketplace, China now also shares with South Korea a mass media saturated with globally circulating symbols of consumer wealth, fashion, and physical beauty. This has led, as it has in South Korea, to newly commoditized and sexualized visions of femininity that appear much gentler and more compliant than the feminine ideals of the preceding generation. The Chinese media still valorize the "superwoman" (*qiangnüren*) for her ability to manage both household and career. However, official party policy no longer denounces the stay-at-home housewife (*jiating funü*) for her lack of public engagement. Instead, women who diligently manage the domestic sphere and their children's education represent an enviable option for wives in well-off, urban Chinese families. Popular culture and public spaces since the 1980s are increasingly pervaded by visual representations of sexually appealing, fashionably dressed, and self-effacing young women (Evans 2002, 341; Evans 2008).

I have mapped out in schematic fashion the shifting constructions of the categories "woman" and "wife" over the last half century in South

---

10. It was not until the 1990s in South Korea that the image of a powerful wife was redefined as working against the interests of the nation (Cho 2002, 187).

Korea and China to convey a general sense of the hegemonic discourses that transect the lives of Chosŏnjok brides in South Korea. I have shown how in the 1960s and 1970s the South Korean ideal of the middle-class housewife appeared diametrically opposed to the Chinese revolution-era ideal of the working wife. At the same time these competing constructions share an underlying assumption that women take primary responsibility for managing the domestic sphere and ensuring the stability of the nuclear household. As China has become progressively interwoven into the global economy, its mass media have become increasingly saturated with the same globally circulating, commoditized images of femininity that have precedence in South Korea. In marrying across national borders, Chosŏnjok brides must traverse constructions of gender that on some levels reinforce and on other levels contradict their personal visions of how to be a good wife, mother, and daughter-in-law. The competing and overlapping ways in which understandings of the domestic and public spheres are gendered in South Korea and China complicate Chosŏnjok women's adjustment to the gendered familial roles and expectations of their marital families.

I now turn to the lived experiences of three Chosŏnjok brides to depict this complexity. The stories were selected not only because they illustrate the range of obstacles migrant brides face within their marital households but also the degree of agency Chosŏnjok women possess.

Yunŏk: A Marriage with Motives

In the story of Yunŏk, the Chosŏnjok woman whose dialogue with the Chinese Public Security official I used to start this chapter, I left off with the official's tongue-in-cheek warning that her South Korean husband would almost certainly abuse her and keep her a prisoner in the home. Yunŏk was amused by these comments and repeated them to her friends in the village at the end of the day, eliciting peals of laughter. I had a more sober reaction. Though the official of course exaggerated, I knew from interviews the previous year with Chosŏnjok brides in South Korea that tensions over division of labor were no laughing matter. What is more, Yunŏk's disputes with her Korean husband-to-be over her clearly stated intentions to work outside the home were widely acknowledged and a common topic of gossip in the village during the long wait for her marriage visa. In this section, I explore the clash of gender and kinship expectations that the villagers correctly predicted would arise once Yunŏk returned to her marital household in Seoul.

Yunŏk, like many other Chosŏnjok women I interviewed, had a history of previous work experience before meeting her Korean fiancé, a taxi driver in Seoul. She had worked first in a factory in Qingdao, China, before traveling to Korea as an "industrial trainee" *yŏnsusaeng* (see chapter 2). The pay in the Korean factory where Yunŏk had been assigned to work was so low she could not pay the interest on the loans her family had taken out to enable her to travel to Korea, leaving her no other option but to break her contract with the factory and take up more lucrative employment elsewhere. She found a job waiting tables in a restaurant, one of the most common forms of employment for undocumented female laborers. While it is common for "industrial trainees" to abandon their designated workplaces for higher paying jobs in the informal economy, Yunŏk was unusually ambitious. After three years of working in the restaurant, she saved up enough capital to open her own raw fish house, using for legal purposes the name of a Korean citizen.

Though her business failed during the economic crisis of the late 1990s, Yunŏk was fond of talking about her success as an entrepreneur, the skillful way in which she managed her staff and earned their respect and affection, and her feelings of accomplishment in having "done something big." If she were to return to the village in China, she claimed she would be "wasting her life with nothing to do but crochet woolen booties and play mahjong." To remain in Korea as an illegal alien involved the risk of deportation and steep fines. Yunŏk explained she could no longer bear the anxiety that swept over her every time she spotted a police officer. Marrying a Korean, she reasoned, would enable her to legalize her status in the country and pursue her entrepreneurial ambitions.

The opportunity to marry a Korean man arose when she received an introduction from a Korean man who had business ties with her father in China. Unlike the majority of women I interviewed who had met their husbands only once or twice on Chinese soil before agreeing to marry, Yunŏk moved in with her Korean fiancé, his mother, and his ten-year-old son from a previous marriage. They lived together for three months before deciding to get married. She thus was familiar with both the family and the country into which she would be marrying. She also knew she would have to overcome her husband's staunch opposition to her working outside the household. He had made it clear that he would marry only on the condition that she stay at home, take responsibility for raising his son, and not go out to work. Yunŏk protested that her personality was not suited for domesticity, that she needed a job not for the money but to feel as though she were leading an "active" life. Taking her at her word, her husband bought her an exercise machine. "He means well," she said, "he just doesn't understand."

Like Yunŏk, many Chosŏnjok women justified their desire to work outside the home by a wider range of reasons than just making money. Some women had children from a previous marriage or other family members back in China they wished to support through remittances out of their own paychecks. Others were dissatisfied with their husband's earning ability and wanted to make a contribution to the household coffers, claiming it was "unnatural" for a healthy person to remain idle in the prime of her working years.[11] Most women, however, especially those without the responsibility of caring for young children or elderly in-laws or those who, like Yunŏk, resisted the domestic duties assigned to them, were just plain bored staying home alone. Yunŏk expressed her profound dissatisfaction with her house-bound lifestyle when I visited her at her marital residence in Seoul: "Korean women are pitiable [*pulsanghada*]. They are prisoners of the home. Most of them are content to lead the life of a housewife. But you and I are different." She told me how she imagined the ideal conjugal arrangement with her husband to be a childless one in which each person pursues his or her own livelihood during the day and partakes in meaningful conversation in the evenings. Yunŏk lamented the isolation of her domestic confinement, complaining that she had no idea what was going on, let alone if it was raining or sunny outside. Like many other Chosŏnjok brides I met, Yunŏk was drawn to South Korea in large part by intense curiosity about life in a "developed country" and was interested in exploring what South Korea had to offer beyond the boundaries of her domestic quarters.

Even farmers' brides, disappointed by the paucity of resources and opportunities in their rural surroundings, valued their work experiences outside the home for expanding their understanding of life in their newly

---

11. I often heard this complaint in China among middle-aged Chosŏnjok who had been laid off from jobs in government-owned businesses and looked to South Korea as their only hope of putting their labor power to good use. Among the Chosŏnjok, the appeal of South Korea lies precisely in its imagined abundance of high-paying jobs.

A Chosŏnjok bride decorates her new one-room, neolocal residence with a poster-sized wedding portrait and a pair of wedding ducks.

adopted country and facilitating their adjustment. Oksŏng, the fisherman's wife I introduced in chapter 1, for example, considered herself very fortunate to have a job shucking oysters. She described how working helped her settle her thoughts, gain confidence in social interactions, and get the chance to observe the way Koreans lived:

> There's a lot of thoughts in your head. If you work outside the home, you don't have any of these thoughts. You don't have any anxieties because you are concentrating on your work. You can talk to people and make jokes and learn Korean, so it's better than staying home, don't you think? I also get to see how people here live. When I first came here, I knew nothing. Since going out to work I've learned a lot. I think if my husband had prevented me from working I might have considered running way. If you have freedom, you can live harmoniously here.

The struggle over a Chosŏnjok woman's right to take up paid employment outside the household that occurred in so many urban families is partly explained as a clash between Chinese and Korean constructions of conjugality. Some urban families, including those without the economic wherewithal to keep a wife out of the workforce, aspired to the middle-class ideal of maintaining gendered spheres of work and home. Kyŏng'ŭn, my twenty-eight-year-old research assistant, revealed her middle-class Korean sensibilities when she urged a Chosŏnjok woman during an interview to be more understanding of her Korean husband's refusal to allow her to work outside the home. "Others would talk about your husband, saying he lacks the ability to support his household [*saenghwal nŭngnyŏk*]," she explained. The husband agreed: "My wife says she wants to work in a restaurant. See, she still doesn't understand. You have to think about how other people would look at me if my wife were to work in a restaurant, you know?" Withdrawing from outside employment to secure a husband's social standing despite the need for additional income made little sense to Chosŏnjok women whose income-earning activities in China would have been part of a wife's normal prescribed role.

In many lower-income families throughout Korea, wives are important and necessary contributors to family economic survival, which suggests that fears beyond simple loss of face induce men to restrict the income-earning activities of their Chosŏnjok wives. Influenced by negative media imagery and locally circulating gossip about Chosŏnjok women who leave their husbands after obtaining citizenship, many husbands struggle with profound fears that their Chosŏnjok brides might run away. South Korean men living in urban areas tended to view the workplace as full of hidden dangers and temptations to which their Chosŏnjok wives, no matter how trustworthy, are particularly susceptible. When a woman works outside the home, many husbands explained, she regularly meets not only other men who might lure her away but also Chosŏnjok female friends who might influence her to desert her husband. Mr. Na of the Research Association for the Welfare of Korean Farm and Fishing Villages likened the anxious state of a man married to a Chosŏnjok woman to a person whose front door has no lock. "You know the security that most people feel when they lock up their homes when they are away? Well, the man who marries a Chosŏnjok woman feels like his door is always unlocked and there's nothing he can do about it. That's why men insist their wives stay at home." Ironically, the rigid gendered split of work and domesticity, which presumably upholds the safety and stability of a wife's place within the home, was one of the most common sources of dissatisfaction among brides I interviewed and a leading cause of divorce or desertion.

In rural areas where villagers knew one another and monitored each other's affairs closely, women moved about with considerably more freedom than in the cities. Chosŏnjok wives in many villages I visited in South Korea had earned reputations for their hard work and devotion to their families. Similarly, Chosŏnjok wives who lived in urban areas were encouraged to work in family businesses where contact with strangers could be monitored by their husbands and in-laws. While nearly all the working couples I interviewed were forced to work exceedingly long hours as they struggled to survive during the "IMF era" (IMF *sidae*), husbands and wives who worked together seemed to have genuine mutual appreciation for the other's ability and willingness to live diligently (*yŏlsimhi sanda*).

Matchmaker Pak, the commercial matchmaker of chapter 2 who draws on his own experience as husband to a Chosŏnjok woman to counsel his clients, urges South Korean men to facilitate the entry of their Chosŏnjok wives into the workforce. Many of the reasons he gave match those given by the Chosŏnjok women I interviewed. "The men don't want their wives to work," he explained. "They want them just to take care of daily necessities. But women in China aren't accustomed to that kind of arrangement. The women are generally very motivated and want to learn the customs of the country by working. They are bored at home and don't understand what they watch on television. They're not used to that kind of life. And if the woman works, she still has to make dinner while the man reads the newspaper. The women complain to me that the men don't help with the housework." Mr. Pak explained how his Chosŏnjok wife learned a great deal about how to interact with others through working at an insurance agency. He said he always advises his clients to find work for their wives or, in the case of farmers, to have their wives work alongside them in the fields.

Yunŏk is an example of a Chosŏnjok wife who chafes at her confinement to the household and the restrictions placed on her ability to make productive use of her entrepreneurial talent and ambition. In contrast to the young, rural brides discussed in chapter 1 who expected marriage itself to deliver them instantly into a life of material comfort, Yunŏk viewed marriage as a vehicle for carrying out her own work-related aspirations by enabling her to capitalize on the economic opportunities afforded by life in a developed country. Compared to the relative independence her entrepreneurial endeavors allowed her before marriage, she complained of feeling trapped by Korean standards of wifehood and motherhood, and, in strong language, confessed her contempt for the young boy in her charge whom she described as unruly, disrespectful, and disliked by the entire neighborhood.

As Yunŏk and I carried on our conversation in the kitchen, we could hear the sounds of an English lesson under way in the next room. Yunŏk continued her rant against the boy: "I don't know why my husband wastes money on a private tutor for him since he doesn't study and doesn't seem to retain anything the tutor teaches him." I got up from the table to take a closer look. A young Korean woman was calling out English phrases while the boy spun around and around, trying in vain to pick out the correct phrase from an array of papers scattered on the floor. I had to agree that the boy seemed confused. When the lesson was over, the tutor suggested that Yunŏk help the boy study by watching the instructional videos with him and answering any questions he might have. Yunŏk explained that she did not speak a word of English. The tutor opened her eyes wide with astonishment. I resisted the urge to intervene and rescue Yunŏk from feeling embarrassed by the tutor's presumption that all housewives in Korea would have been educated in at least a modicum of English for the sake of overseeing their children's studies. Before leaving the house, the tutor advised Yunŏk that it would still be a good idea for her to sit alongside the boy for moral support while he watched the English videos.

When the tutor left, Yunŏk expressed her disapproval of the way South Korean children depend upon their mothers to supervise their studies. "Chinese children are much more independent," she declared, pointing to her younger brother's son in China who attends school in the city and comes home to the village only on the weekends as an example of a model student. Yunŏk boasted that her nephew is an excellent student and does his homework without his mother's prompting and prodding. I recalled visits to Yunŏk's sister-in-law's one-room house where Yunŏk's nephew sat quietly in one corner, studiously bent over his books, seemingly immune to the chatter of his mother's houseguests. Yunŏk added that she was not opposed to studying English and computers as Korean housewives are expected to do but feared she lacked the rudimentary skills to join even an introductory-level class. I sensed that Yunŏk's reluctance to follow her husband's wishes and devote herself to full-time motherhood stemmed not only from her desire to pursue her personal ambitions but from her apprehension about her ability to perform the role of the middle-class, Korean-style "education mother."

Yunŏk reflected on the irony of her situation. Her husband had been the one initially to have reservations about getting married. He had proposed that they continue living together out of wedlock, but Yunŏk insisted that they marry. After three months, her husband relented, and they spent the following year living apart while processing the paperwork that would legalize their union. Now that they were finally reunited as husband and wife, Yunŏk was beset with regrets. The villagers in her hometown had speculated that the marriage would not last. Still, I was taken aback to hear Yunŏk herself, just weeks after legalizing her marriage, speak of divorce as a solution to her dilemma. While she believed that her husband sincerely "loved" her, she said she did not return the same degree of emotional attachment. She imagined that over time she would cultivate feelings of affection for him but not if he continued to forbid her to work. Unless her husband yielded, Yunŏk vowed that she would divorce him after obtaining citizenship.

One month later, Yunŏk was waiting tables in a restaurant. The threat of divorce, the only leverage she possessed, had been enough to dismantle her husband's opposition. For the time being, at least, Yunŏk had achieved what she desired through marriage: a legal entrée into the working world of a major metropolitan city. Yunŏk's relationship with her marital family members was secondary to this goal, by her frank admission. Chosŏnjok and South Koreans alike distinguished between the "purity" of rural-bound brides who naively believed that marriage would deliver them from poverty versus the "cleverness" and opportunism of women like Yunŏk for whom marriage was not an end in itself. These women were pejoratively spoken of as having married "with motives" (*you mudi de*).

Yŏnjae: A Love Marriage

Whether their motives were clearly defined or not, nearly all the Chosŏnjok brides I met explained their marriages in terms of strategic upward mobility. Yŏnjae was unique in that she claimed to have married for love (*yŏnae kyŏrhon*). She met her husband, Jinwŏn, for the first time in a restaurant in Shenyang, China. Yŏnjae was visiting her older sister who was working as a hostess in the restaurant. Jinwŏn managed the restaurant, which was owned by his father, a former taxi driver from South Korea. With the opening of Chinese markets to South Korean investors, large numbers of South Korean petty entrepreneurs had opened small businesses (mostly restaurants and massage parlors) in northeastern China and staffed them with Korean-speaking Chosŏnjok workers. These business operations provided one of the primary contexts for Chosŏnjok women and South Korean men to meet each other "naturally," without the mediating influence of a marriage broker.

Yŏnjae remembered being unmoved by the initial encounter with Jinwŏn. A poised, well-spoken, and attractive twenty-six-year-old, Yŏnjae was accustomed to deflecting the unwanted attention of male suitors. But Jinwŏn was not easily dissuaded. He invited Yŏnjae and her sister to rent a room in his father's house near the restaurant. The sisters accepted the offer, preferring the downtown location to that of their parent's home on the outskirts of the city. Living under the same roof, Yŏnjae and Jinwŏn established a friendship. Several months later, Jinwŏn asked Yŏnjae to marry him. "He and his father were both very good to me," she explained. "And I felt sorry for him because he grew up with a cruel stepmother. I thought if I treated him well I could make up for the pain he had suffered as a child." Motivated by a combination of kindness and pity, she agreed to marry him against the wishes of her own parents who had higher marital aspirations for their college-educated daughter. In Yŏnjae's eyes, her husband's humble family background did not amount to a flaw. She professed to judge a man based on his character alone, not his money.

Yŏnjae may not have looked to her husband for monetary support, but like Yunŏk she sought to take advantage of the opportunities her Korean passport presented. Not long after her arrival in South Korea, Yŏnjae conducted Internet searches, circulated her resume, and knocked on doors. In a matter of days, she found a job in a trading company as the in-house consultant on China-related commerce. What she lacked in training, she made up for in her bilingualism, assertiveness, and charm. She worked extremely long hours, took frequent business trips to northeastern China, and earned a salary nearly twice that of her husband, now an operations manager in a meat-packing company. She was exhilarated by her lucrative and fast-paced career. But her enthusiasm for her new life was severely dampened by her embattled relationship with her in-laws.

According to Yŏnjae, her parents-in-law had treated her well while she was dutifully caring for her husband's ailing grandfather in the final months before his death. The relationship became strained after Yŏnjae entered the workforce, and her father-in-law asked her to hand over a portion of her monthly salary. She simmered in silence as Jinwŏn turned over his paycheck in full each month to his parents. Grudgingly, she complied with her in-laws' wishes. When her father-in-law refused to give her spending money for a business trip to Pusan, Yŏnjae retaliated by taking back exclusive control over her purse strings. This incident marked the end of amicable relations in the household. Yŏnjae described the daily onslaught of insults and accusations she was forced to endure—pointed barbs regarding her ineffectualness as a daughter-in-law and her dirtiness and laziness as a "Chinese person" (*Chungguk saram*).

To escape the constant fighting with her in-laws, Yŏnjae pressed her husband to establish a separate conjugal residence. Yŏnjae knew her husband was in a difficult position, caught between his desire to please his wife and a deep-seated fear of defying his father. "I feel sorry for my husband," she explained, "but I told him that if he doesn't stand up to his father and move out, I will divorce him and go to Japan or Hong Kong, as I've always dreamed of doing."

For both Yunŏk and Yŏnjae, the ultimatum of divorce was a remarkably effective strategy in bending the will of their husbands. One month after the above conversation, Yŏnjae called me to help her choose new kitchen appliances for the tiny basement apartment she and her husband had rented with Yŏnjae's earnings. Yŏnjae was enjoying the freedom of her independent household and took a new interest in playing the role of homemaker. She took a leave of absence from work to set up the new household. While she busied herself in the kitchen, she talked of her plans for the future. She still intended to go to Japan or Hong Kong one day and pursue her studies. When I asked about her husband, she replied that if it was his wish to follow her, then they would remain together.

Mira: Dutiful Housewife

Kyŏng'ŭn (my research assistant) and I traveled four hours by train, from Seoul to the southern city of Pusan, to meet Mira. We stood in the rain on the corner where Mira had instructed us to wait until a petite woman came rushing up to us with a smile and an umbrella. We followed Mira down a narrow alleyway and into her husband's home where she treated us with customary hospitality to steaming cups of instant coffee, doctored with heaping spoonfuls of sugar and powdered creamer. As she handed us our coffee, she apologized for the modest conditions in which she lived, adding that despite her dreary surroundings she considered herself really quite "fortunate" (*xingfu*). For the better part of the afternoon, twenty-eight-year-old Mira would tell us the story of her marriage to a South Korean factory worker, eight years her senior, and how, unlike many Chosŏnjok brides in similar circumstances, she had come to accept her role as a round-the-clock housewife and daughter-in-law in the home of her in-laws.

On the way to Mira's bedroom where we would conduct our interview, I caught a glimpse of Mira's ailing father-in-law, bundled in quilts on the heated floor of his room. She closed the sliding doors to her room where the three of us sat down in privacy, cross-legged on the floor around my tape recorder. Mira seemed cheered by the presence of houseguests on a rainy afternoon, even odd ones such as Kyŏng'ŭn and I must have seemed. She was forthcoming with the details of her life, and I returned the favor at the end of our open-ended conversation, responding with equal candor to Mira's own inquiries about my thoughts on similar topics of marriage, mobility, and personal aspirations.

During our interview, Mira explained that, as the eldest son, her husband needed to find a wife who would be willing to live with and serve his parents. "His parents were afraid they might not be able to find that kind of woman in Korea," she said. Mira's mother-in-law took the initiative in finding her son a bride when she gave his picture to an unlicensed Korean matchmaker, Mrs. Yi (described in chapter 2), to take to China. Mira saw the photograph, which she recalled seemed "okay" (*kuench'anda*) when, following in the footsteps of her older cousin, she sought out Mrs. Yi's services in Shenyang. The example of her older cousin was, by her own account, a powerful incentive, combined with the stories she had heard about Chosŏnjok friends who were married and "living well" in South Korea. Mira's husband had seen a picture of her before signing up for a marriage tour, but, fearing he would not get along with or be able to communicate with a Chosŏnjok bride, her husband needed further convincing. "Just meet her," Mira reported the matchmaker had said to him. "It's the trend now to marry a Chosŏnjok woman. Just try it." Still skeptical, her husband embarked on a trip to Shenyang with two other bachelors from Pusan.

Mira claimed not to think much of her husband upon first meeting but spoke of how her husband had been impressed when she greeted him at the airport in Shenyang smartly dressed in a pair of clean, white pants. "My husband thought that all Chinese women must be 'country bump-kins' [*ch'onsŭrŏpda*], but compared with other Chinese women he really liked my style." Mira showed us a photograph of herself that day stand-ing beside the other two Chosŏnjok women who had been paired with the men from Pusan. "Look," she said pointing to one of the women in the picture, "*she's* a 'bumpkin.'" There were dozens of pictures in Mira's album chronicling the many places the three couples had visited in the course of their week-long "group date." Mira spoke nostalgically of their brief, two-part "courtship," one week together in China to cement their decision to marry followed by a second six-week-long return trip to China to complete the necessary paperwork. Though only two and a half years had passed since they first met, Mira reminisced as if it were decades ago, about how "handsome" (*shuai*) and "sharp minded" (*nalsae poida*) her hus-band had been (despite his disappointingly short stature), remarking that in the interim he had "gotten older," no longer as "clean-cut" as he used to be. Mira also boasted of how she had felt comfortable strolling arm and arm with her husband during their days in China, unlike her cousin who, according to Mira, had avoided the hand-holding attempts of her South Korean fiancé.

Throughout the interview, Mira remained positive and upbeat about her experience of married life, giving particular emphasis to the caring and considerate nature of her husband. While many Chosŏnjok women reported feeling disappointed by the standards of living provided by their rural or working-class husbands, Mira claimed that her circumstances, material and otherwise, were precisely as her "straight-talking" (*tokparo malhanŭn saram*) husband had described them, giving her no reason to ex-pect anything other than the kind of existence she was currently leading. Without prompting, Mira enumerated her husband's positive traits and the many occasions on which her husband treated her kindly:

My husband takes me to the karaoke [*norae pang*]. He helps with the house-work. He feels sympathy with me when I cry.... He's very considerate. He brings me a *papsang* [miniature table for eating on the floor] and serves me food.

She continued:

When I met my husband, I did not really like him at first. I thought he was too short. He's one meter, sixty centimeters and I'm one meter fifty-six centimeters. But he treats me much better than a tall man might have. He works for a company that makes boxes for cookies and pizzas. His coworkers think very highly of him and he has many friends. He makes a living. I know we aren't going to starve, so that makes him good groom material [*choŭn sinlanggam*]. He works very hard, but best of all, if I'm sick, he brings me flowers. I love flowers. If we go somewhere and I want to pick flowers, my husband says, "No, let me buy some for you."

No matter what direction I steered the interview, it always came back to Mira's descriptions of her husband's thoughtful treatment of her. Examples of her husband's benevolence included his considerate habit of sleeping in a separate room on nights when he returned home with the smell of alcohol on his breath. Mira also spoke of her husband's unconditional compliments on her cooking and her habit of waiting for her husband to return from work each night so that they might eat dinner together as a couple. Her husband was usually mindful to call her on nights when he would need to stay late at work, but should he forget, Mira said that he would apologize profusely "before I even have the chance to get angry." Aside from these quotidian courtesies, her husband also treated Mira to occasional holiday outings to the beach and trips to the karaoke. In Mira's estimation, the quality of her conjugal relationship surpassed that of her husband's brother who was married to a South Korean woman, as well as the marriages of other Chosŏnjok brides she knew in South Korea. "I have friends who married Koreans, and generally speaking, the husbands don't trust their wives. Some [husbands] come home at lunch time just to make sure their wives haven't run away. Things are okay that way with us."

According to Mira, the matchmaker initially expressed concern that someone as "clever" and "self-sufficient" as Mira would be apt to desert her husband. I too observed that Mira seemed to radiate a quiet confidence, as did Kyŏng'ŭn who remarked after the interview that Mira struck her as exceptionally quick-witted (*nunch'i pparŭda*). Six months into her marriage, Mrs. Yi called her on the phone to congratulate her for persevering with her marriage and not running away. "My husband's friends tell him he has a good wife," she said proudly. "I'm not naive and pure like they thought I would be. They say to my husband, 'You better watch out. She's a clever one. She might run away and marry someone better.' I tell them, 'I'll run away with my husband on my back.'" The image was meant to be humorous, but I also found it touching, a tribute to how much Mira seemed to genuinely care for her husband.

Despite the closeness of her marital bond, Mira described enduring long and lonely house-bound days, forced to attend to her bedridden father-in-law while her husband and mother-in-law went out to earn a living. "Since coming to Korea, I don't have anything to do. I do not have a job, so sometimes all I can really do is sleep. I've become an idiot [*pabo*]." The personal freedom of Mira's mother-in-law to come and go far exceeded her own. Mira recounted how some nights her mother-in-law would not come home from work until the next morning. Whereas other Chosŏnjok women like Yunŏk resisted the physical and psychic limitations of their assigned domestic duties, Mira surprised me by reserving any form of negative commentary on her relationship with her in-laws. When asked about her in-laws, Mira emphasized her good fortune in having a mother-in-law who tells her up front when she makes a mistake and then "turns her back and doesn't bring it up again." Of her father-in-law, she said, "he is very sick, so there is no nagging [*chansori*] from him."

Later that evening, in the relaxed setting of our motel room, where Mira was given permission by her husband's family to join us for a take-out dinner and an evening of Korean soap operas, Mira let down her guard and confessed to occasional feelings of regret over having married to South Korea. She talked of the difficulties she faced in caring for her sick father-in-law and how her aversion to Korean food combined with a failed pregnancy had left her in a profoundly weakened state of health. She sighed repeatedly and mused that she might have had a less difficult life had she stayed in China.

Despite these confessions of melancholy, Mira took pride in her ability to weather the challenges ahead of her, an ability she attributed to her strong character shaped through an earlier life of suffering and hard work. "I worked a lot in China and I suffered a lot in China, so I can handle [the difficulties of married life in South Korea]. But [Chosŏnjok women] who have never really suffered before have more trouble adjusting. I just made up my mind to be strong," she explained. As an indication of her natal family's poverty, Mira explained how an adopted son-in-law (*teril sawi*) had been brought in to the family for her older sister. For fifteen years he lived in her father's household before marrying Mira's sister and moving back into the home of his parents. Among other deprivations, Mira lamented her lack of education, having had to give up going to middle school because it was too great a distance for her to walk every day. Though she had worked in the fields from an early age, the death of her mother when she was fourteen accelerated her entry into the world of wage work and adult responsibility. She found a variety of ways to make money and used her earnings to pay for her older sister's wedding expenses. "That's how I got such a strong disposition [*sŏngjil*]," she said. "Even though I wasn't formally educated, I have *nunch'i* [an intuitive sensibility]. I was forced to become very clever in China.... I'm a person who knows what I want and I'm not afraid to say it."

Mira recounted a story about how her "strong disposition" stood in the way of her father's ability to get remarried. "My father went to a fortune teller when my mother died. She said there was a second wife for my father. I was so angry [when I heard this] that I went home and smashed a window. Rumors spread that I had a very difficult personality. That I was too *lihai* [formidable]. Because of me, because I am so *lihai*, my father could never get remarried."

Mira now looks to her husband as a model of emotional stability and tenderness:

> He is soft-hearted [*maŭmi yakhada*], so he doesn't get angry. When my husband went to China for the first time and saw that the marriage paperwork was taking such a long time, he became very angry. I worried that his disposition [*sŏngj'il*] must not be very good. But after coming to live here I found out that my temperament is much worse than his.... My husband is very good to me, so I'm trying hard to be a better person myself.

Mira, who seemed just as resourceful and driven as Yunŏk and Yŏnjae, might have picked herself up and looked for better opportunities elsewhere, as Matchmaker Yi and friends of her husband's family feared she might. Instead, for the time being at least, she had made up her mind to persevere beside her good-natured husband. While it is impossible to say for sure, it seems that Mira's affection for her husband was a powerful enough incentive to overlook the less favorable aspects of her marital situation.

In a casual conversation with Yŏnjae and two South Korean male friends, she gave advice on how kindness and empathy on the part of a husband could go a long way toward making a wife more willing to carry out the domestic duties expected of her:

> I've seen this happen with so many couples.... If the wife stays at home and takes care of the kids and the house, there is no understanding on the part of the husband about the difficulties involved in her responsibilities. So when he comes home, he is very demanding and wants only to be taken care of. If men were more sensitive to women's concerns and didn't take it for granted that women are supposed to cater to their every whim, and even offered to help women around the house, then women would be bending over backward to treat their husbands well.

Some women I interviewed claimed to be able to "soften" the patriarchal attitudes of their husbands. One farmer's wife, for example, boasted proudly about having trained her husband to bring her a glass of water should she request one. "What was once an unthinkable request for a woman to make to her husband has now become a habit with us," she explained.

For forty-four-year-old Yumi, another bride I had interviewed in Seoul, more meaningful communication with her husband might have smoothed over their differences over the division of labor in their household. Yumi broke down in tears in a coffee shop as she described the difficulties in her marriage that had led her to separate from her Korean husband and move in with her aunt who was living in Seoul at the time. She pointed to her husband's refusal to allow her to work outside the home as the main source of her unhappiness. However, she also criticized the rigid manner in which her husband enforced the division of labor and his inability to express affection toward her. "When my husband comes home, he expects everything to be ready and waiting for him." Having spent the day at home without human contact, she explained how she longed for meaningful conversation with her husband at the end of the day. "But my husband does not answer me when I try to speak to him. He doesn't know how to express affection. He doesn't treat me with tenderness [*bu teng wo*]."

Juju: A Runaway Bride

Juju, a thirty-four-year-old woman from Mudanjiang who appeared briefly in chapter 2, married a Korean man after her first marriage in China ended in divorce. She joined her older sister who had obtained Korean citizenship through a fake marriage to a South Korean man and was working in Seoul with her real husband from China. Though Juju spoke no more than a few words of broken Korean, she had been continuously employed since she arrived in Seoul in 1996, first in a restaurant and then in a jewelry store that catered to Chinese tourists. When I met Juju, she was working long hours in the jewelry store and spending most of her evenings away from home socializing with her older sister and other Chosŏnjok migrant workers she had befriended after arriving in South Korea. Whereas many Chosŏnjok brides complained of being closely guarded and forbidden by their husbands to work, Juju seemed to enjoy an unusual amount of personal freedom in her marriage.

When I asked her about it, Juju voiced her dissatisfaction with her husband. "He is ten years older than I am," she complained. "He is more like a father than a husband. We don't share any interests. He doesn't understand me at all, so he just lets me do as I please." Looking at the wedding portraits above their bed, I agreed that they seemed an unlikely match.[12] She appeared radiant and beautiful. He looked weathered, sullen, and old by comparison. "If he had any abilities [*nengli*], I could overlook his personality flaws," Juju explained. "He works hard at his construction job, but he has no ambition, no skills, and no mind for business. Every day is the same—he goes to work, comes home, eats, watches television, and goes to bed."

Unlike her husband, Juju was continually brainstorming for ways to turn a profit. By her own admission, high wages had lured her to South Korea in the first place. The numbers seemed high when she heard them in China, she explained, but she had not accounted for the high cost of living in South Korea. She was exhausted by the long hours at work, frustrated by the slow pace of capital accumulation, and angered by her employer's discriminatory treatment toward Chosŏnjok. Like many Chosŏnjok with South Korean passports, she sought to turn a faster profit by peddling goods back and forth across the Sino-Korean border. She enlisted my help

---

12. See Adrian (2003) for an in-depth look at the significance of wedding portraits in Taiwan.

in determining which sorts of consumer goods from South Korea would find a ready market in China.

Juju told me in confidence that she often contemplated leaving her South Korean husband. "I feel sorry for him," she said, "so it's very difficult to leave. It would be much easier if he beat me or drank heavily. But I know that he really loves me and he's good to me. I guess I have *chŏng*[13] for him." As the months passed, however, I watched a restlessness continue to brew inside her. Each time I saw her, she had devised a new scheme to relieve her unhappiness. In one of them, she considered going back to her first husband in China and their twelve-year-old daughter. Six months later, after I returned to Seoul from fieldwork in China, Juju had mustered the nerve to leave her Korean husband. She was living with a heavyset Chosŏnjok migrant worker in his forties who had been courting her steadfastly throughout the course of my fieldwork. While she had earlier denied any romantic interest in this man, Juju now claimed to have discovered a great deal in common with him, not the least of which was his entrepreneurial spirit. Juju, it seemed, had found a partner in business, if not in romance. She proudly offered me one of her new business cards emblazoned with both their names and a picture of a rare breed of dog that she and her new mate would be exporting to China.

Maneuvering across Power Geometries and Gender Logics

Yunŏk, Yŏnjae, Mira, and Juju, like many other Chosŏnjok brides, were motivated to leave their villages and marry into South Korea out of a sense of independence, adventure, entrepreneurialism, and a longing to lead a "modern" life in a "developed country." As women, their transnational mobility was enabled by their gendered positioning—both in terms of the demand for brides in the South Korean "marriage market" and in terms of the specifically female niche they occupied in the South Korean labor market, as nannies, waitresses, factory workers, bilingual service workers, and entrepreneurs, among other occupations. Many of these gendered opportunities for work and/or marriage abroad, as I explore further in the second part of

---

13. Koreans use the term *chŏng* to refer to the emotional bond between spouses that develops over time as a result of shared life experiences. Unlike the Western notion of romantic love, *chŏng* encapsulates the full spectrum of human emotion and grows more intense with the passage of time.

this book, were the exclusive preserve of women, giving them a uniquely female means of transcending the limits of their marginal positioning as they perceived it, both within the Chinese national economy and vis-à-vis South Korea as well as other centers of wealth and development overseas.

If cross-border marriages appealed to women who possessed the will and strength of purpose to try to change their lives, their personal goals and ambitions were often thwarted by South Korean kinship conventions that circumscribed a wife's activities outside the household and enforced hierarchies of gender and generation within it. As I have argued, the restrictions imposed on Chosŏnjok women by their husbands' families was further intensified and rationalized in light of the media-spun imagery of the "runaway bride" and the apprehension it inspired in the minds of their husbands. Chosŏnjok brides, many of whom possessed a cultural model of a wife's role as equally engaged in spheres of work and home, constructed the compulsory female domesticity they encountered in South Korea as a form of gender oppression.

The stories of Yunŏk, Yŏnjae, and Mira bring into sharp relief the gendered conflicts and cultural contradictions with which upwardly mobile, entrepreneurial-minded Chosŏnjok brides must contend. In the case of Yunŏk, Korean kinship norms conspire with her husband's fear of abandonment to prevent her from working outside the household. Though she regards her husband as basically well meaning and affectionate, his expectations for Yunŏk as a wife and mother are fundamentally at odds with the vision of gender and marriage she brought with her from China. Yŏnjae, by contrast, enjoys unfettered access to the formal economy. However, problems arise in the realm of the household economy when her desire to manage her own finances collides with her in-laws' expectations of how a daughter-in-law should behave. Mira, the round-the-clock housewife and caretaker of her bedridden father-in-law, also perceives her marital circumstances to be narrowly confining. For a woman who early on in life had proved her capacity for hard work and self-sufficiency, enduring the boredom and isolation of her domestic routine has not been easy.

Were I to end here, I might conclude like Gilmartin and Tan (2002) that although in many cases women might be active with respect to the initial decision to participate in marriage migration, their agency is ultimately compromised by the patriarchal family regimes into which they marry. Invoking Doreen Massey's (1994) frequently cited concept of "the power geometry," I might also conclude that Chosŏnjok women are ultimately not "in charge of" their mobility. Evidence that other stakeholders seek to exert control over Chosŏnjok women's mobility abound. As I showed in chapter 1, the South Korean government, eager to resuscitate the rural economy with a steady flow of brides from China, stood to gain, politically and economically, from the productive and reproductive labor of Chosŏnjok women. Chapter 2 described the crucial role that marriage brokers on both sides play in moving brides across borders and the sizable profit they can make in the process. It is also impossible to deny that Chosŏnjok brides—though the overwhelming majority may enter marriages of their own volition—ultimately depend upon South Korean men to achieve the mobility they desire.

This chapter has taken a close look at the "power geometries" and conflicting gender logics that Chosŏnjok women encountered in moving between Chinese and Korean settings. But, just as important, it also considers *how women responded to them.* The life sketches suggest that a woman's fate is not inevitably sealed with marriage or the patriarchal conventions imposed by her husband's family. The tactical forms of power wielded by Chosŏnjok women call for a reexamination of Massey's concept of "power geometry" and its corollary that, to borrow Smith and Guarnizo's (1998) popular terminology, "transnationalism from above" necessarily prevails over "transnationalism from below."

Nearly all the women I interviewed espoused what they defined as "Chinese" notions of kinship and gender relations against which they evaluated the ways of their "Korean" families. Some women acted upon their egalitarian visions of what married life could and should be like to resist practices and ideas they found objectionable. Both Yunŏk and Yŏnjae, for example, used the threat of divorce to negotiate favorable outcomes. Yunŏk's husband eventually bowed to her demands that she work outside the home, while Yŏnjae pressured her husband into defying his parents and establishing a separate household. Contrary to studies that emphasize the intensification of male privileges and the exacerbation of gender inequality through transnational mobility, the successes of these women illustrate the potential for Chosŏnjok women to resist and, to some degree, overcome the gendered inequalities that impinge upon their sense of personal freedom.

If some Chosŏnjok women risk destabilizing their marriages to push for change, others appear resigned in their daily routines to abide by the cultural rules of their South Korean families. Mira accepts the domestic role assigned to her by her marital family, despite her proven ability and inclination to achieve in other spheres. Though it is impossible to say for sure, I suggested that Mira's feelings of affection toward her husband and the gentle way he treated her may have been a powerful factor shaping Mira's acquiescence to a less than ideal arrangement. Given the pragmatic considerations that propel women into transnational marriages, the popular and academic tendency is to overlook or even discount the role that human emotion plays in these marriages (see Constable 2003a). The stories of fake marriages turned real, which I explore in the second part of the book, illustrate how love and romantic attraction can surface in unexpected ways in marriages contracted on purely pragmatic grounds.

In contrast to the other women in this chapter, Juju faced no apparent constraints on her personal freedom, living apart from her in-laws and married to a man who made no attempt to monitor her comings and goings. Yet Juju was unhappy in her marriage, feeling as though her husband lacked the financial capabilities and drive she deemed necessary. Moreover, unlike Mira who socialized easily with her husband despite their considerable age difference, Juju considered the ten-year age gap with her husband unbridgeable. Desiring a partner both financially savvy and socially more compatible, Juju took the most radical course of action available to her: she took her Korean passport and left her marriage in pursuit of better marital and economic opportunities.

There are no statistics to indicate the number of marriages that end this way. It is equally difficult to determine how many women enter marriages intending to divorce after they obtain citizenship. However, one thing is clear: many Chosŏnjok women are determined and capable of taking advantage of new forms of mobility, either maneuvering within or directly challenging the "multiply intersecting power hierarchies" (Mahler and Pessar 2001, 446) and gender logics that stand in their way. I would need testimonies from a statistically significant sample of brides over a much longer time to identify with any degree of certainty what factors influence whether a transnational bride chooses to resist or acquiesce to the kinship conventions she finds objectionable. The small sample of women I have included in this chapter points to the importance of difficult-to-measure factors such as women's personal proclivities, initiative, resourcefulness, and quality of emotional bonds with their husbands.

Part II

MIGRANT WORKERS, COUNTERFEIT KINSHIP, AND SPLIT FAMILIES

4

Faking Kinship

For the first part of this book I conducted fieldwork on the move. I roved the length and breadth of South Korea following leads to transnationally married couples and their families from various walks of life and regions of the country. While some conversations evolved into ongoing relationships, many were fleeting encounters that lasted but a few days or in some cases a few hours, always directed by the pointed and probing questions of my research agenda. By contrast, my fieldwork in China, which informs the second part of this book, was more localized, composed of relatively sedentary day-to-day observations and conversations that mostly took place in the homes of the families that had generously "adopted" me. If in South Korea I was forced to operate as an investigative reporter following a beat, in China I felt more like a foreign exchange student, well provided for and watched over by two doting mothers, one rural and one urban, who shared custody over me.

Occasionally I chafed at the constant surveillance maintained by my well-meaning guardians as they closely monitored my social contacts and comings and goings, no matter how trivial or close to home. A hike in the mountains encircling Creek Road Village where my rural family lived or an aimless stroll through the marketplace behind the concrete apartment building where I spent weekends in Mudanjiang City were perceived as occasions warranting a chaperone. This was to ensure my safety, my hosts explained. I suspect, however, they were also safeguarding the well-being of their own families by monitoring any unwanted attention or outside relationships their foreign houseguest might bring to their own household. But while they sought to shield me from the world outside their circle of friends, family, and acquaintances, these women quickly and unreservedly drew me into the intricacies of their inner lives.

As I shuttled back and forth between the mud-thatch dwelling of my rural "mother" and the newly renovated apartment of my urban "mother," hereafter referred to as Country Ajumma (Aunt) and City Imo (Auntie),[1] I witnessed the remarkable lengths to which these particular women and those around them were willing to go to cross the border into South Korea. This chapter charts the emotionally charged exploits of my host "mothers" in their respective quests to enter South Korea on the basis of falsified kinship identities. Following the rhythm of my fieldwork encounters, I tack back and forth between the two settings, rural and urban, describing the events as I witnessed them unfold. In so doing, I hope to convey a sense of the drama, the unpredictable twist and turn of events and emotions that

---

1. Imo and Ajumma are the terms I used to directly address them. *Imo,* which might be translated as "auntie," refers specifically to one's mother's sister but is also an affectionate term that children use to address adult female friends of the family. *Ajumma* (the informal form of *ajumŏni*), though it colloquially also means "aunt," is the teknonymic term of address for one's elder brother's wife. It is also the generic term of address for all married women, much like "Ms." or "Ma'am." The different degrees of intimacy conveyed by these terms of address should not be interpreted as reflecting the degree of closeness I felt toward the two women. I felt equally close to both women. It is, rather, more reflective of their relationship with one another and the order I became acquainted with them. I was living with City Imo when I requested that she help me find a host family in the nearby countryside. Imo located Country Ajumma by way of a friend's introduction. Imo fancied herself my primary caretaker and as such asked me to address her by the intimate term "Imo." Through subtle actions and expressions, City Imo conveyed the impression that she was "loaning" me to Country Ajumma on a temporary basis and that my primary allegiance should remain to her family. Imo assigned a young woman named Kyuyŏng (the daughter of the friend who introduced us to Country Ajumma) to stay with me in Creek Road Village and escort me back and forth to Mudanjiang. This woman had grown up in Creek Road Village addressing "Country Ajumma" as "Ajumma." It only seemed natural that I follow suit.

arise as prospective migrants negotiate with brokers, family members, fortune-tellers, Korean embassy workers, and government officials at every level of the Chinese bureaucracy.

In juxtaposing the story of Country Ajumma, a poor widow whose financial troubles are compounded by a series of personal tragedies, with the story of City Imo, an educated professional who had managed thus far to provide her family with many of the trappings of a middle-class lifestyle, I also wish to highlight the extent to which Chosŏnjok located at extreme ends of the socioeconomic spectrum at the millennial turn had come to regard going to South Korea as the most effective strategy of upward mobility. There is a presumed connection in many countries, including South Korea, between illegal border-crossing activities and poverty. The two stories in this chapter show how the market in fake kinship identities and forged documents penetrated every level of society from desperately poor farmers to well-established, urban professionals.

Country Ajumma set her sights on purchasing the identity of a Chosŏnjok bride's mother, a common means of evading South Korea's restrictive visa regulations. The widespread practice of traveling to Korea in the guise of a "paper mother" was in part an outcome of South Korea's immigration policies that facilitated the exodus of Chosŏnjok brides while permitting the parents of married-out brides to visit South Korea on the occasion of a daughter's wedding. Despite the prevalence and social acceptability of falsifying kinship relations, as Country Ajumma's story illustrates, carrying out such a strategy required so many resources (financial, political, familial), not to mention resourcefulness, that it was often beyond the grasp of the poorest segments of Chosŏnjok society.

City Imo, by virtue of her husband's ancestry, was positioned to take advantage of another type of kinship relation sanctioned by South Korea's visa and immigration legislation—that of the "separated family" member (*isan kajok*). If marriages between South Korean men and Chosŏnjok women were celebrated in South Korea as a symbol of restoring ethnic homogeneity to a divided nation, the nationally televised and pathos-laden reunions of families historically separated by national division constituted the ultimate embodiment of the dream of reunification.[2] The historic role

---

2. See Grinker 2000 for an in-depth discussion of how the divided family has become a symbol of the divided nation in South Korea. See also Kim 1998; Foley 2003; and N. Kim 2010.

played by Korean nationalists in Manchuria in resisting Japanese colonial rule created an additional sense of obligation on the part of the South Korean government to open its doors to the lineal descendants of these celebrated national heroes.

Despite the legitimacy of her kinship connections, however, City Imo's migration strategy, like that of Country Ajumma, necessitated forgery and the use of a broker. Her story gives us a glimpse into the world of brokering and the vast black market that emerged to distribute the privileges of working in South Korea to those who lacked the necessary genealogical connections to enter the country or, as in the case of City Imo, simply needed help dodging certain aspects of South Korea's stringent immigration laws. The perceived injustices of the South Korean government's policies as well as its efforts to make the visa application process ever more complicated for all categories of migrants spurred the Chosŏnjok to continually invent new ways of subverting these restrictions. By tracing in step-by-step detail the plots of two migrant mothers to enter South Korea with falsified documents, I hope to illuminate the possibilities and limits of illegal migrants' ability to resist state control as well as to draw attention to the brokers and "networks of complicity" (Sadiq 2009) on which their success depends.

Korea Wind

While living in northeastern China, I had no need to ever raise the subject of migration to South Korea. It was a daily preoccupation for Imo and Ajumma, their family members, close friends, acquaintances, and most people I chanced to meet. No matter how large or small the gathering, how intimate or public the setting, how sustained or fleeting the exchange, the conversation at some point would inevitably veer toward the latest visa regulations governing travel to South Korea, the going rates of purchasing a fake kinship identity of one sort or another, stories of successful border crossings, or tales of broken families and broken dreams. That the two women who took me into their homes both happened to be in the throes of transacting schemes to foil the gatekeepers to South Korea was not a coincidence. Had I chanced to live with any other Chosŏnjok family in the region, I almost certainly would have had an equally privileged vantage point from which to observe the effects of "Korea Wind" (*han'guk param*), the fetishistic desire to travel to South Korea drawing Chosŏnjok of every level of society into its whorl.

Occasionally I encountered someone who, for various reasons, consciously resisted the direction of the popular tide. Kyuyŏng, the feisty young woman whom Imo had assigned to live with me in Country Ajumma's house,[3] proclaimed on a regular basis her disdain for South Korea for "taking away her mother" (her mother had gone to Korea as a "paper bride") and robbing the Chosŏnjok population of its collective self-esteem. Yet despite her defiant attitude, Kyuyŏng admittedly looked forward to the remittances her mother would periodically send from Seoul that enabled her to afford fashionable clothing and join her friends in the recreational pleasures that Mudanjiang City had to offer. On the eve of my departure from China, I was shocked to learn that Kyuyŏng herself had succumbed to Korea Fever (*han'guk yŏl*) and had purchased a fake kinship identity to cross the border.[4] Thus it appeared that no Chosŏnjok living in northeastern China was immune to the effects of Korea Wind.

By the estimates of many I spoke with in Creek Road Village, every Chosŏnjok household had on average at least one member who had worked or was presently working in South Korea. Many households were trying to find a way to send a second member of the family to South Korea. For many of the families of migrants, the fruits of their labor were channeled into various forms of conspicuous display. Anyone strolling along the dirt paths that wend through Creek Road Village could readily distinguish the houses built with money earned in South Korea. The houses

---

3. Imo insisted that Kyuyŏng act as my chaperone, assistant, and companion while I lived in Creek Road Village. Kyuyŏng had contracted tuberculosis while working as an interpreter for a Japanese firm in the port city of Shenzhen and had returned home to convalesce. She was living in her father's home in Mudanjiang City where, apart from a couple of friends, she had few diversions to distract her from boredom. She enthusiastically agreed to live with me at Ajumma's house. Because of her bubbly personality, sharp wit, and extensive social networks in the village, her informal assistance and, more important, her friendship sustained me throughout my field research.

4. Kyuyŏng had crossed the border as a "second-generation compatriot" (*tongp'o isae*). South Korea extends citizenship rights to Chosŏnjok who were born on South Korean territory ("first generation compatriots") and their children. In Kyuyŏng's case, both she and her "parent" had forged their identities.

of those who had "been to" were colorfully tiled, two-story structures, often fortified with sturdy iron doors, encircled by even picket fences, and warmed by modern heating systems. These newly built houses stood out like trophies against the surrounding mud-thatch village architecture. Oftentimes, a household with one or more family members working temporarily in South Korea might choose to leave the village altogether to live in one of the concrete high-rise apartment buildings in nearby Mudanjiang City, which had come to symbolize for most villagers the highest level of cleanliness, convenience, and "modern" living locally available. Still other return migrants preferred to remain in their one-room, fire-heated, mud-thatch dwellings while adorning their homes with high-status consumer goods, such as color television sets and stereos. These tangible commodity markers, which not only permeated the tightly clustered residences of the Chosŏnjok but set them apart from the houses of their Han Chinese neighbors on the opposite side of the village,[5] were visible testaments to the wealth that could be amassed in South Korea.

The reputed rewards of working in South Korea were also commonly measured in straightforward monetary calculations. One year of hard labor in South Korea was alleged to yield 100,000 RMB (with an exchange rate of 8.27 RMB per U.S. dollar, roughly U.S. $12,000), a staggering figure when compared to a year's local wages, which for a factory worker amounted to roughly 4,800 RMB (400 RMB per month) at the time of my research.[6] Another way of conveying the profitability of a work stint in South Korea was the popular claim that after five years of toiling at a dirty, dangerous, and difficult (3D) job in South Korea, one could earn enough money to pay off the steep debts incurred in the process of migration, buy a new house, and live comfortably without having to lift a finger for the next ten years in China. Though migrants complained of having to endure the worst possible work conditions and treatment by their Korean employers, the promise of a house for a soon-to-be married son, a superior education for one's children, the erasure of a debt incurred from a past business

---

5. The Chosŏnjok and the Han Chinese socially and physically segregated themselves on opposite sides of the main road in the village, jokingly referred to by some as the "thirty-eighth parallel."

6. My use of "RMB" (*renminbi*) and "yuan" interchangeably when referring to Chinese currency is consistent with local practice in China.

A newly renovated home in a Chosŏnjok village, built with money from a stint of migrant labor in South Korea.

venture gone awry, or a nest egg for retirement were among some of the powerful motivators for leaving home in order to work in South Korea.

Xiagang and Failing State Enterprises

The undisputed wage differential between northeastern China and South Korea would have been alluring even in the best of times. But the socioeconomic outlook for many families in northeastern China at the start of the new millennium was fraught with uncertainty and insecurity. If some succeeded in forging new lives in China's permissive market economy, many floundered as the party state withdrew its famous promise of the "iron rice bowl," which under the planned economy guaranteed all urbanites at least a modicum of housing, food, health care, schooling, and employment. This left growing numbers of citizens and state-owned companies to fend for themselves in an intensely competitive and increasingly global marketplace. *Xiagang* or "unemployment," a Chinese word I had never encountered before in my previous travels throughout

China, was now on everyone's lips. This economic predicament, which resulted partly from the unrestricted influx of cheap migrant labor to the cities and partly from the pressure of market forces to streamline state enterprises by cutting wages and workers, had even given rise to a new genre of "unemployment literature" or *xiagang wenxue,* which detailed the travails of China's rapidly growing population of unemployed factory workers.

Alongside the economic dislocations, economic reform[7] has also fostered tremendous growth and opportunity to certain regions of the country, particularly along the eastern seaboard. Recognition of the regional disparities only served to intensify the feeling among northeasterners that they were being denied equal access to the benefits of China's opening (*kaifang*). Formerly the center of heavy industry and weapons manufacturing during the Communist Revolution and throughout the Mao era, Heilongjiang is struggling to transform its infrastructure to meet the contemporary market demand for consumer goods and services. While Korean investment in the region has created employment opportunities, particularly for Korean-speaking Chosŏnjok residents,[8] experts believe the region's best hope for economic expansion depends not only on the resuscitation of its own economy but those of neighboring Russia and North Korea, with the ultimate objective of establishing a special economic zone that would extend across Northeast Asia.

Until such a long-term and difficult-to-imagine goal might be realized, Chosŏnjok and Han Chinese residents alike are looking outside the region for ways to improve their circumstances. Young people in Mudanjiang who managed to find secure employment complained that local wages were insufficient to afford basic goods, such as housing. I spoke with the principal of a Chosŏnjok school on the outskirts of Mudanjiang City. He claimed that

---

7. Initiated in 1978 under Deng Xiaoping, economic reform entailed an array of government policies designed to move China away from a centralized planned economy toward a market-based one. The steadily expanding market unleashed new hopes and desires, but also created polarization between the rich and the poor, unleashed an enormous stream of rural migrants to the cities, and deprived urban workers of employment security.

8. By the late 1990s, South Korean businesses were no longer solely dependent on Chosŏnjok workers for their bilingual skills. South Korea has produced a growing number of Chinese speakers, while China has produced Korean speakers (H Kim 2010, 27). The "xinxianzu" or "New Koreans," as the bicultural, bilingual children of South Korean residents in China are called (28) will also be poised to take jobs in Korean businesses away from Chosŏnjok workers.

if he continued working for the next fifty years at his current job, which carried a respectable salary by local standards of 800 yuan per month (less than U.S. $100), he would still be unable to afford to buy his own house. His parents advised him to keep his secure employment while they labored in South Korea in his stead for the funds he needed. Other young people shunned the possibility of working for meager wages in China, knowing what their labor power could potentially fetch on the Korean market. One thirty-year-old man, whose wife divorced him to marry a South Korean man and left their toddler behind to support, turned down an opportunity to earn 300 yuan per month doing factory work. He said he preferred to remain a "blind wanderer" (*mangliu*) until he could find a way to get to South Korea. Middle-aged people who had been forced into early retirement or laid off without pensions by failing state-owned enterprises claimed that working in South Korea was quite simply a matter of survival (*weile shengcun*).

I now turn to the chronology of events, decisions, and dilemmas that constituted Country Ajumma's plan to migrate to South Korea as the fictive mother of a bride.

Ajumma: "The Important Thing Is That I Be Able to Make Money"

Country Ajumma looked at first glance more than a decade beyond her forty years because of her thick mass of prematurely silver hair, a symbol of the endless suffering she claimed to have endured in her life thus far. She regularly referred to herself as "the most pitiable person in the village." "Have you ever met anyone as unfortunate as I?" she asked me on the day I moved in with her and her two adolescent sons. I was unsure how to answer, or even if the question was meant to be anything other than rhetorical. I would soon learn, in the course of the next three months together, the unlucky details of her personal history. She readily shared them while going about the household chores or sitting next to me, cross-legged on the *kang*, crocheting pair after pair of woolen booties, a favorite pastime of the village women through the frigid months of the year.

Country Ajumma traced the beginning of her misfortune to her marriage. Like many young Chinese people contemplating their marital options in the early years of economic reform, Country Ajumma wrestled with whether to follow the dictates of her parents in choosing a partner or her own personal passions. In the end, she listened to her mother who fiercely protested Ajumma's first choice: a man with five younger brothers. Her mother had warned that a man with so many younger brothers to look after could only pose a burden to his future wife. There had been a second suitor. I did not probe for reasons why this man had also failed to win parental approval, but Ajumma recounted how her mother had staged a hunger strike in protest. In the end, perhaps frustrated by the difficulties in finding a candidate who would please all parties, Ajumma resigned herself to marry her parents' choice: a man from Creek Road Village whose shortness of stature was offset by his attractive face. The latter attribute, Ajumma reflected bitterly, was of little consequence for her future happiness: "I wouldn't have cared if he were ugly. It would have been enough if he had been of sturdy constitution and could have farmed and made some money." Ajumma was referring to the liver cancer that had plagued her husband for the last seven years of their marriage and eventually turned her into a widow at the age of thirty-three. The ten years of marriage that had preceded her husband's illness, by Ajumma's account, had been no better. Her mother, she said, was forever racked with guilt for having married her daughter to a man of such ill temper.

In the years immediately following her husband's death, Ajumma received repeated offers to marry South Korean men. While pursuing my fieldwork in South Korea, I had come across Chosŏnjok widows and divorcees in their fifties and sixties who had married South Korean men in the hopes of acquiring companionship and financial security in their later years.[9] Ajumma, by contrast, explained how she had been restrained by *nunch'i,* a concern for how her actions might appear in the eyes of others. At the time, she feared that remarrying so soon after her husband's death would have aroused public censure. Now she said she deeply regretted

---

9. An article in the Korean-language *Heilongjiang News* describes a fifty-year-old woman who suffered a string of unfortunate events: her husband died of liver cancer, her son was imprisoned in Mudanjiang, and her daughter had gone to work in Russia three years earlier, leaving her son behind and failing to ever call home again. When the woman's grandson injured his leg, this was, she is quoted as saying, the "last straw." She placed her grandson in the care of her younger sister and married a seventy-year-old South Korean man, sight unseen, in the hopes of being able to send money back home to support her grandson.

not seizing the opportunity to marry a South Korean man when the offers abounded. It had become increasingly difficult for Chosŏnjok to enter South Korea as either wife or worker. Government restrictions and IMF-era privations had the effect of curtailing both marriage tours to China and "industrial trainee" recruiting. With South Korean bachelors no longer showing up by the busload to their hometowns, Chosŏnjok women were forced to rely upon their personal networks for introductions. If she could find a South Korean man now, she would put her morals aside, as long as he had money, Ajumma declared. Playing devil's advocate, I cautioned her that marriage to a South Korean man, if not chosen carefully, could bring her misery of the sort she had suffered while married to her first husband. "Well, if he were no good, I would divorce him!" she retorted matter-of-factly. "The important thing is that I be able to make money. I've given up on any chance of my own happiness." Her only interest in life, Ajumma explained, was to make enough money to save her two teenage sons from a fate as miserable as her own.

In her narrative, Ajumma cast herself as a victim of her parents' matrimonial meddling, setting her on a course of marital unhappiness, poverty, and early widowhood. Whereas she portrayed herself as once conscientiously adhering to the rules of social decorum in deferring remarriage until a respectful length of time following her husband's death, she now declared herself free of moral obligations and personal desires in the name of selflessly serving the needs and desires of her children. South Korea, she firmly believed and the neighbors concurred, was the key to her family's salvation. Every now and then, however, doubt would creep in and unsettle Ajumma's resolve to find a panacea in South Korea. Assuming that I had some privileged insight into reality, Ajumma would turn to me for reassurance: "Is it *really* true that you can make a lot of money in South Korea?"

As much as she bemoaned her lot in life, Country Ajumma had a cheerful disposition and an easy smile. She kept her one-room house immaculately clean, scrubbing the vinyl-coated surface of the *kang* several times a day. She got up at five o'clock every morning to light a fire under it so that the house would be comfortably warm by the time Kyuyŏng, Ajumma's sons, and I, roused by the sizzle of breakfast cooking in the *kama* (a large, shallow, iron pan set into a woodstove) some two hours later, rolled off our sleeping mats and put them away tidily.

The mud-thatch hut that Ajumma cleaned so fastidiously was not her own. On my second morning in the village, we sat gingerly on the *kang,* still scorching hot from having been freshly lit, and cracked sunflower seeds while Ajumma told me the story of how she had sold her house[10] to treat her older son's mysterious illness. "*Lao Tianye* [Old Heavenly Grandfather] is unfair, isn't he? He has given me an unfair share of troubles," Ajumma began with customary self-pity. The first time I set eyes upon nineteen-year-old Chŏlsu, Ajumma's eldest son, I immediately detected that something was wrong with him. His movements were jerky and uncoordinated. His tongue, which appeared unnaturally red, darted in and out of his mouth. He spoke in slurred speech and laughed at inappropriate moments. Ajumma explained how Chŏlsu had been hit by a car while riding his bike along the main road in the village two years earlier. At first the boy seemed unharmed, but as time wore on he increasingly exhibited loss of control in his speech and actions. With the money Ajumma obtained from the sale of her house, she took her son to see doctors in Yanji City, the capital of the Korean Autonomous Prefecture in neighboring Jilin Province. Traveling as far as Beijing, she persisted in her search for a cure until her money ran out. In the end, no doctor had succeeded in diagnosing, much less treating, Chŏlsu's peculiar condition.[11]

---

10. The house in which Ajumma lived originally belonged to a Chosŏnjok family who had gone to work in South Korea. The family borrowed money from a Han Chinese man in the village to fund their passage to South Korea. As collateral, the family gave the man the deed to their house. Now the Han Chinese man was renting the vacant house to Ajumma in what is apparently a common arrangement in the village and just one of the ways in which the Han are profiting materially from the out-migration of Chosŏnjok villagers. In addition to high-interest moneylending to Chosŏnjok migrants, Han Chinese also rent farm land from migrant Chosŏnjok families. With increased landholdings, Han Chinese farmers are able to increase their earnings from agriculture. Many Chosŏnjok contrasted the laborious income-earning and patient money-saving practices of the Han to the Chosŏnjok predilection for speedy capital accumulation and lavish spending. If the Chosŏnjok praised the Han for their thrifty ways, many also concluded that their lives were uninteresting (*chaemi ŏpda*).

11. In the opinion of a fortune-teller whom Ajumma and I visited in Mudanjiang, Chŏlsu was possessed by a ghost. The fortune-teller said he could exorcise (*song*) the ghost if Ajumma provided him with the date when her son first fell ill. The exorcism would require the possessed person to somehow affix to his body a piece of paper inscribed with Chinese characters (*fu*) for a designated period of time before burning the paper, mixing the ashes with water, and drinking the mixture. The fortune-teller claimed to have recently cured a young girl of paralysis using this method in just four days. Ajumma did not appear convinced. Moreover, she was unable to recall the exact date of the onset of her son's illness. The fortune-teller offered to try to perform

"I wanted to kill myself and my sons as well," Ajumma said, recalling her desperation at the time. "I felt I had no means of carrying on [*meiyou huolu*]." But a concerned neighbor reproached her for her self-pity and at the same time urged her to find a way to get on with her life. The neighbor was Yunŏk, the thirty-something, entrepreneurial-minded woman I described in chapter 3, who had returned to the village to process her marriage visa to a South Korean taxi driver. Ajumma recounted how Yunŏk had made her a generous offer. Once the paperwork was finalized for her marriage, Yunŏk would be authorized to invite her parents to South Korea for up to ninety days on the occasion of her wedding. These parental rights to visit a married-out daughter, if not used by the bride's actual parents, could be sold for a large sum of money on the black market in China. Since Yunŏk's mother had previously entered and worked in South Korea through her connections to a South Korean relative,[12] she was willing to sell her travel privileges, identity card (*shenfenzheng*), and household registration (*hukou*) for the price of 50,000 yuan. In addition, Ajumma would need to pay 10,000 yuan to have a broker forge her name on the documents. In the final step in the process, Ajumma would travel fourteen hours by train to the Korean consulate in Shenyang with Yunŏk's uncle, who had purchased the paper identity of Yunŏk's father. If Ajumma and the uncle could deliver a convincing performance as husband and wife during the interrogation process and if their forged documents passed scrutiny, only then could Ajumma and the uncle proceed together to South Korea, parting ways after they crossed the border.

It first struck me as callous for Yunŏk to expect money from Ajumma given their close friendship and Ajumma's patently destitute condition. At the time, however, I was unaware of how vast and institutionalized the market in paper kinship relations had become. Ajumma and Kyuyŏng immediately corrected my underestimation of Yunŏk's generosity, explaining

---

the exorcism without this crucial bit of information, assuring Ajumma that she need only pay him whatever amount she was able to afford. Ajumma said she would think about it but seemed uninterested in pursuing the matter.

12. Some Chosŏnjok visitors are genuinely, and sometimes exclusively, motivated to reunite with separated family members. It is my sense, however, that the vast majority, even when they do have a desire to reestablish connections with South Korean relatives, set off for Korea with the intentions of overstaying their visas in order to work for a number of years, as Yunŏk's parents had done.

that it was sufficiently charitable for Yunŏk to have chosen Ajumma to be the purchaser of her mother's identity, since a host of Yunŏk's blood relatives were jockeying for this privilege.

What is more, they assured me, 60,000 RMB to become the paper mother of a Chosŏnjok bride in South Korea was considered a bargain.[13] Ajumma's younger brother had traveled to Korea as the fictitious father of a fictitious bride. For this type of complicated forgery in which both the identity of the bride and the parents had to be manufactured, Ajumma's brother had paid a much larger sum of money. Ajumma explained that since she would have authentic documents—copies of Yunŏk's marriage certificate, copies of Yunŏk's and her husband's identification cards, and a letter from the couple stating the date of their (fictitious) wedding ceremony[14]—the costs and risks incurred would be minimized. Given the illegalities involved in this type of migration strategy, however, there remained the risk of a broker absconding with the money or a government official extorting a large sum of money to authorize (often transparently) forged documents, both commonplace occurrences. Chosŏnjok brides often complained of being forced to pay bribes to local Chinese officials even when their paperwork involved no falsifications. As a precautionary measure, Chosŏnjok migrants who entered South Korea with the assistance of a broker had recently begun the practice of assigning a relative in China to pay the broker only *after* the migrant had phoned home with the news that he or she had arrived safely.

Ajumma's anxiety over how she would raise the money to pay Yunŏk mounted steadily with each passing day. There was urgency to raise the money before May 27, the wedding day which, though arbitrarily chosen

---

13. One day Ajumma walked in on a conversation that made her question the desirability of Yunŏk's offer. Two former classmates of her son were sitting on the *kang* inside her house talking about a woman they knew who had contracted a paper marriage with a South Korean man for 60,000 yuan. Ajumma's eyes bulged in disbelief. "If it cost as much to go as a paper mother, wouldn't it be better to arrange a fake marriage?" she wondered aloud. A paper wife, unlike a paper mother, is eligible for the ultimate prize of Korean citizenship and its attendant privileges of working for an unlimited period without the constant fear of deportation. The boys agreed that paper marriage was indeed the best way to go and expressed frustration that this route was only open to women.

14. Because this was a second marriage for both Yunŏk and her taxi driver husband-to-be, the couple chose to forgo the expense and effort of a formal wedding ceremony.

by Yunŏk, had already been recorded on the official letter of invitation. That date was just six weeks away.

Ajumma enumerated the various sums of money involved in her migration strategy, as if sharing this information with me might help spur ideas about where to borrow the money. Ajumma would give 25,000 yuan to Yunŏk's mother up front in return for her household registration and identity card. She would then need to pay a broker 10,000 yuan to forge her own name on these documents. Once Ajumma arrived in South Korea, she would be required to pay the remaining 25,000 yuan to Yunŏk. Ajumma intended to borrow this final payment from her younger brother who was currently working in Seoul. She explained how one year ago she had borrowed money from a Han Chinese man in order to help her younger brother pay a broker to get him to South Korea. "Now it is *my* turn to borrow from him," she explained. Then Ajumma's thoughts turned to her older brother. Several days ago she had received the disappointing news that her older brother had obtained, through a broker, an invitation to travel as a paper father to South Korea. The costs of this transaction, Ajumma figured, eliminated him as a potential money lender. Without a house and no more than three *mu* (roughly one-half acre) of land to her name, Ajumma had no collateral to offer to a bank or a private money lender. To add insult to injury, in the house next door, her brother-in-law's daughter was in the midst of processing paperwork to marry a South Korean man. Since the bride's mother was already working in South Korea, this meant the mother's visitation rights would be available for purchase by one of the bride's female relatives. Ajumma noted with a mixture of sarcasm and sadness that she would be last in line in the family to be considered for such a precious commodity. To her friends and family who knew the intricacies of her plight, Ajumma would require nothing short of a miracle to raise the money she needed to purchase Yunŏk's mother's identity.

Imo: "I Need Only Put in a Few More Years in South Korea"

I pause in telling Ajumma's migration saga to describe events that were simultaneously unfolding, along similar lines, in the geographically and economically more privileged household of City Imo. Like Country Ajumma,

City Imo was in the throes of carrying out a migration strategy that involved acts of forgery and deception. And like Country Ajumma, City Imo made no effort whatsoever to hide from me the illegalities involved. To the contrary, she encouraged me to record every intimate detail, convinced that an outside audience would view the laws she was bending as excessively rigid, the system she was navigating as corrupt, and the indignities that Chosŏnjok endured to overcome these obstacles as worthy of compassion, not criticism.

With an urban household registration, professional training as a nurse, and earnings from a seven-year stint of wage labor with her husband in South Korea, City Imo's socioeconomic situation was infinitely more secure than Country Ajumma's. Imo's desire to go to South Korea a second time was born not of desperation but the desire to ensure the future academic and professional success of her two children.

One year before I came to live with her, Imo had left her husband to labor alone at his construction job in Taegu, South Korea, while she returned to Mudanjiang to help her older child, Binmu, prepare for the entrance exam to study at Harbin's Academy of Chinese Medicine. Imo boasted about the nutritious meals she cooked, the steady supply of energizing snacks she prepared, and the constant encouragement she provided to enable her daughter's round-the-clock study regime during the year leading up to the exam.[15] If she passed the exam, Binmu would become the first member of her family to ever attend graduate school. To impress upon me the magnitude of this goal and the maternal sacrifices required to achieve it, Imo recounted how she had warned her daughter she would "kill herself" if, after all her maternal efforts, Binmu failed the exam. A bespectacled, serious-minded young woman with apparent nerves of steel, Binmu did not disappoint her mother. When I asked her about having to perform under the pressure of her mother's ultimatum, Binmu said she was thankful for her mother's honesty, noting how much greater the pressure would have been if her mother simply had told her, "It doesn't matter, just try your best."

---

15. The selectivity of university entrance examinations in China (as in other East Asian nations) has long necessitated this kind of intensive preparation on the part of students. However, in China the role of a full-time "education mother" who micromanages every aspect of her children's study schedule is a post-economic-reform phenomenon made possible by newly emerging forms of wealth and linked transformations in models of motherhood.

Now that Binmu had entered graduate school and settled into her dormitory in Harbin, Imo said she could return to South Korea "with peace of mind." Yet at the same time, Imo expressed dread about the prospects of resuming the exhausting work regime and condescending attitudes of her fellow workers in South Korea. Imo described having endured such indignities for seven years while working as a waitress there. Like Country Ajumma and vast numbers of other Chosŏnjok mothers I encountered, Imo's model of motherhood was constructed upon the willingness to migrate in order to bring a better future to her children. Yet she frequently lamented that the prime years of her life had been spent in South Korea in the absence of her children. Having grown up in the care of their maternal grandmother, her children would only know their mother as "an old lady," Imo noted sadly, alluding to what Parreñas (2001b, 370) calls the "pain of mothering from a distance" (cited in Piper and Roces 2003, 14) (explored more fully in the next chapter). "I need only put in a few more years in South Korea" was a refrain she repeatedly invoked to reassure herself.

Citing the lack of local employment opportunities, Imo (perhaps to convince herself as much as others) portrayed her decision to go back to South Korea as "not a choice" but the only way to "make money for the children." She and her husband were no longer able to return to their original career paths in China. Her husband's work unit had not survived economic reform, and Imo had knowingly forfeited her nursing career at the local hospital when she left to earn South Korean wages. "I can't be a nurse now because the hospitals [in Mudanjiang] are only willing to hire young people. I can't make money working for a wage in China [because the pay is insufficient]. I can't start a business, because I don't have the heart to cheat people. And I'm too young to retire." In their late forties, she and her husband were still capable of performing labor-intensive work abroad. "So, you see, I have no choice but to go to Korea," she concluded in what seemed like an effort to resolve her own feelings of ambivalence about returning to South Korea, as much as to elicit support from her two listeners—me and the upstairs neighbor who had wandered in to chat [*laoke*]. "I'm willing to *die* for my children," she intoned dramatically.

Judging from Imo's material surroundings, the money that she and her husband had earned in South Korea had been parlayed into creating a more comfortable lifestyle for their family. They owned two apartments, one of which was rented out to supplement their income. The newer of the two apartments had been given an impressive makeover by Imo's teenage son, Bongnam, who demonstrated his unusual flair for interior design when his parents gave him the remittances and carte blanche to redecorate the one-bedroom apartment. Bongnam was fond of boasting about how he had personally selected everything from new linoleum flooring (which he meticulously swabbed on his hands and knees at least once a day) to new window treatments and moldings. A large color television was the focal point of their spartanly furnished living room. Running hot water was another luxury that many neighbors in the same apartment building could not afford. Though the furnishings, or lack thereof, were in keeping with the cultural proclivities of the Chosŏnjok to sit, sleep, and eat on the heated floor, a calendar with glossy, poster-sized photographs of Western-style interiors hung prominently on the living room wall. These pictures symbolized the generalized notions of modernity and cosmopolitanism that Bongnam and his mother were striving for in their own particular style, if not directly in emulation of the West. Imo, for example, extolled the virtues of Corning dishware, which she had learned to appreciate while living in South Korea. While considered quality cookware, Corning is more closely associated with mundane domesticity than cosmopolitanism in the United States. Imo, by contrast, was sure, via the images and practices she encountered in South Korea, that owning a set of "plain white" Corningware dishes would add the perfect touch of elegance and sophistication to her newly modernized kitchen.

Lest I convey the impression that Imo was lavish in pursuing her materialist notions of modernity, I should note that, to the contrary, Imo adhered to a strict budget. She spoke with a mixture of criticism and envy about Chosŏnjok return migrants who used their newfound wealth to indulge in personal extravagances, such as jewelry and fine clothing. Imo recounted a story about a gold bracelet she had seen on display in a jewelry store window near her workplace in Taegu. So enchanted had Imo been with this bracelet, she would go out of her way each day on her way home from work to gaze at it longingly. This obsession, she said, went on for weeks until she managed to put the bracelet out of her mind. In telling me this story, Imo wished to impress upon me her ability to rein in her admittedly acquisitive desires. At the same time, in describing her self-restraint, Imo set herself apart from the excessive consumer practices of other Chosŏnjok migrants such as her sister, whom Imo described disapprovingly (but not without a hint of jealousy) as having returned from South Korea "with a gold ring on nearly every finger."

Imo saw herself as using her resources more sensibly than "others" by investing in the education of her children. This decision speaks to the relatively privileged economic status she had already achieved, as evidenced by not only her newly renovated urban residence but also by the academic abilities and aspirations of her children. Given her studious nature, Binmu's success in pursuing the rigors of an education in Chinese medicine seemed assured. The direction of Bongnam's future education, however, had yet to be decided. Imo spoke frequently of her plans to send her son to dental school and her long-term goal of opening a dental clinic for him with the money earned from her next sojourn in South Korea. While Bongnam expressed his preference to study abroad in pursuit of a more glamorous career in hotel management, his intentions to earn a professional degree of some kind were never in question.

Aside from her depiction of herself as a sensible money manager in times of widespread conspicuous consumption, Imo also justified her desire to accumulate more capital in South Korea by citing her intentions to use her earnings to help others beyond her own family. This desire to "do good" in the world, she believed, stemmed from her and her husband's essentially altruistic nature and the immense gratification she feels when helping others (I sensed in some respect that I was one of her "projects"). Until she could amass the capital needed to carry out large-scale works of charity, she busied herself in the meantime by using her training as a nurse to administer free, intravenous vitamin injections to local residents in need of a boost to their immune systems. For a few hours nearly every morning, the living room floor was strewn with the supine bodies of middle-aged women who had come to take advantage of Imo's skills and benevolence.

Imo's longer-term strategies of upward mobility and philanthropy would require some artful dodging of the law. Even so, she considered herself in much better stead than most illegal migrants to South Korea. Unlike Country Ajumma who traced her ancestry to North Korea, Imo had solid kinship connections in South Korea on her husband's side of the family. Her husband's first cousin in Taegu (her husband's mother's brother's daughter) had originally sponsored Imo and her husband to travel to South Korea on a family visitation visa eight years ago.[16] Though only valid for ninety days, the family visitation visa offered an important means to Chosŏnjok with living relatives in South Korea to enter the country. Once there, Chosŏnjok "visitors" could overstay their visas and earn money as undocumented workers for as long as they remained undetected by the authorities.

Imo and her husband were fortunate in having South Korean relatives who were willing to help them enter the country to make money. Many Chosŏnjok migrants were reluctant to ask their South Korean relatives for this kind of assistance. One middle-aged mother in Creek Road Village, for example, explained how, despite the existence of bona fide relatives in South Korea, she preferred to outright purchase a family visitation visa and enter South Korea in the guise of the fictive relative of someone she did not know. This method, she said, was preferable to suffering the "embarrassment" of asking her elderly relatives to go through the bureaucratic red tape involved in issuing an invitation.

Imo, on the contrary, had boldly asked her South Korean relatives to issue a *second* invitation, which under the circumstances was in violation of South Korea's immigration law. At the time of my research, migrants who exceeded the limits of their visas were legally prohibited from re-entering the country for a period of five years. Five years was too long for Imo to wait. She felt she had tarried long enough in Mudanjiang and was eager

---

16. Article 777 in the Korean civil law code (*minbŏp*) defines the parameters of the kinship group. The law identifies three categories of kin: (1) agnates (*hyŏlchok,* literally "blood relatives") up to eight degrees of genealogical distance (*palch'on*); (2) affines (*inch'ŏk,* literally "kin of mate") up to four degrees genealogical distance (*sach'on*); and (3) spouse (*ch'injok*). (I am grateful to Sin Seungnam for obtaining this information for me from the Ministry of Unification [T'ongilbu].) The closest genealogical distance is that between parent and child, which constitutes one degree. The kinship distance between two individuals is calculated by adding up the number of parent-child links that connect them to a common ancestor. Siblings, for example, are two degrees apart because they are each one degree from their parents. First cousins are four degrees apart, second cousins are six degrees apart, and third cousins are eight degrees apart. The significance of eight degrees for establishing the outer limits of the agnatic kin group in the contemporary legal code may stem from the traditional convention of defining the outer limits of the lineage and ritual-performing group as an eight-degree segment (Janelli and Janelli 1982, 107–8). It is still unclear to me why the boundaries of the ritual-performing group are drawn at eight degrees. Janelli and Janelli point out that the practice of reciprocal participation in the domestic rites of collateral kin is a tradition unique to Korea. It is not ordained by neo-Confucian orthodoxy, which places more emphasis on family unity than agnatic solidarity (182).

to join her husband in South Korea. She imagined her husband to be frittering away their hard-earned money by eating in restaurants and buying alcohol and cigarettes. As if it were common wisdom, Imo explained that without a wife's help and supervision, a man could not be trusted to save money while living abroad.

Imo explained the ins and outs of her scheme to get around the "five-year rule." She would bribe an official in a nearby rural township to change her last name, age, and city of residence as it appeared in her passport, identity card, and household registration. She would then ask her husband's South Korean relatives to issue an invitation using this new alias. By traveling as "Kim Miyŏn," a woman in her fifties from a neighboring rural township, instead of as forty-eight-year-old Ko Miyŏn from Mudanjiang City, she hoped to fool immigration officials into thinking this was her first visit to South Korea. She would also meet the new age requirement established by the Korean government that year, prohibiting Chosŏnjok family members less than fifty years of age from entering South Korea on family visitation visas. The whole package would cost her roughly 30,000 RMB, including bribes to local officials. Her relatives would have to put up another 1,000 RMB on their end. Imo was confident she could earn the money in South Korea to pay them back in just one month's time.

Imo knew all too well the risks of relying on a broker to carry out these types of forgeries. Her younger brother had been cheated out of 60,000 RMB several years ago when he tried to purchase a business visa (*sangwu*) to enter South Korea. Imo was still trying to help him recuperate his financial loss so that he might try his luck again. Imo explained to me, with an almost smug sense of assurance, that, unlike her brother's plan, hers was foolproof. The key to her success, as Imo saw it, was a close friend of hers who had connections to a high-level official in the Public Security Bureau. Just then the phone rang, interrupting her boasting. There was a problem with her visa. Imo rushed out of the house in a panic, leaving me with the impression that her plan was more precarious than she had assumed.

That evening, Imo returned with her sense of confidence restored. She regaled us with tales of her skillful handling of her run-in with an official at the Public Security Bureau. She described how she had managed to maintain a calm demeanor despite the fluttering of her heart and the amount of money at stake. She was pretending to be a woman from the countryside and had deliberately dressed for the part, donning an old sweater she had borrowed from a friend. She was proud that she had remembered "to hunch her shoulders like a country woman." But because she had forgotten to ruffle up the edges of her newly forged household register, it looked suspiciously unworn. The official processing her documents had detected this oversight and accused her of submitting a fake household registration. Imo explained how she discreetly tiptoed backward out of the room, allowing her politically connected friend who had accompanied her to negotiate with the Chinese official in private. Her friend managed somehow to resolve the crisis.

Now Imo needed only to wait until the end of the week when "Kim Miyŏn's" passport would be ready. Once the passport bearing the name of her alias was in hand, Imo could proceed to the South Korean consulate in Shenyang to apply for a family visitation visa. Imo enjoyed a moment's relief in having proceeded thus far in the game, but then she began to worry about how she would convince the immigration officials at the South Korean consulate that she was the age she was claiming to be. In Beijing, it was rumored, South Korea–bound migrants could undergo a surgical procedure to add wrinkles to their foreheads. The wrinkles were said to naturally dissolve several weeks after the migrants had safely crossed the border. With no such services available on the local market, Imo would have to depend on the subtleties of body language and grey hair dye applied strategically around her temples to lend credibility to her charade.

Other elements such as good fortune, though beyond Imo's control, were not simply left to fate to decide. Like many Chosŏnjok migrants I met, Imo consulted a fortune-teller the next morning to determine the most auspicious day for her departure to South Korea. The fortune-teller, Mr. Zhao, was a stout and well-spoken Han Chinese man who claimed to tell fortunes "by the book," not by virtue of any innate powers of prognostication. After performing a series of calculations, Mr. Zhao concluded that Imo would encounter problems if she attempted to get a visa this year. "Best to go next year," he advised. Imo became distressed and explained how she had already paid a large sum of money for documents that were only good for three months. Mr. Zhao had a solution. He dipped his calligraphy brush into a clam shell of red ink and painted some characters on a small sheet of paper, instructing Imo to wear the paper close to her body for protection and to burn it after her mission had been accomplished.

Ajumma: "I Wish South Korea Would Just Explode"

Upon my return to Creek Road Village, I learned that Country Ajumma had also sought the advice of a fortune-teller to help determine an auspicious date to enter South Korea. Ajumma was encouraged by the fortune-teller's words. Not only was this year a good year for travel, the old lady had told her, but a *guiren* or benefactor would appear who would provide Ajumma the help she needed to finance her journey. Ajumma went about her day, muttering to herself, "I wonder who the *guiren* is?"

A trip to a second fortune-teller corroborated the first. I sat beside Ajumma as the fortune-teller mapped out the waxing and waning of her life's fortune. He characterized her early years straight through to her mid-forties as a period of misfortune. In her mid-forties, her luck would turn and get progressively better. He predicted that Ajumma would come to possess a great sum of money, not as a result of hard work but as a result of meeting a *guiren*. Ajumma asked if he could predict the last name of the *guiren*. The fortune-teller scribbled down a list of characters. Pak was at the top of the list. Pak was the last name of Yunŏk, the neighbor who had invited Ajumma to travel to Korea in the guise of her mother. This remarkable concurrence filled Ajumma with a sense of optimism.

That evening Ajumma shared the news of the fortune-teller's predictions with a group of curious friends and relatives back in the village. Her listeners laughed and Ajumma smiled broadly as she contemplated the remote possibility of her misery turning into great fortune. Though she regarded it as a farfetched idea, Ajumma seemed more determined than ever to find a way to reach South Korea. Over the next few days, she continued to rack her brain for a way to borrow the money she needed to pay Yunŏk, all the while hoping for her *guiren* to appear.

With nowhere else to turn, Ajumma decided to make a pilgrimage to the rural homes of her older siblings to see what kind of assistance or information they could provide. She offered to bring me along, thinking I might like to see how Chosŏnjok live in other parts of Heilongjiang Province. Ajumma's *ŏnni*, or older sister, lived in a tiny village of about

two hundred people, mostly mud-thatch houses in varying states of disre-
pair. With Ajumma's younger brother in Seoul making money, her older
brother having departed the day before for South Korea, and her youngest
brother's whereabouts unknown to the family for years,[17] Ŏnni was the
only sibling in the family who intended to stay put. Ajumma explained
that Ŏnni's body, weakened by a lifetime of hard labor, was no longer capable of withstanding a stint of migrant labor in South Korea. An energetic
two-year-old granddaughter had been placed in the charge of Ŏnni and
her sixty-year-old husband, further ruling out the possibility of Ŏnni leaving the confines of her village. Ŏnni complained that her daughter, who had
given birth to the little girl while working in a factory in Beijing, had disappointed her twice over: first by marrying a Han Chinese man, and second by giving birth to two girls. Having let down her family by not being a
boy, the baby girl was considered a pointless transgression of the one-child
policy and was spirited away soon after birth to her grandmother's village
so that her parents, who continued to eke out a living in Beijing, might
escape the legal repercussions of their excess childbearing.

Though Ajumma realized Ŏnni was already sufficiently burdened by
the physical demands of caring for a toddler, Ajumma felt she had no one
else to turn to for the favor of caring for her two sons in the event that
she made it to South Korea. With promises to send money, Ajumma presented this arrangement as beneficial to both families. Ŏnni agreed without hesitation. The second purpose of Ajumma's visit was more delicately
posed, the matter of asking her brother-in-law to lend her 10,000 yuan to
finance her journey. Ŏnni's husband promised to see what he could do.
Two days later we set out by train for our next destination: the home of
Ajumma's older brother's wife, or *olk'e*.

When we arrived at Olk'e's house, the atmosphere was tense. Just minutes
after Ajumma and I walked through the door, the phone rang, triggering a

---

17. According to the story Ajumma tells about her youngest brother, he shunned a life of
farming in order to try his luck in the outside world (*chuang zai waimian*). Unable to make a stable
living, he arranged for his girlfriend, for whom he allegedly cared very much, to marry a South
Korean man. According to Ajumma, his girlfriend preferred to remain with Ajumma's brother,
but the brother insisted that the South Korea man would be a better provider for his beloved. The
brother regrets his decision. He is now a "wanderer" (*liulangzhe*) who resurfaces every few years
on Chinese New Year. Ajumma worries about his welfare and would like to find a way to send
him to South Korea to join the rest of her siblings.

familiar scene I had watched unfold in other households anxiously awaiting news on whether a family member's forged documents had passed the final point of inspection at the South Korean border. In this case, the phone call was from Olk'e's husband (Ajumma's older brother) who had departed the day before as the paper father of a Chosŏnjok bride. From Olk'e's shrieks of joy, the answer was clear. She quickly passed the phone to Ajumma so that she could congratulate her brother. The house suddenly erupted into a raucous celebration of relief and joy.

The nervous expectation leading up to the awaited phone call followed by the cathartic reaction to good news was strikingly reminiscent of the scene I witnessed just weeks before at City Imo's house. Imo had been waiting for a phone call from her younger brother who, after being swindled by a broker the first time, was relying on the costly services of a broker once again to help him cross the border in the guise of a businessman. Imo paced the living room floor on the day of her brother's departure, muttering prayers that her brother's forged documents might hold up under scrutiny. Nearly every hour she would check the clock and wonder aloud where her brother might be at that precise moment. When she finally received the confirmation phone call that evening, Imŏ was so wound up with exhilarated relief she could hardly sleep.

I learned from the scene at Olk'e's house, however, that *all* family members did not necessarily greet news of a safe border crossing with unequivocal celebration. Ajumma tried to be happy for her brother and his family, but his success in reaching South Korea seemed only to highlight her own inability to muster the resources for such an undertaking. In a more direct way, Ajumma's brother's departure for South Korea ahead of her robbed her of the possibility of relying on him in the near future for financial assistance, given the magnitude of the debt he had amassed in purchasing a fictive identity. It was not until Ajumma phoned Ŏnni to pass along the news of their brother's safe arrival that Ajumma revealed her conflicted emotions. Ajumma hung up the phone, visibly disturbed. The jubilant atmosphere in the house died down as Ajumma informed us of the news she received over the phone: Ŏnni's husband had failed to come up with the 10,000 yuan she had hoped to borrow. Ajumma complained of a headache and announced that she wished "Korea would just explode." "That way I wouldn't have to expend so much energy day after day in trying to get there." She then turned to Olk'e, apologetically, and noted that her sister-in-law was probably unhappy to hear her wish for the decimation of Korea. "After all," she said with barely concealed envy, "Korea is now *your* family's pipeline to riches."

The highly charged emotions and range of reactions experienced in the aftermath of a relative's departure for South Korea speak not only to the high-risk stakes involved in purchasing fictive identities but also to the interfamilial politics involved in deciding who gets to go first. Because of the enormous amount of money required to buy one's way into South Korea, it is often necessary for extended families to pool their resources. The obligation to help send younger siblings to South Korea constitutes an overwhelming burden to some Chosŏnjok, who are struggling to improve the lives of their nuclear family members. Imo, for example, characterized her life in Mudanjiang as "mentally exhausting" as a result of having to help her four younger siblings strategize and pay for a means of reaching South Korea. As difficult as her work regime had been in South Korea, Imo found herself longing to return to the relative simplicity of her life there. "In Korea," she said, "all I knew was work and sleep for the sake of my own children."

At the same time, the necessity of having to rely on family and friends for assistance can be equally, if not more, stressful. Ajumma occasionally fantasized about having a daughter of her own to marry off to South Korea. That way, she said, she would have no need to purchase the identity of Yunŏk's mother or solicit money from her siblings to pay for it. Moreover, Ajumma's feelings of resentment and abandonment in the wake of her younger brother's departure for South Korea highlight the rivalry that can occur as a result of this type of interfamilial strategizing. Competition is the flip side of cooperation as families decide who should be the recipient of their limited, combined resources. In the next chapter I look more closely at the gendered basis of migration decisions, particularly as they pertain to whether a husband or a wife should proceed first to South Korea.

Months later, when it came time for me to say good-bye to Ajumma and return to South Korea, Ajumma had not made any headway in her search for financial backing. Later I found out from Yunŏk, who had by this time taken up residence with her South Korean husband in Seoul, that Country Ajumma's quest had taken a turn for the worse. On the eve of my departure from Creek Road Village, Yunŏk's mother asked me to deliver a bag of Chinese medications to her daughter in Seoul.[18] Yunŏk suggested that I bring it to the upscale *kalbi ch'ip* (a barbeque ribs restaurant) where she was working as a waitress. She seemed happy to see me and very eager to talk. After getting clearance from the restaurant manager, she agreed to let me treat her to *kalbi* for lunch while she poured out her version of the events gone awry.

Yunŏk grew visibly agitated as she recounted the story of how Country Ajumma had botched her chance to go to South Korea as Yunŏk's paper mother: Country Ajumma hired a broker (Ajumma's brother-in-law's wife's younger brother) to forge her name onto Yunŏk's mother's identity papers. The Public Security Bureau (PSB) later recognized the documents as forgeries and levied steep fines on the broker, Country Ajumma, and Yunŏk's mother. As if that had not been bad enough, Yunŏk continued, the PSB confiscated her family's household registration (*hukou*). Yunŏk was very angry over the loss, saying that it would require several thousand RMB to recover it. Yunŏk blamed Country Ajumma for not choosing a broker wisely and for not taking responsibility for the consequences. "She [Ajumma] keeps saying 'duibuqi, duibuqi' [sorry, sorry], but that really doesn't do anyone any good, does it?" Yunŏk said irritably. Once her family regained possession of the *hukou,* Yunŏk vowed she would sell it to someone else.

Imo: "Fake Is Realer than Real"

Unlike Ajumma's, Imo's forged documents had passed inspection at the local and regional levels of the Chinese bureaucracy. The day had arrived for her to subject them to the final test at the South Korean consulate in Shenyang. Imo invited me to accompany her on the overnight journey by train, thereby relieving her son, Bongnam, of having to do the escorting and saving Imo the cost of an additional traveler. I enthusiastically accepted the invitation to follow Imo on the legendary pilgrimage to Shenyang, the penultimate destination for all prospective migrants in the northeastern

---

18. Yunŏk explained that the medications were to help her recover from an abortion she had recently undergone against the wishes of her Korean husband. I presume that Yunŏk wished to avoid any additional complications in her marriage until the couple had worked out their differences regarding Yunŏk's desire to work outside the home (see chapter 3).

region before entering South Korea. Some, like Imo, had reached this critical juncture in the bureaucratic process using forged documents. Others were who they claimed to be. Ultimately it was up to the Korean immigration officials, on the basis of a brief but rigorous interrogation, to separate the genuine article from the impostor. Though Imo had faith in the quality of her forgeries, under her clothing she wore the strip of paper given to her by Fortune-teller Zhao for an extra measure of good luck.

After fourteen hours on a crowded train, Imo and I disembarked in Shenyang station the next morning. Imo reminded me not to blow her cover and instructed me to help her scan the throngs of people milling about the station for a woman bearing a sign with her fictitious name on it. Imo spotted the sign right away, chuckling at the strangeness of pretending to go by a different name. The woman, in her thirties, holding the sign ran the *minbak ch'ip* or boarding house where we would be staying. The *minbak ch'ip ajumma* (*minbak ch'ip* matron) as Imo called her, or MCA, as I refer to her here, herded us into a waiting taxi, which immediately deposited us and our luggage in front of the Korean consulate. As soon as we disembarked, the MCA pressed a visa application form into Imo's hand and urged her to fill it out on the street corner as quickly as possible. The MCA shuffled hastily through Imo's paperwork before ushering her into line, which by early morning was already wrapped around the building.

Hours later, the consulate doors opened. There was a shudder of activity as people jockeyed for position, angrily defending their places in line as they pushed through the front doors. I had heard from others and read newspaper accounts of the long lines of Chosŏnjok applicants, several blocks long, which formed daily outside the consulate building and of an alleged ticket system that enabled people to hire a proxy to reserve their space in line. As a newcomer to the scene, Imo had not yet learned how to work the system. I grew weary sitting on the ledge of the consulate building, minding our suitcases, while Imo waited in line, only to return three hours later, saying that the doors had closed for a lunch break and that we would need to return an hour later to stand in line again.

We trudged down the road to the *minbak ch'ip* to survey our accommodations and grab a quick bite to eat. Our *minbak ch'ip,* located on the third floor of an apartment complex near the consulate, was one of many such businesses that had sprung up with the recent opening of the Korean consulate in Shenyang to accommodate the continuous stream of

Chosŏnjok visa seekers entering the city each day from far-flung locations across northeastern China. Offering services above and beyond the usual low-cost room and board of an ordinary *minbak ch'ip,* MCAs draw upon their insider knowledge to coach clients through the complicated visa-application procedures. This service is not considered supplemental but rather an integral part of what the customer is paying for. For example, Imo found fault with the MCA when, after waiting the better part of the day in line, her application was turned down because she had neglected to include a copy of her Korean relatives' certificate of residency with the rest of her paperwork. Imo considered it the MCA's responsibility to make sure all her documents were in order, and she blamed the woman for not taking the time to check her paperwork more carefully when she dropped us off that morning in front of the consulate. (Fortunately, the mistake was resolved with a phone call to Imo's relatives in South Korea. They immediately faxed the required document, and Imo, frazzled but relieved, returned to the consulate later that afternoon.)

The MCA provided other vital services as well. Without an MCA or other broker, as Imo and I later discovered, it was next to impossible

Lively interactions take place in a *minbak ch'ip* in Shenyang, China, where Chosŏnjok migrants seek room, board, and advice on how to gain entry to South Korea.

to purchase a train ticket out of Shenyang because they were regularly bought out by enterprising middlemen. And because *minbak ch'ip* housed large numbers of migrants and brokers in communal quarters, they also served as an important meeting ground and conduit for information on both official and "black market" matters, including the latest changes in visa regulations, the going prices for manufacturing fictive identities and other services, and advice on what to do and what not to do during the oral interrogation that is a routine part of the visa-application procedure. In other words, staying with a reliable MCA who has solid connections could help eliminate some of the hassles and anxieties involved in the application process, and in some cases it could mean the difference between having one's application accepted or rejected.

Through my conversations with some of the dozens of MCAs hovering around the consulate recruiting clients, I learned that many of them were women, drawn to Shenyang sometimes from distant locations to take advantage of this unique business opportunity created by Korea Fever. Some spoke of their businesses as a viable money-making alternative to migrating to South Korea. One twenty-eight-year-old MCA whom I met outside the consulate said she did not wish to go to South Korea because she was neither willing to perform "dirty and difficult" labor nor subjugate herself to a South Korean boss. Her husband, on the other hand, was no help to her at home, she said, so she "sent" him to South Korea instead. The freedom of controlling her own income and spending it as she liked was, in her opinion, one of the greatest benefits of running a *minbak ch'ip*. Our MCA also expressed similar complaints, stating that her husband was "useless." She moved to Shenyang from neighboring Heilongjiang Province with her sister. They rented a three-room apartment near the consulate, hired a cook, and were instantly in business.

Our first day in Shenyang had been grueling, but it ended on a positive note. Imo submitted her documents in full to the Korean immigration officials before the end of business hours. What is more, Imo felt confident that she had answered the official's interview questions cleverly and convincingly. Imo was especially proud of the way she answered the question "What does your twenty-year-old daughter do for a living?" Saying that her daughter was handicapped increased the sympathy value of her case, Imo explained. But despite all the factors in her favor, Imo was riddled with anxiety during the three-day wait for her visa to be processed. At the back of her mind were the cautionary words of Fortune-teller Zhao. What is more, every day we heard rumors and firsthand testimony from guests at the *minbak ch'ip* of the capriciousness of Korean immigration officials in whose hands rested the fate of every migrant.

Imo was so consumed with worry that she withdrew from the lively social interactions that occurred in the evenings at the *minbak ch'ip*. My presence had generated a great deal of curiosity and attention, particularly from the brokers and businessmen who were staying there. One broker invited me to take in an aerial view of the city from the top of Shenyang's television tower, followed by late-night snacks in the bustling night market below. Another, a man known as Old Piao—one of the many brokers I had chatted with outside the consulate while waiting for Imo—took me on a guided tour of Shenyang's historic sites. Imo stayed behind on every occasion, saying she was too anxiety-ridden to join us. It was uncharacteristic for Imo to allow me out of her sight much less to fraternize with strange men. To step out of my role as Imo's daughterly charge while she brooded over the uncertain fate of her passport gave me twinges of guilt. Nevertheless, I seized these opportunities to learn as much as I could about the business of brokering. Later I found myself in the bizarre situation of being called upon to use my new *guanxi* (connections) when Imo herself developed an urgent need for brokering assistance, as I describe below.

There were many types of Chosŏnjok brokers making money off Korea Fever, from the marriage brokers I discussed in chapter 2 to the MCAs in Shenyang to the multitude of brokers involved in buying and selling (and forging) identities across the northeastern region. Shenyang, I discovered, was the hub for brokers all and sundry. As the northeasterly site of the Korean consulate in China (prior to its opening, Chosŏnjok migrants were forced to travel to the Korean embassy in Beijing), Shenyang is the place where brokers congregate while looking for new recruits or taking care of visa-related business. I was taken aback by the overt manner in which brokers in Shenyang proffered their services in the vicinity of the consulate. Some men I met at the *minbak ch'ip* elusively described themselves as "businessmen" and declined to elaborate further when asked. For the most part, however, those I chanced to meet during our brief stay in Shenyang were willing to discuss in surprising detail the ins and outs of their trade.

Old Piao described a hierarchy of brokers, in which "small" ones did the footwork for the "big" ones by traveling back and forth to South

Korea in search of citizens willing to issue invitations to fictive Chosŏnjok relatives. Because of their connections and because they are careful to leave South Korea before the expiration of their three-month visitor visas, brokers can repeatedly reenter the country without the complicated and costly forgeries required by those like Imo who have overstayed their visas. At the top of the hierarchy are brokers in Shenyang with high-level political connections to the South Koreans who work in the consulate. Old Piao explained, speaking from his own experience, "It is essential that these connections be continually nurtured, by dining and drinking with the South Koreans. It's hard work." By all accounts, South Korean consulate workers stand to benefit the most from these illicit transactions. One broker urged me to record the precise figures he had obtained by virtue of a personal connection (his friend was dating a South Korean secretary who worked at the consulate): "Write this down," he said. "The secretaries alone in the South Korean consulate made 400,000 RMB in bribes in the last four months."

* * *

At last the day to pick up Imo's passport arrived. It was raining, and the long line of people pressed close to the building for protection. I waited with Imo an hour and a half before a uniformed man with a bull horn announced that those in line to pick up their visas could enter the building. Once inside, it was a free-for-all to reach the thirteenth floor where the visa processing center was located. Some people ran up the flights of marble steps, trying to gain a lead. Others raced to the elevator. I left Imo in the tenth floor stairwell to wait it out alone while I returned to the street corner to mingle with the brokers and MCAs in the chilly rain. It was 5:30 p.m. by the time Imo re-emerged, a look of desperation on her face. "Yu Kayŏng!" she called out my Korean name. "What am I going to do? I was rejected!" Imo showed me the indelible stamp in her passport that stated that she must wait sixty days before reapplying. Her voice was trembling. She was in a state of panic. "You must go in there and tell them I am for real," she pleaded.

As I tried to calm her and reason with her that my testimony was not likely to carry much weight, we were approached by Old Piao. Eager to help a friend of the *miguk agassi* or "American Miss" as he called me, he offered to take a look at the documents Imo had submitted. Imo figured she had nothing further to lose, so we followed him back to his *minbak ch'ip*. There he scrutinized Imo's documents while squatting on the floor, pulling on a cigarette. Old Piao identified the following three errors:

1. The letter of invitation from Imo's South Korean relatives contained a word *[saenghwal sukso]* that was not typically used by South Koreans. The use of this word, according to Old Piao, was a red flag to immigration officials that the letter had been written by a Chosŏnjok and not a South Korean citizen.
2. The thumbprint was too dark. A common mistake, Old Piao said.
3. The genealogy was not perforated at the bottom like an official genealogical document, betraying the fact it was a forgery.

Imo considered these points. It was possible that she had made a poor word choice when she wrote the letter on behalf of her relatives. Old Piao's comment about the thumbprint struck us both as odd. But most disconcerting was that Imo had no idea what "perforations" he might be referring to.

Just then a middle-aged couple burst through the front door of the *minbak ch'ip*. They were elated. The woman had just been granted a visa to South Korea, even though, as she boasted for all present to hear, she had been pretending to be a fifty-six-year-old when her true age was forty-four. Her husband praised her on the finesse with which she had handled the interviewer's questions. "One little slip could have spelled disaster," she agreed, wiping her brow and beaming broadly.

Witnessing this scene only exacerbated Imo's feeling of dejection and indignation. "You see what kind of place China is now?" she said to me. "Fake is realer than real!" She implored me to expose this injustice to the outside world, using her own experience as a case in point. "The fakes are allowed to go [to South Korea], while the real ones are rejected!" she continued to rage. I dared not point out that Imo had applied for a visa using an assumed name and a number of forged documents. What was "real" from Imo's perspective was that she had bona fide relatives in South Korea who had extended her a legitimate invitation. I recalled Old Piao making a similar observation that those who seek admittance to South Korea on the basis of falsified documents often have a better acceptance rate than those with genuine documents and genuine kinship connections. Those who submit unadulterated documents often do not feel the need to check them over with a fine-tooth comb, he explained. The tiniest error, even an honest oversight by a local official, could lead to rejection. What is more, he explained, those with verifiable kinship relations to South Korean citizens sometimes feel less compelled to memorize the minutiae of their genealogies. For this reason, they are more apt to falter during the oral interrogation phase of the process.

Imo, prone to hyperbole, announced that she was bleeding internally from stress. It frightened me to see Imo in such a state of emotional disarray. Not knowing what else to do, I offered to contact another broker. I pulled Kich'ang's business card from the small collection I had amassed while waiting for Imo outside the consulate. Kich'ang was the broker who had boasted of having a friend with a connection to a secretary in the consulate. I called him on my cell phone, and he agreed to meet us the next day at his mother's *minbak ch'ip*.

That night a good omen appeared to Imo in a dream. She explained that in her dream, she and a group of others stood at the edge of a large puddle of mud. One by one, the people in front of her leapt effortlessly across the puddle. When it came time for Imo to cross, she landed smack in the middle, mud up to her ankles. Someone reached out to her and pulled her out of the mud and brushed off her shoes. Imo, who had a history of prescient dreams, felt certain that this dream signaled the arrival of a *guiren* who would help her find a way to get to South Korea. She called her son in Mudanjiang to share this reassuring vision.

Shortly thereafter, Bongnam called back with details regarding the identity of the *guiren* in the dream. Imo was proud that her teenage son had had the wherewithal to consult a fortune-teller on his own in order to further illuminate the meaning of her dream. According to Bongnam, the fortune-teller had said that "the fourth person" would help his mother. Imo thanked her son for the valuable information and thought for a while. Then she nodded. Imo pronounced me as number one, Lao Piao as number two, Kich'ang as number three. "Kich'ang's *guanxi* [his contact in the Korean consulate]," Imo exclaimed, "must be the fourth person!"

"She Could Buy an Official"

Kich'ang introduced us to a skinny Korean woman in her twenties, casually dressed in jeans and a T-shirt. Her complexion was pale and her appearance unadorned except for a pair of wire frame glasses and a slender gold chain around her neck. She leaned forward on her chair with her hands on her knees, flexing her scrawny arms outward in an oddly double-jointed fashion. This was the fabled secretary who worked on the thirteenth floor of the consulate. Given her access to the computer files, she claimed to have the power to erase Imo's record from the database, enabling her to reapply immediately for a visa to Korea, notwithstanding the stamp in her passport requiring her to wait two months. "What counts is what's in the computer," she said in a mellifluous Seoul accent. However, to be safe, she added, Imo would need to pay bribes to immigration officials in Shenyang and Seoul. She quietly stated that the bribes would cost Imo 50,000 yuan.

For a moment, Imo was carried away by the thought of what money could buy. She was face to face now with someone within the seat of power at the South Korean consulate, and she wished to know the extent of this woman's influence. With no paperwork required besides a passport, for the right price the young secretary claimed she could "buy an official" (*mai yige guan*) to let just about anyone through the gates of South Korea. Imo's eyes rolled with excitement as she recited the names of her friends and relatives who were struggling back in Mudanjiang to get there. "My brother's wife!" she exclaimed. "She could go to South Korea!"

In a society where fake and real were increasingly indistinguishable and corruption was pervasive, preoccupations with morality must have seemed inappropriate to Imo, if not downright foolish. Eventually, however, the prices for "buying officials" had a sobering effect. Imo regained her composure, and we departed for Mudanjiang the next day.

Shortly thereafter I returned to Seoul. Imo phoned two months later to tell me that her second attempt to apply for a visa in Shenyang had also ended in rejection. I referred her to a South Korean friend, Kang Chansuk, whose volunteer work assisting Chosŏnjok migrants in South Korea is described in chapters 1 and 2. Later Imo explained how Chansuk had identified an error in her genealogy. Having fixed the mistake, Imo was making preparations for her third trip to Shenyang. I visited her for the last time in Mudanjiang several days before her departure. Though suffering from a bad cold and taking intravenous vitamin treatments several times a day to energize herself for the journey, Imo's sense of confidence and optimism was stronger than ever. She was convinced that this time she would sail effortlessly through the application process. Before leaving she considered one last visit to Fortune-teller Zhao, but Bongnam, reminding her of his poor track record, sternly advised against it.

When I returned to Seoul, I phoned Mudanjiang to find out the outcome. Imo's perseverance had paid off. Soon she would be on her way to join her husband in South Korea.

Imo's and Ajumma's migration schemes, which I was privy to watch unfold, and to some extent participate in, capture the frustrations, anxieties, and logistical complexities involved in planning and carrying out what had become, among the Chosŏnjok at the turn of the millennium, a widespread practice of falsifying kinship connections and/or documentation to enter South Korea. To succeed, potential migrants needed not only to mobilize personal connections with officialdom at multiple levels (local, regional, and transnational) but also to mobilize kinship ties, both locally and abroad, or manufacture them when they did not exist. Though Imo possessed considerably more kinship, political, and financial capital than Ajumma, she suffered the frustration of having to pay expensive bribes to local officials, the anxiety that her bribes would not be accepted or that her masquerade would not be convincing, and doubts about whether her dates of travel were auspicious. Alongside the stress of preparing for and preventing the myriad possibilities for logistical error lurked the existential dilemma of whether the financial rewards of working in South Korea justified the angst of long-distance motherhood and the feeling of having squandered the vigor of her waning middle years on a menial job in South Korea. As the eldest sibling in her family, Imo had the added responsibility of financing the migration schemes of her younger brothers and sister.

Ajumma's scheme, by contrast, was beset by extreme financial deprivation from the beginning. Before she could even begin to contemplate the logistical challenges of posing as Yunŏk's fictive mother, she first had to raise an enormous sum of money to purchase the opportunity to try. Her story highlights the feelings of despair and jealousy that arose for those without the financial wherewithal and kinship capital to join the popular exodus to South Korea. Nevertheless, Ajumma found her *guiren* in the end. As I did for Imo, I referred Ajumma's case to my Korean friend Kang Chansuk. Under the auspices of her church in Seoul, which actively recruited Chosŏnjok migrants to its congregation, Ms. Yi appealed to the South Korean government to allow Ajumma to seek medical treatment for her son at a hospital in Seoul. Ms. Yi understood that Ajumma had intentions of overstaying her visa to work in South Korea and only asked that Ajumma promise that her son would promptly return to Mudanjiang after receiving treatment. Ajumma agreed to this condition, and her visa was successfully processed. After being examined at a hospital in Seoul, Ajumma's son returned to China without being cured, while Ajumma stayed on to work illegally as a waitress in South Korea for nearly a decade. Sadly, Ajumma was called back to Mudanjiang in 2007 on the occasion of her son's death. With the money she earned in South Korea, she was able to buy a house in Creek Road Village, but tragedy continues to follow her. In a later e-mail from Kyuyŏng (April 3, 2010), I learned that Ajumma's younger son has come down with the same mysterious illness that cut short the life of his older brother. Without money to hospitalize him and without a means of returning to South Korea to work, Ajumma is apparently beset by the same desperate circumstances as when I first met her eleven years ago.

Imo's and Ajumma's stories not only illustrate the personal anxieties that affected would-be migrants and their families. They also reveal much about the social upheavals and uncertainties of the time and place in which they were living. The desperation of these two women to reach South Korea and the legally transgressive strategies they employed emerged from the context of China's abrupt transition to a market economy, its accompanying social dislocations, and the particular shape of the prevailing opportunity structure. Their awareness that mobility opportunities can be short-lived, opened and closed as they are by the vicissitudes of global politics and global capitalism, engendered a sense of urgency among the Chosŏnjok to act swiftly to take advantage of the gains in status and wealth that their connections to South Korea (real or fabricated) might bring. The 1997 Asian financial crisis combined with South Korea's vacillating immigration policies and public opinion regarding the Chosŏnjok only served to intensify the perception that those who do did not act immediately to enter South Korea might not be given a chance in the future.

The South Korean government's ever-changing and increasingly stringent policies governing Chosŏnjok access to South Korea had also fostered a rather cynical view of state power among the Chosŏnjok. As discussed in chapter 2, many Chosŏnjok migrants were angered by the incongruities they perceived between the South Korean government's rhetoric of ethnic and familial reunification and its exclusionary immigration policies.

From a purely pragmatic perspective, many Chosŏnjok acknowledged the challenges the South Korean state faced in dealing with the large numbers of Chosŏnjok migrants pushing their way across its borders. As Ajumma observed, if South Korea were to indiscriminately admit every Chosŏnjok who applied for a visa, "the small country would explode." At the same time, she was severely critical of the South Korean state for not being more compassionate toward its Chosŏnjok "compatriots" once they arrived on Korean soil. Ajumma urged me to write about the cruelty of the South Korean government's policy of deporting illegal migrants with no regard for how long they had been in the country. "It is okay to deport [a Chosŏnjok migrant] who has been in Korea for five or six years," she said. By Ajumma's calculations it would take a migrant at least one or two years to pay back the enormous debts required to "buy" his or her way into South Korea. To deport a Chosŏnjok migrant before the end of this critical period was, in Ajumma's words, "tantamount to murder."

It bears noting that Chosŏnjok migrants also bristled at the Chinese state's attempts to contain them within its borders, a stance that, like that of the South Korean government, struck many as inconsistent with official PRC rhetoric. Given China's curtailment of the socialist distribution system and the state's ideological endorsement of capital accumulation and geographic mobility, many Chosŏnjok felt the Chinese government should have facilitated rather than constrained their efforts to earn money in South Korea. Drawing on the example of South Korea's model of economic development and its continued high rates of emigration, one elderly return migrant I met in Harbin chastised the PRC government for not appreciating how the Chosŏnjok exodus to South Korea could boost the future growth and development of the Chinese economy. "South Korea developed precisely because so many people left the country," she explained. "That way the population was reduced and people brought money back into the country. Now it's our turn to develop, so people must leave the country.... There's no other way to develop." A migrant bride I befriended in South Korea went so far as to call the Chinese government's attempt to curtail the transnational travel of Chosŏnjok citizens an infringement of human rights. "The United States doesn't impose restrictions on its citizens like that," she complained. "The Chosŏnjok are very competent [*nenggan*], and the Chinese government is not allowing them to realize their potential. It is a form of oppression."

Given these sentiments, the market in fake kinship identities might be seen as an attempt by migrants to subvert categories of migratory control in both the Chinese and Korean states. If the rules are unfair, why should they have to play by them? As we have seen, a legion of hierarchically organized brokers had emerged to help mediate the troubled relationship between migrants and government bureaucrats. Through the use of these brokers, many Chosŏnjok migrants attempted to turn the restrictive categories of immigration to their own advantage. Their efforts were so successful that, as Imo put it, "the fakes" were granted visas while "the real ones" were rejected. Thus, South Korea's stringent immigration policies and procedures, originally designed with the intentions of limiting the number of Chosŏnjok entering the country with falsified documents, actually had the opposite effect. The irony that "fake" kinship connections were sometimes a better bridge to South Korea than "real" ones is testament to the power of migrants to resist those "in charge" of migratory flows, contrary to Massey's (1994) oft-cited concept of "power geometry."

By contrast, Ajumma's failure to find a reliable broker reminds us that migrants needed at least a modicum of money and social connections to navigate the bureaucratic gauntlet that stood in their way of reaching South Korea. What is more, as Ajumma's comments about the constant fear of deportation suggest, no matter how successful migrants were in subverting the immigration process, the Korean government wielded the ultimate power to punish them for their transgressions and was capable at any moment of reasserting control over its borders.

In his well-argued and provocative book, *Paper Citizens* (2009), Sadiq examines the use of fake documents in illegal border crossings. He highlights the paradoxical role that documents play as the primary gatekeeping tool of the state. On the one hand, the implementation of compulsory documentation "from above" makes it easier for states to monitor, classify, and control the movement of people within and across national borders. On the other hand, "networks of complicity," as Sadiq calls the dense, ethnic, and/or historically based relationships that both extend into state bureaucracies and transcend state borders, "corrode the gatekeeping functions of the state" (53) by helping illegal immigrants acquire and use forged documents to bypass state regulations. The secretary in the South Korean consulate and the PRC official who accepted Imo's fake passport are both examples of complicitous state actors bending laws or turning a blind eye to accommodate the use of forged documents by would-be migrants. These actions "from below" undermine the territorial sovereignty of the state, even as states try to regain control by implementing ever more numerous and technologically more sophisticated forms of compulsory documentation. Sadiq sums up the irony of the situation: "In short, documents give states power for social and political sorting and thereby order, and yet it is the documents themselves that undermine this fig leaf of order and security" (135). Echoing the lessons learned by Imo as she watched "the fakes" sail through the final rounds of documentary inspection and interrogation at the Korean consulate, Sadiq writes, "As long as local government agencies cannot tell the difference between legal and fake paperwork, fake documents ensure incorporation into a host just as well as legal documents" (110).

The stories of Imo's and Ajumma's struggles to outwit South Korea's bureaucratic apparatus also shed light on the culturally and historically specific tensions between capital and kinship in the Korean diaspora. From the perspective of the South Korean government, Imo, Ajumma, and the multitude of Chosŏnjok like them who either draw upon legitimate kinship connections or fabricate them in order to work illegally in South Korea violate more than just the nation's immigration laws. They are perceived to violate the very meaning of "family" and its metaphoric association with the sacred goal of reunification. In part 1 of this book, I examined how the economic motives of migrant Chosŏnjok brides called into question the sincerity of their conjugal intentions. Similarly, the undisguised economic opportunism of separated family members is perceived by South Koreans to undermine the sincerity of their familial intentions. The result is a climate of mistrust in which *all* Chosŏnjok applying for a family visitation visa (or any other category of visa), no matter how legitimate their claims, are suspected of having forged their genealogies. We shall see in the following chapter how these bureaucratic contours and unlawful entailments posed a challenge to everyday norms of family life on the Chinese side of the border.

5

FLEXIBLE FAMILIES, FRAGILE MARRIAGES

When Imo realized she would need to return for a second five-year stint of hard labor in South Korea to finance her children's education back home in China, she gave serious consideration to arranging a fake marriage. Many of her already-married friends and relatives had contracted paper marriages with South Korean men, and she envied the freedom of mobility and unfettered access to the South Korean labor market that their marriage-visas-turned-citizenship-rights afforded. But in the face of strong objections from her husband and two teenage children, Imo reluctantly gave up pursuing the matter.

As Imo would later discover from other women who had used fake marriage to maneuver across the South Korean border, this migration strategy often had unintended repercussions for their real marriages to Chosŏnjok husbands. Imo explained how early on she had naively assumed, along with many of her friends, that a fake marriage was a simple, straightforward exchange of money for citizenship status. A conversation with her younger sister-in-law who had recently returned to China after having arranged a fake marriage to a South Korean man confirmed the worst suspicions of Imo and her family members.

"I asked her what it was like to go through a fake marriage," Imo recounted. Her sister-in-law responded that she was required to live with the South Korean "husband" for twenty days in order to convince immigration authorities of the authenticity of their marriage. "What did you do there for twenty days?" Imo probed. The sister-in-law told her that she had picked grapes on the man's farm. "Picked grapes for twenty days?" Imo asked in disbelief. I thought I knew what Imo was insinuating through her incredulous tone but wanted to make sure: "Was your sister-in-law coerced into sleeping with the South Korean man?" "That," said Imo, "is the big question! My feeling is that she certainly had to have slept with him. And it has affected her relationship with her Chosŏnjok husband ever since."

In this chapter I explore the range of geographically dispersed family configurations and legally transgressive strategies that Chosŏnjok married couples pursued in exchange for a transnational livelihood in South Korea. Previous anthropological studies have emphasized the resilience of transnational families and the maintenance of intimate kin contact across vast distances. I do not dispute their findings, but my aim here is to highlight the extraordinary risks that Chosŏnjok were pressured to take with their marital relationships. The cases I present demonstrate how particular forms of transnational family dispersal engender moral ambiguities and cultural conundrums regarding proper gender roles and responsibilities within the family. Specifically, I look at how the gendered division of mobile and nonmobile labor in the split transnational household (whether the husband migrates alone, the wife migrates alone, or a married couple migrates together) reinforces, reprioritizes, or reshapes previously taken-for-granted dimensions of conjugal and parent-child relationships.

Mother-Abroad and Father-Abroad Families

Patterns of dispersing and localizing family members, the number and type of geographic sites involved, the frequency of reunions, and the duration of family separations vary widely across national and international space, and even within particular migration circuits. The work of anthropologists studying transnational families in diverse locations suggests that transnational family making is a complex project, largely contingent on the ways local practices and imaginings of gender, family, nationality or race, class, and mobility articulate with global markets and the "bureaucratic contours" (Chalfin 2010) of the two or more nation-states involved. Ong (1999), for example, describes how historically evolved ethnic and instrumentalist family practices intersect with the larger institutional and ideological context of the nation-state and global capitalism to reinforce long-standing patterns of "mobile masculinity and localized femininity" among overseas Chinese entrepreneurial families. Ong describes contemporary Chinese transnational investors, or "astronauts" as they are called in Hong Kong and Taiwan, maneuvering across nation-states in search of economic opportunities, while dropping off their wives and "parachute kids" (the term used when they are unaccompanied) in politically stable parts of the world to earn residence rights and pursue their educations (127).

In contrast to these male Chinese investors, the growing demand for migrant domestic workers in "global cities" throughout the world (Sassen 1991) has encouraged women from less privileged locations across Asia, Latin America, and the Caribbean to venture overseas as the primary breadwinners of their families. The live-in nature of their work and the immigration restrictions they encounter often force migrant mother domestics to leave husbands and children behind for extended periods while caring for the children of their employers.

This transnational family arrangement differs from Chinese astronaut families not only in the gendered reversal of movers and stayers but in the transgressive effects it has on local gender norms. In the Philippines, where men have traditionally held a monopoly on breadwinning and mobility, migrant mothers must cope not only with the strains of family separation itself but with the social stigma of being labeled a "bad migrant mother" who "abandons" her children (Parreñas 2001b). Contrary to media portrayals of their transnational families, Parreñas argues, migrant mothers "overcompensate for their physical absence" and reconfigure the meaning of mothering by becoming "martyr moms" who attempt to nurture their children from a distance (Parreñas 2005, 103). Other migrant mothers, like the Latina domestic workers in a study by Hondagneu-Sotelo and Avila (2003), respond to similar pressures by expanding the definition of motherhood to value maternal breadwinning overseas.

In South Korea, where ideals of intensive, round-the-clock mothering also prevail,[1] the recent phenomenon of mothers laboring overseas as "education managers" (SJ Park 2006) of their children's early study abroad (*chogi yuhak*) (that is, before college) while fathers remain rooted in their white-collar jobs in South Korea, is no less controversial. On the one hand, "wild geese families" (*kirogi kajok*), as these education-focused, transnational families are called, can be seen as reinforcing—even intensifying—existing ideals of the "sacrificial mother" and the "breadwinning father," though spouses perform these traditional roles on opposite shores. On the other hand, with increasing popularization of early study abroad into the 2000s, the goose mother has had to defend against familiar charges of familial or maternal excess as well as class privilege (Abelmann and Kang 2011).[2]

The Chosŏnjok split transnational households I describe in this chapter encompass a variety of organizational arrangements and also provoke certain internal debates and moralizing discourses about family and gender norms. In the cases I examine, already-married Chosŏnjok couples with dependent children maneuver to send one or more members of the household to South Korea to work for substantial periods of time. The expense and effort involved in obtaining an entry visa were so vast, as we have seen, that migrants typically had to work five or six years in South Korea before they could see a return on their investment. Some sought to take maximum

---

1. While highlighting the emphasis placed on idealized notions of female domesticity in contemporary South Korea, I do not mean to elide the diversity of mothering arrangements and female subjectivities available to women. In addition to full-time housewives, South Korea is also home to increasing numbers of career women, many of whom hire migrant domestic workers to take care of household responsibilities normatively assigned to them. At the time of my research, Chosŏnjok women were performing these surrogate caretaking roles in many South Korean households. See Lan 2003 for a balanced look at the complex relationship between madams and migrant domestics in Taiwanese households.

2. The critique against goose mothers is fueled in part by the growing recognition during the first decade of the twenty-first century that in South Korea's increasingly competitive and deregulated market, early study abroad is a necessity that only the well-to-do can afford (see Kang and Abelmann 2011). A typology of "bird fathers" indexes the disproportionate ability of wealthy families to realize this global project and afford periodic plane tickets for fathers to visit their families. "Eagle daddies" have the financial wherewithal to visit their families any time they desire. Less well off "penguin daddies" endure material deprivation and prolonged separations to support their children's early study abroad. "Sparrow daddies" must forgo altogether the possibility of global education for their children (Presidential Council on Nation Branding [PCNB], February 16, 2010).

advantage of their hard-won foothold in the Korean marketplace, staying ten years or more before reuniting with their children and/or spouses back in China. While the necessity of splitting the family to take advantage of income-earning opportunities in South Korea was rarely questioned, debates centered on which variant of the transnational family would be least transgressive of family norms and most sustainable over time.

Should a mother or father or both journey to South Korea on behalf of the family? The decision was far from straightforward. The gendered structure of the South Korean labor market in conjunction with relatively flexible ideas about motherhood in China helped create a situation in which Chosŏnjok women were just as likely as men to become the overseas breadwinners for their families. For purposes of analysis, I have broken down Chosŏnjok transnational family arrangements into three main categories: families in which the husband migrates and the wife remains at home with the children, families in which the wife migrates and the husband remains at home with the children, and families in which the husband and wife migrate together and a caregiver (usually a close relative) raises the children. Each arrangement posed a different set of challenges and revealed different meanings, priorities, and tensions with respect to gender, generational, and conjugal dynamics.

Far-Flung Fathers and the Female-Headed Household

The deployment of men to work in South Korea and the localization of women at home to care for the children constituted one variation in the organization of transnational Chosŏnjok families. I start with a description of the lives of three nonmigrant wives,[3] highlighting the loneliness, isolation, and general malaise these women experienced while waiting for their husbands to return home. Familial arrangements in which men migrate for paid labor and women mind the domestic sphere back home

---

3. Time did not allow me to locate and interview their husbands in South Korea. Men's perspectives on what it means to be a father and husband in this particular transnational family arrangement would certainly enrich our understanding. See Pribilsky 2004 for a nuanced account of men's perspectives on transnational family life as Ecuadoran migrants in New York. See Lee and Koo 2006 for an examination of the perspectives of middle-class South Korean fathers on their role in wild geese family (*kirogi*) arrangements.

conformed to long-standing Chosŏnjok ideals that conflate motherhood, reproduction, and domesticity. And yet most people in China define the roles of wife and mother neither exclusively in terms of domesticity nor in opposition to productive employment. Staying at home in China thus restricted Chosŏnjok women from acting on the full range of culturally prescribed roles for wives and mothers.

Though wives (and husbands) who remained in China had the option of joining the local workforce, in my observations most seemed to prefer to live exclusively off remittances from migrant family member in South Korea. One reason was that stable employment was difficult to find in northeastern China at the turn of the millennium, when the transition to a market economy and the accompanying pressures on state-owned enterprises had resulted in massive urban unemployment. But, perhaps more significantly, Chosŏnjok attitudes and expectations regarding the value of their labor made them reluctant to work for Chinese wages— which seemed meager compared to what they could potentially earn in South Korea.

An article in the *Heilongjiang News* (Pak 2000) entitled "An Exceptional 'Living Widow'" treats the income-earning efforts of a migrant's wife as a rare and newsworthy phenomenon. Despite her husband's objections that he could earn in twenty days in South Korea what she could earn in one year in China, the wife featured in the article resolutely lives off the meager wages she earns as a farm laborer while stashing away her husband's remittances for a future home-building project. The article praises the woman for her "exemplary" behavior, observing that most so-called living widows (*saeng kwabu*), with husbands in distant locales earning money, abstain from hard labor, living exclusively off their husbands' paychecks and perhaps even indulging in extramarital affairs.

The ever-present specter of an extramarital affair posed a serious challenge for physically separated spouses. For many women, the priorities of wifehood and motherhood seemed to be in conflict, creating an insoluble dilemma for women who wished to serve as the primary caregivers for their children while also preserving the quality and viability of their marriages. As a springboard for discussing these tensions, I introduce three sisters-in-law I met in a small Chosŏnjok village outside Harbin, all of whom were raising children in the absence of their migrant husbands. The three sisters-in-law were married to the youngest three of six brothers.

I refer to them as Fourth Sister-in-Law, Fifth Sister-in-Law, and Sixth Sister-in-Law. The first and third brothers had died young. While living in Harbin, I befriended the oldest living brother's wife, Second Sister-in-Law ("Mrs. Cho," as I call her), who worked in a Korean-language news-paper agency where I spent countless afternoons scouring back issues for articles on Chosŏnjok migration to South Korea. Mrs. Cho and I had many discussions about the disruptive effects of Korea Wind on Chosŏnjok fam-ily life. One weekend, she took me on a journey to her husband's home-town, where I met her three sisters-in-law.[4] The conversations we had there highlighted the difficulties of maintaining marital relationships at a distance and, by contrast, the taken-for-granted nature of parent-child relationships. Interestingly, I learned that for Chosŏnjok mothers the deci-sion *not* to migrate could sometimes be harder to justify than the decision to stay home and care for the children.

Mrs. Cho considered herself and her husband part of a privileged mi-nority that did not have to rely upon South Korea to enhance their family's financial well-being. Her husband, the only one of his six siblings to attend college, had a secure, managerial position at the Korean-language newspa-per agency in Harbin where Mrs. Cho also drew a steady salary. In resist-ing the popular trend to travel to South Korea to make money, Mrs. Cho perceived herself as "more fortunate" than "ordinary people" whom she perceived as "blindly" flocking to South Korea, unguided by any specific goal or long-term vision of their future. Instead of South Korea, Mrs. Cho staked the future economic mobility of her children on the educational and employment opportunities offered by Japan, widely perceived to rank

---

4. The primary purpose of my visit was to interview a former student of Mrs. Cho in the village who had married a woman from North Korea. Six brides from North Korea were living in this particular village. These brides were of interest to me because they were linked, at least demographically, to the migration of Chosŏnjok brides out of China to South Korea. The exodus of Chosŏnjok brides had created a bride shortage in the local Chosŏnjok marriage market, which in turn had generated a demand for brides from North Korea. Since the North Korean fam-ine which began in 1995, an estimated 100,000–400,000 North Korean migrants, many of them women and children, have crossed the so-called rivers of death (the Yalu and Tumen rivers) into Chinese territory where, if they remain, they live in fear of deportation by Chinese authorities (Cho 1999; Chung 2008; S Kim 2010, 49; Shipper 2010, 22). Of these border crossers into China, only 16,000 have managed to reach South Korea by way of the underground railroad, as the cir-cuitous overland routes that pass through the Gobi Desert or the jungles of Laos are called (S Kim 2010, 49).

a step above South Korea in the economic hierarchy of nations. After an initial investment of U.S. $6,000 to pay tuition for her daughter's first year at a Japanese university, Mrs. Cho proudly reported that her daughter had managed to secure a scholarship to finance the remainder of her college education. Her son's accomplishments gave her even more reason to boast. Working in Harbin as an interpreter for a Japanese real estate investor, he had earned enough money not only to pay for his first year of tuition at a Japanese university but also to outfit his older sister in Japan with a new computer. Given the academic and entrepreneurial achievements of her children, Mrs. Cho explained, she and her husband saw "no need" to endure the drudgery of working in South Korea.

The sense of uncertainty that enveloped the lives of the families of the sisters-in-law in the village contrasted sharply with Mrs. Cho's optimistic outlook. Fifth Sister-in-Law recounted regretfully how she had been married a mere thirty days when her husband left to make money in South Korea, eight years ago. She was pregnant when he left. "The father has *never* seen his eight-year-old daughter," Mrs. Cho stated emphatically, suggesting that the facts alone spoke volumes about the sadness of the situation. Shortly after her husband left, Fifth Sister-in-Law moved back to her natal village where she raised her daughter until she was of school age. I expressed surprise that her in-laws did not request that she remain close by, but Fifth Sister-in-Law simply shrugged and said her parents-in-law had other sons to look after them.

Her daughter would have started elementary school at the Chosŏnjok school in her husband's village, but with only three students in the first grade that year, the school had been forced to close. Chosŏnjok student shortages and school closings due to high rates of outward migration were so pervasive in villages across northeastern China that concerned Chosŏnjok intellectuals had recently declared a national crisis in ethnic education (Chŏng 1995, 226). Rural parents with financial means could either relocate to the nearest city to give their children an urban (and most likely Han Chinese) education or remain in the countryside and send their children to boarding schools in the city. Because of her preference for country living and her desire to keep her daughter close at hand, Fifth Sister-in-Law decided to shuttle back and forth between the village and the nearest city, about an hour away by taxi. With the remittances her husband was sending from South Korea, Fifth Sister-in-Law could afford to rent an apartment near her daughter's school. On weekends, mother and daughter would return to the Cho family village where Fifth Sister-in-Law said she feels most at home. "The city is boring," she complained. "The only attraction is the department store, and since I have no money to spend, it's not interesting."

Fifth Sister-in-Law said this as she split firewood with an axe to light a fire under the kitchen stove. The crackle and scent of burning wood prompted further commentary. "City food and water does not taste good," she continued. "In the country, vegetables are fresh, and they taste much better cooked in the *kama*." "There is nothing like the smell of burning wood," Mrs. Cho noted with approval, adding that after she retires she would like to go back to living in the country. The other two sisters-in-law, who lived in neighboring houses in the Cho family village, soon arrived, one after the other, to help prepare breakfast. I watched the busy shadows of the women in the smoke-filled room, marveling at their ability to maneuver through the dense fog of smoke.

Fourth Sister-in-Law had spent twenty years living with her husband before he departed for Korea. She had two daughters in their early teens

Readying the *kang* (fire-heated platform) for mealtime in a Chosŏnjok home in China.

Carrying home supplies to make *ttŏk* (rice cakes), Chosŏnjok village in northeastern China.

who attended the Chosŏnjok school in the Cho family's hometown; they had been born before the shortage of students became severe. The daughters showed little interest in their American houseguest, or anything else for that matter. They lounged lethargically on the *kang,* looking rather bored. Both of them were noticeably plump with broad features and heavy brows and lashes, which I guessed must have been inherited from their father. At meal time, the daughters sprang to life. They both ate with fervor, heaping vegetables into their rice bowls and mixing them with spoonfuls of sauce, creating a concoction that they spooned noisily into their mouths. I noted that Fourth Sister-in-Law did not interfere with their zealous eating habits. To the contrary, she encouraged them to eat to their hearts' content. Even the liquor-filled candy I had brought as a gift, a delicacy from Harbin meant to be savored, was promptly polished off by the girls. Fourth Sister-in-Law spoke little except to say that she was fed up with living the village. When I probed into the source of her dissatisfaction, she muttered that she would simply like to distance herself as far as possible from Sixth Sister-in-Law whose incompetence she said was driving her mad.

Sixth Sister-in-Law was apparently the black sheep in the family. The other women, Mrs. Cho included, made regular reference to her and her husband's "incompetence." The husband had reportedly borrowed thousands of dollars from Fifth Sister-in-Law to finance his trip to Korea, and this was a source of tension between the two families. No one had confidence that Sixth Brother would ever succeed in earning money in South Korea, so it was unlikely that he would ever pay back the loan. Even Mrs. Cho treated Sixth Sister-in-Law without much regard. Instead of referring to her by name, Mrs. Cho referred to her in the third person by pulling her lip to one side, mimicking the harelip which marred Sixth Sister-in-Law's face. Mrs. Cho laughed when I asked her to stop and agreed instead to call her "mangnae," meaning youngest. Sixth Sister-in-Law had one son who showed up irregularly at meal times. He sat slumped in the corner with his head down, avoiding eye contact with his female-dominated family. His features were delicate, unlike his mother's, but his good looks were eclipsed by the unhappy, withdrawn expression that seemed fixed upon his face.

On the day of our departure, Fourth Sister-in-Law and Fifth Sister-in-Law and their three daughters waited with Mrs. Cho and me on the *kang* for our taxi to take us back to the bus station. I had wanted to ask the women how they felt about their husbands' prolonged absence from the village but had suppressed my curiosity for fear of further dampening the somber mood. In the final moments of my visit, I drew up the courage to broach the question in the form of a rhetorical commentary: "It must be very difficult for you women to live for such extended periods without your husbands in the village." Both women complained that raising their daughters alone was not easy and that they suffered from loneliness. But the ensuing discussion centered upon the plight of Fifth Sister-in-Law, whose eight-year separation from her husband was the most prolonged among the three wives and was exacerbated by the short duration of the couple's postmarital co-residence and the fact that the father had never laid eyes upon his daughter.

Speaking as if it were the first time the matter had been aired, the others expressed concern that Fifth Sister-in-Law's marital relationship had reached the limits of what it could be expected to endure. "It is unlikely that your husband has lived alone for eight years after just one month of married life together," cautioned Mrs. Cho. Fifth Sister-in-Law explained that her husband had not made enough money to return to China. When I asked her about her family's monetary goals, she stated that she and her husband had no particular objective in mind. Mrs. Cho was as interested as I to understand this apparent contradiction. She pressed for an explanation. Fifth Sister-in-Law, after an awkward silence, came forward with a confession. She spoke of how she had lent a large portion of the money her husband had remitted from South Korea to her three brothers so that they could purchase falsified documents and apply for their own entry visas to South Korea. Fifth Sister-in-Law recounted how her husband often called her on the phone in a drunken state of anger to reproach her for having given his hard-earned money to her brothers, who seemed unlikely to be able to pay him back.

Mrs. Cho bestowed some stern but well-meaning, sisterly advice. "Your husband's anger is justified," she said. In her opinion there was only one course of action to be taken: Fifth Sister-in-Law should go to South Korea herself and help her husband earn back the money she had lent to her brothers. Fifth Sister-in-Law protested that she could not leave her daughter, but Mrs. Cho countered that Fourth Sister-in-Law could easily absorb a third daughter into her household. "The children all play together anyway," she reasoned. "It's time that you go to South Korea yourself. Help your husband make money more quickly, and then bring him back home."

A Good Mother Makes Money, a Good Wife Resides with Her Husband

When Mrs. Cho urges Fifth Sister-in-Law to join her husband in South Korea to help him make money for the family and leave her children in the care of a close female relative, she sends several messages about the meaning of mothering and conjugality. I suggest she is reflecting a widely expressed Chosŏnjok sensibility. First, Chosŏnjok do not regard it as essential that biological mothers be the caregivers for their children. Under ordinary circumstances, it is the responsibility of the Chosŏnjok wife and mother to manage the domestic sphere, including the care and nurturance of her (biological) children. When the economic well-being of the family and the exigencies of the global economy compel her to choose between her productive and reproductive responsibilities, a Chosŏnjok woman is pressured by the weight of public opinion to choose the former.

Though Fifth Sister-in-Law claims that her care-giving responsibilities toward her daughter prevent her from traveling to South Korea, Mrs. Cho dismisses this logic. She suggests placing the child in the home of Fourth Sister-in-Law as if it were an uncomplicated transaction requiring no further deliberation or negotiation by any of the parties involved. Operating under similar economic pressures and cultural norms, many Chosŏnjok brides who marry South Korean men choose to send their children to live with their maternal grandparents in China while the parents devote their time and energy to earning a living in South Korea. Reliance upon extended kin networks to raise the children was also common among Han Chinese couples who sought employment in Chinese cities far from home. While I do not want to undermine the sense of loss or pain involved in these parent-child separations, the point I make here is that mothers in China who migrate for work and leave their children behind are not categorically labeled "bad mothers." To the contrary, as we shall see, the migration of mothers is considered an understandable, if not noble, sacrifice made by mothers on behalf of their children.

Second, Mrs. Cho's advice to Fifth Sister-in-Law underscores the centrality of the conjugal relationship and the difficulties of sustaining it across transnational space. The decision whether Fifth Sister-in-Law should stay at home with her daughter or join her husband in South Korea involves not simply a choice between productive and reproductive labor but also a choice between residing with her daughter and residing with her husband. While people regarded it as socially acceptable to place a child in the care of another "mother" for years at a time, the possibility of another "mate" stepping in, either temporarily or permanently, to fulfill the emotional and physical desires of a spouse was not to be taken lightly. The parent-child relationship, no matter how strained by separations, was generally not talked about as being in danger of dissolving. The husband-wife relationship, by contrast, was understood as less capable of weathering extended physical separation.[5]

---

5. Interestingly, the "wild geese" families in South Korea described earlier in the chapter appear to be based on the opposite assumption: that marriages are indissoluble whereas children require active maternal labor to thrive.

The possibility of marital infidelity among separated spouses loomed large as a topic of conversation and personal preoccupation. In the case of one couple I knew, the husband's unfounded suspicions that his migrant wife was having an affair in South Korea haunted him so profoundly that it eventually led to their divorce (and the wife's eventual remarriage to a South Korean man, whom she met after the fact). But in many cases, the specter of infidelity could not be dismissed as mere paranoia. It was a fact of life that touched the lives of friends, neighbors, and relatives. During my trip to Ajumma's natal village, described in the previous chapter, Ajumma's nephew led me on a tour of the village. I followed him up a small but steep mountain, from the top of which we took in a bird's-eye view of the entire village. Ajumma's nephew, looking down on the tiled rooftops below, much to my surprise, identified the homes of men and women who had been unfaithful to their migrant spouses as if it were the most significant characteristic distinguishing one house from another. In Mudanjiang City, tales of adultery were even more pervasive. As I walked through streets with Imo, my host mother, she would whisper in my ear the personal details of the passersby: This one is having an affair. That one's wife never came back. Imo seemed especially moved by the plight of a neighbor who hawked bottles of water in the streets outside our apartment, chanting *"Kuangquan shui!"* (Spring water!). Deserted by his Korea-bound wife and left with no other means to support his three sons, this man's voice reverberated each morning throughout the neighborhood as a reminder to all residents of the hardship faced by those whose spouses never return from South Korea.

Nonmigrant Spouses Can Dance Too

The migrant male worker involved in an extramarital affair overseas while his wife's fidelity back home is closely guarded by her in-laws is a familiar stereotype in societies where men hold the monopoly on mobility. But this is no longer the case among the Chosŏnjok; perhaps it never was. Wives migrate just as often as, if not more often than, their husbands, so women can engage in extramarital affairs while living and working in South Korea apart from their husbands. Chosŏnjok workers socialize with one another to relieve the loneliness and sense of alienation they often experience in South Korea, and the resulting friendships can easily evolve into romantic relationships in the relative anonymity and heady atmosphere of life in a "modern," metropolitan city. Living in South Korea also brings Chosŏnjok women in contact with South Korean men. Unlike their male counterparts, Chosŏnjok women may attract a marriage proposal from the swelling ranks of South Korea's eligible bachelors—an option that is more appealing to some than returning to the lives (and husbands) left behind in China.

Women instigated extramarital affairs overseas, but the more surprising finding was that nonmigrant women in China also entered into liaisons while their husbands were away, mostly with Chosŏnjok men whose wives had migrated to South Korea but also with South Korean men who were living or traveling in China. Far from being "disciplinable subjects of the family regime," as Ong (1999, 20) describes the localized wives of overseas Hong Kong transnational capitalists, Chosŏnjok women exercise great freedom over their own decisions and actions in the absence of their husbands. Fifth Sister-in-Law, for example, relocated to her natal village after her husband left for South Korea, eliminating the possibility of her in-laws keeping a watchful eye over her or meddling in her affairs. (I do not know whether this figured into her motivations for moving, but the important point here is that she had the autonomy to do so.) Fifth Sister-in-Law also exercised control over the money her husband earned, lending it, against her husband's wishes, to her brothers. Though it was the husband's fidelity and not her sister-in-law's that Mrs. Cho suggested was in question, the fact of the matter was there were few restraints on Fifth Sister-in-Law's behavior during her weekly stints in the city, where she lived beyond the gaze of the villagers in her husband's hometown.

In Mudanjiang, one of the major meeting grounds for men and women with spouses working in Korea was the local dance hall (*wuting*). A neon sign bearing the Chinese characters "wuting" in bold script hung at one end of the outdoor market directly behind the Chosŏnjok apartment complex where I lived with Imo's family. There were two dance sessions each day, one at six in the morning and the other at seven in the evening. After the morning session ended, dance hall patrons would spill out into the morning market (*zaoshi*), which by that hour was already bustling with people. High-heeled women clad in formal and sometimes showy attire, teetering gingerly around the mud puddles in the marketplace, could be readily picked out.

Imo pointed to those who patronized the dance hall as a sad testimonial to the destructive influence that Korea Wind had wrought upon local families, and she regarded them with pity. According to Imo, they were victims of broken relationships: husbands and wives whose spouses disappeared, often without explanation, after leaving to work in South Korea. Imo saw these men and women, disillusioned and brokenhearted, as seeking an escape from their feelings of abandonment. Rather than a place for finding new and enduring companionship, the dance hall, in Imo's opinion, provided at best only a momentary palliative for the brokenhearted and at worst diverted them from facing up to the hard task of putting their lives back together.

Imo's close friend Sujin was a regular patron of the dance hall. According to Imo, Sujin's husband had made and lost a small fortune doing business in South Korea. The sudden loss of financial security was soon followed by the dissolution of her marriage. Sujin's husband announced he was moving in with his lover, a Chosŏnjok woman he had met in South Korea. As Imo described it, Sujin underwent an "extreme transformation" in the wake of her personal misfortune. Whereas before Sujin had preferred to remain quietly at home, leading a life of thrift as a housewife and mother, now she had shed the extra weight from her formerly plump and sedentary figure and had taken to wearing stylish, form-fitting dance hall attire. What is more, she had found a steady dance partner, a man whose wife had gone to South Korea to make money. This man's wife was rumored to have faithfully remitted money back home every month for three years. But in the fourth year, the money suddenly stopped coming. The cessation of money in such cases was a well-understood sign that the wife had switched her allegiance to a new partner in South Korea.

In the meantime, the abandoned husband had met Sujin in the Mudanjiang dance hall. He was a soft-spoken man from the countryside, tall, suntanned, and handsome. Sujin was an urban housewife with a new desire to appear sexy and attractive. To see the two of them together, as I did when Imo invited the couple over for dinner before the start of their dance session one evening, one could not help but notice the playful innuendos, the significant glances and smiles, which suggested they were quite taken with each other and, for the time being at least, exhilarated by one another's company. After the couple had left the house, Imo admitted they were a match as far as appearance was concerned. Imo remained doubtful,

however, about the long-term viability of their relationship, perhaps because of the rural-urban status that divided them or perhaps because their
relationship had been initiated in the dance hall, a venue commonly associated with "transient eroticism."[6] Imo sympathized with her friend but did
not entirely approve of her new lifestyle. If she were in her friend's shoes,
Imo said, she would not dance, she would work. "I would work in whatever job I could find—as a nanny, a dishwasher—whatever it would take to
continue to support the development of my children and their education."
Of course, a life of self-sacrifice and deferment of personal gratification for
the sake of her children was precisely the route Imo herself had chosen. In
criticizing her friend and other dance hall regulars, Imo may have been
seeking to validate the relative asceticism of her own lifestyle.

At Sujin's urging, Imo reluctantly agreed to go to the dance hall one
evening to watch her friend dance. I was invited to tag along. Imo sat
stiffly with her arms crossed in one of the chairs against the wall, and I sat
beside her, watching the waltzing couples spin by us, one after another.
The room was dark and dingy, lit only by sparkling disco balls. At several
points between dances, the disco balls were dimmed, allowing couples to
indulge in small intimacies under cover of darkness. In the front of the
room, a man banged out old-time Korean songs on an electric keyboard
to which the couples marched and twirled with solemn expressions on
their faces (except when the sight of me would catch their eye and mo-
mentarily break their concentration). Sitting on the side of the dance hall,
Imo made eye contact with four acquaintances, all of whom she claimed
had been abandoned by their husbands. Imo commented on how embarrassed they must be to be seen dancing with strange men. Yet all four
women greeted Imo with broad, un-self-conscious smiles. Imo also took
note of how young, well made-up, and nicely dressed they all looked. (By
contrast, people on the street regularly greeted Imo by commenting on
how much she had appeared to have aged as a result of working in South
Korea.) Imo insisted on seeing the well-groomed demeanors of the danc-
ers as merely a facade. "These people are not *really* happy," she leaned

---

6. I borrow this term from Farrer who uses it to describe the interactions that take place inside dance halls and discotheques in contemporary Shanghai. He writes, "[R]ather than spaces for
constructing permanent erotic relations, discos and social dance halls were usually seen as spaces
for avoiding them" (2000, 234).

over to whisper in my ear. "They are devastated inside by their failed marriages."

Farrer (2000, 247), writing about dance halls in Shanghai where middle-aged men and women socialize in the absence of their spouses, argues that much of what happens inside the dance hall can be described as "an escape from the boring routine of work and family chores into an alternative but pleasurable routine of dance." Similarly, Imo described the very first commercial dance venues in Mudanjiang City, which she said emerged in the mid-1980s, as providing what she called "pure" (in the sense of wholesome [*dancun*]) entertainment for married, middle-aged people who worked together. "People in the same work unit would go at the end of a long work day to release the stresses of the workplace and unwind," Imo reminisced. She traced the origins of the practice of dancing with one's colleagues to the early 1980s, years before the first commercial dance halls appeared in Mudanjiang. At the conclusion of each monthly meeting of the work unit, the meeting hall would be converted into a dance space. Imo described how the faces of the women would turn red from embarrassment when they stepped onto the makeshift dance floor at the invitation of male colleagues. After a while, they grew accustomed to this sort of coed recreation. Imo remembers feeling pressured by her superiors at the hospital to join them in their collective outings to the dance hall. It wasn't until Korea Wind, explained Imo, that the dance hall became known as a place where the spouses of migrants indulged in social improprieties.

Farrer offers a compelling explanation for why participants in Shanghai dance halls found it relatively easy to accept the "low-key extramarital dalliances" of others. The suspension of social norms inside the dance hall was possible, he argues, precisely because it occurred against the backdrop of the "comfortable, everyday world of work unit and family life" (2000, 248). In Mudanjiang, however, the dislocation of market reform had rendered large numbers of people jobless, and the mass exodus to South Korea had shaken the foundations of everyday family life. Unlike the dance hall patrons in Shanghai, those in Mudanjiang, for the most part, did not have spouses waiting at home for them at the end of the evening. Everyday norms in Mudanjiang were suspended not simply in the dance hall but in the world outside as well, so that intimacies inside the dance hall could no longer be comfortably defined by their separation from the routine of work and family.

Fake Marriages and Gender Reversals

Mothers on the Move

Chosŏnjok wives were often sent solo by their families to make money in China while their husbands remained in China with the children. Chosŏnjok women enjoyed two important advantages over their male counterparts which made them good candidates as overseas breadwinners in their families. First, the employment opportunities for migrant women in South Korea were simply more diverse and more appealing than those for men. Though still locked into traditionally feminized occupations such as nannies, waitresses, factory workers, and bilingual service workers, Chosŏnjok women were often able to obtain room and board from their employers, enabling them to save significant amounts of money. Many Chosŏnjok men, by contrast, were limited to construction work, which was not only dangerous but subject to seasonal and weather-related disruptions. The ability of Chosŏnjok women to find jobs that allowed them to live frugally and work steadily thus made it financially prudent to send a wife rather than a husband to South Korea.

Chosŏnjok women also had more immigration options as a result of their gendered position in the Korean marriage market. As we have already seen, obtaining an entry visa to South Korea was a costly and risky undertaking which, more often than not, involved brokers, bribes, and the forging of kinship identities. Chosŏnjok men as well as women regularly entered South Korea in the guise of "separated family members." But a Chosŏnjok woman had the additional advantage of being able to contract a paper marriage to a South Korean man. If the Chosŏnjok woman were married,[7] she would need first to pay a broker to remove her name from her husband's household register and forge a new identity card (*shenfenzheng*) that testified to her unmarried status.[8] Chosŏnjok widely referred to this practice as getting a fake divorce in order to arrange a fake marriage.

---

7. It is my impression that fewer unmarried Chosŏnjok women chose this option, but more research would need to be done to verify this. A woman who has never been married risks damaging her reputation by entering a fake marriage, making her appear less desirable when it comes time to find a "real" marriage partner.

8. The going rate at the time of my research to erase evidence of a woman's marriage was 5,000 RMB.

A reporter describes a departure scene he witnessed in Shenyang airport between a Chosŏnjok man, his wife, their daughter, and his wife's "new [Korean] husband." The wife has signed a contract in which she promises to return to China after making a certain sum of money in Korea. As the Chosŏnjok wife and the Korean "husband" disappear into the airplane bound for Seoul, the husband looks concerned. According to the reporter, "the Chosŏnjok man feels like knocking out this brazen Korean man with his fist and seizing back his wife." As the man trudges away with tears in his eyes, his daughter consoles him, saying, "Mother went to earn money to buy me new clothes and a new book bag."[9]

Unlike all other categories of visa, a marriage visa entitled the bearer to citizenship rights and the attendant privilege of working for an unlimited period in South Korea without the constant fear of deportation that plagued undocumented workers. A paper bride with South Korean citizenship gained the ability to shuttle back and forth between her job in South Korea and her family members in China. While expensive, complicated to arrange, and emotionally fraught, it was an investment with rewards that lasted a lifetime.

As I learned in a conversation one morning over breakfast with Imo, this migration strategy often had unintended repercussions for relations between spouses that were equally long-lasting. According to Imo, people used to be naive about the potential sexual indiscretions involved in a fake marriage. However, at the time of our dialogue on fake marriage, Imo said this had become a well-known fact, and thus any woman who contracted a fake marriage was knowingly "polluting" herself and her marital relationship. While it was not the focus of my investigation, Imo and others made frequent reference to the inability of Chosŏnjok husbands to come to terms with the fact that their wives may have had sexual relations with a South Korean man in the course of arranging a fake marriage. Imo picked up a white teacup from the table and pointed to a spot on it as a metaphor for something that had once been pure but had become dirty (*tŏrŏpda*). Now that she knows cohabitation is a necessary part of contracting a fake marriage, Imo says she would not be willing to go through with one.

---

9. Peil soke ssain "wijang kyŏrhon" [Illicit marriages beneath a veil]. *Heilongjiang News.* September 16, 1995.

When visiting the homes of friends and relatives, Imo was fond of recounting the story of a woman whose fake marriage to a Korean man unexpectedly landed her in a legal and ethical predicament. When the woman arrived in South Korea, the paper husband threatened to withhold her residence permit and report her to the police if she did not agree to move in with him. "What fake marriage?" Imo quoted the man as saying to his unwitting bride. "I was for *real*!" In each version of the story, the woman was said to have fled the man's home "so fast that she had no time to put on her shoes." In Imo's opinion, the woman had acted nobly: she sacrificed the opportunity to obtain Korean citizenship in order to keep her body "pure." In telling this cautionary tale, Imo appeared to be warning other women about the potential dangers of fake marriages. With each retelling, it also occurred to me that she may have been seeking validation for her own decision to resist the popular tide and the rewards of Korean citizenship by not pursuing a paper marriage. While Imo believed strongly in the virtuousness of her self-restraint, she could not help but lament on occasion "how convenient it must be to be able to move back and forth."

The acts of marital infidelity that Imo cautioned against were either coerced or simply considered a perfunctory part of arranging a paper marriage. The opposite scenario in which the South Korean groom and Chosŏnjok bride, in the course of negotiating the terms of a sham marriage, unexpectedly experience genuine feelings of attraction for each other was a widely acknowledged possibility as well. Stories of "fake" marriages and "fake" divorces turned "real" circulated throughout the Korean-language media in China as well as by word of mouth. One 1997 *Heilongjiang News* article estimates that eight or nine out of ten "fake divorces" turn into real ones, despite intentions to resume married life after the wife earns money in South Korea (Sin and Hwang 1997).

Though I was unable to directly interview any Chosŏnjok women who had forsaken their Chosŏnjok husbands in China for their "paper" counterparts in South Korea, I heard many secondhand accounts of neighbors, friends, and relatives who had done just that. One story I heard while living in Creek Road Village involved a Chosŏnjok woman who had arranged a paper marriage to a South Korean man without the knowledge of her husband or young daughter. Periodically the woman would call home, claiming to be working in the Chinese city of Qingdao. The villagers explained that the woman's original intentions were to sever ties with the Korean paper husband and send money home to her daughter in China. But the woman ended up giving birth to a child in South Korea and switching her allegiance to her fake-turned-real family.

In retelling this story, the villagers did not specify the reasons motivating the woman's change of heart. We can only speculate whether it was inspired by feelings of romantic passion toward the paper husband and/ or by feelings of alienation toward her husband in China. Perhaps it was the birth of a child in South Korea that influenced her decision to turn her back on her family in China. Some Chosŏnjok brides I interviewed who married South Korean men through legitimate channels pointed to the birth of a child as a pivotal factor cementing their decision to remain in an otherwise difficult marital situation. Chosŏnjok women also were careful to avoid pregnancy if they were contemplating running away. Juju, the "runaway bride" featured in chapter 3, for example, confided that she was using an intrauterine device (IUD) without the knowledge of her husband until she had made up her mind whether to stay in her marriage. Recall also that Yunŏk (chapters 3 and 4) terminated a pregnancy without informing her husband in order to keep the door open to the possibility of a clean break.

A local newspaper article on fake marriage requires us to consider the possibility that the woman from Creek Road Village who gave birth to a child in South Korea may have been coerced into having sexual relations with her paper husband. The article presents the testimony of a thirty-year-old woman who contracted a fake marriage with a fifty-year-old grandfather (*harabŏji*). After two years of working in a restaurant in Seoul and waiting for her Korean citizenship, the woman discovered she was pregnant. The woman is quoted as saying, "The Korean man said he would not divorce me unless I shared a bed with him for a night, otherwise he would report me." The reporter points out that the law is on the side of the "husband," since the couple is lawfully married.[10]

As the following sketches illustrate, romantic passions did not have to run high—or exist at all—for a Chosŏnjok woman to reconsider the impermanence of her fake marriage contract, especially if the woman was already divorced or in desperate circumstances. One Chosŏnjok migrant worker in Seoul told me a story about her friend who arranged a paper marriage to a

---

10. Ibid.

Korean man after getting a (real) divorce from her Korean husband. After she arrived in South Korea, she discovered that the Korean man was very kind (*hen shanliang*). The migrant worker pointed out that her friend "did not love the man, but had developed feelings for him [*you ganqing*]." He was a poor man with no family of his own, and the woman was said to "feel sorry for him" and therefore had a difficult time leaving him. At the time of the telling, the woman had reportedly given birth to a son and was still living with her husband. In another story, told to me by a Chosŏnjok bride in South Korea, a young unmarried woman contracted a fake marriage in order to escape her troubled family circumstances in China. The Korean man reportedly fell in love with her, and after she arrived in South Korea he proposed that they get married "for real." Though the woman was said not to return the man's adoration, she agreed to marry him in hopes of attaining the stable family life she had lacked growing up in China.

Each of these scenarios points to ways feelings—whether romantic attraction, empathy, or sense of security—can surface unexpectedly in fake marriages. Here "fake" as it is used by the Chosŏnjok in discussing paper marriages and paper divorces refers to the short-lived, purely instrumental nature of the transaction, the lack of emotional and long-term commitment that ordinarily is presumed to constitute a conjugal relationship. A fake marriage is not meant to endure. A fake divorce is intended to be reversed at some time in the future. A real marriage, by contrast, connotes permanence, stability, exclusivity. In theory, arranging a fake marriage and fake divorce does not violate these matrimonial ideals. The couple that files for a fake divorce is presumed to change only the legal status of their marriage, not the quality of their relationship; a fake marriage is presumed to exist only on paper. But in practice, as we have seen, the process may entail certain breaches of propriety that ultimately impinge on the quality of the original marital relationship. With little if any leverage at their disposal to bring their wives back home and with fewer options for outward mobility, Chosŏnjok men whose wives enact fake marriages often find themselves in a vulnerable position.

Stay-at-Home Husbands

No matter what means their wives use to migrate to South Korea, Chosŏnjok husbands who are left in China face the challenge of adjusting to their new status as the primary managers of the domestic sphere. When women assume the role of primary or even sole breadwinner in the family by migrating to South Korea, they conform in certain respects to existing constructions of femininity or motherhood. Chosŏnjok men who become the primary overseers of the domestic sphere, however, must work harder to build alternative constructions of masculinity and fatherhood that correspond to their new responsibilities. While it is not uncommon in China for men to assist with child rearing and routine household chores, among the Chosŏnjok the domestic arena is still considered the preserve of women.

Men in Creek Road Village whose wives had migrated to South Korea by arranging a fake marriage were deemed worthy of pity by their fellow villagers. One stay-at-home husband I had gotten to know well was the father of Kyuyŏng, the young woman I introduced in the previous chapter who was assigned as my companion and assistant while living at Country Ajumma's house. An affable, benevolent-looking man in his early forties, Kyuyŏng's father lived off the remittances his "fake ex-wife" sent regularly from South Korea. This income allowed the family of three—Kyuyŏng, her teenage brother, and her father—to relocate to an apartment in Mudanjiang City where the schooling was better for her brother. Kyuyŏng's father's primary occupation was the upkeep of their apartment, including cooking, laundry, routine housecleaning, and the supervision of his son's studies, which he appeared to handle efficiently and without complaint. In the afternoons, he seemed to enjoy his leisure time often filled with mahjong and friendly chats with his neighbors—many of them women—in the apartment complex.

Despite the apparent aplomb with which Kyuyŏng's father managed these new fathering arrangements, others voiced their sympathy for him. Country Ajumma expressed concern that Kyuyŏng's father's marriage might not survive a fake marriage and the couple's extended physical separation from one another. According to Ajumma, the villagers were speculating about Kyuyŏng's father's fidelity. Most seemed to think he would be justified in having an affair given his wife's prolonged absence. "It's not natural for a couple in their forties to be separated for so long only to be reunited in old age. What's the point? A couple should stay together," Ajumma proclaimed, echoing commonly held sentiments about the importance of conjugal togetherness. According to Ajumma, what made the situation for Kyuyŏng's father especially deplorable was the fact that his twenty-two-year-old daughter did not step in and take over responsibility for the housekeeping and care of her younger brother. Not only would this arrangement have been strategically preferable in freeing Kyuyŏng's father to join his wife in South Korea and contribute to the family's income, Ajumma implied that it also would have been culturally preferable to reassign domestic duties to the eldest daughter, thereby sparing her father the stigma of performing "women's work."

On another occasion, Ajumma poked fun at a neighbor for his poor housekeeping skills and feminized status as "househusband." This gangly, long-faced man whose wife had left for South Korea nearly four years before as a fake bride wandered almost daily into Ajumma's house glumly

Chosŏnjok men waiting for their migrant wives to return or to send money for their own passage to South Korea.

looking for ways to idle away his time. One evening he arrived to recruit Ajumma for a game of mahjong that was already under way at his house. Ajumma suggested that I come along too so that I might survey the disorder of his household. "He lives like a pig [*twaeji*]," she teased. "The house is a complete mess now that he is the 'mother' in the family. We should call him Twaeji Ajumma [Mrs. Pig]!" The man pretended to kick Ajumma in response and laughed good-naturedly. Most of the time, however, he wore a despondent expression. After four years of working in South Korea, his wife still had not managed to raise the 50,000 RMB he needed to pay a broker to get him to South Korea. The man said his wife claimed she had been ill, but rumors were spreading that his wife must be having an affair. "He does not even have a television set to show for all his wife's years of work in Korea!" one neighbor observed. "His son is not studious and will not attend college or even high school. So what in the world is his wife doing in South Korea?" said another critic. All seemed to agree that the man himself was to blame for not taking a stronger stand with his wife.

As these cases illustrate, men whose wives migrate to South Korea and leave them behind to mind the domestic sphere are considered weak and vulnerable. Like the nonmigrant wives examined earlier, nonmigrant husbands are economically dependent upon the remittances of their spouses and possess virtually no leverage to ensure the sexual fidelity of their sojourning mates. The real and imagined indiscretions that take place in the course of contracting a fake marriage place additional stresses on the (real) marital relationship, which often must continue to be negotiated well after the fake marriage is dissolved and the Chosŏnjok couple is reunited. Finally, men who stay at home to raise the children and perform household labor are stigmatized in the eyes of others for performing tasks normatively prescribed to Chosŏnjok wives and mothers. (Gender logics can shift according to cultural context; see chapter 3 for further discussion.)

Couples Who Migrate Together: Transnational Parenting

Many Chosŏnjok seemed to regard the ideal transnational family arrangement as one in which a couple combines overseas earning power and preserves the sanctity of their marital bond by migrating together. The strategy of sending one spouse first while the other stays behind to care for children is in many cases intended as a temporary stage in a long-range plan to reunite as a couple in South Korea as soon as the first spouse earns enough for the other's illegal passage. This was precisely the strategy enacted by Kyuyŏng's parents. Two years after her mother migrated to South Korea through a paper marriage, her father followed suit. My most recent e-mail correspondence with Kyuyong, ten years after my departure from the field, confirmed that her parents to this day continue to live and labor together in Seoul. As far as I know, the forlorn "househusband" who was taunted for his poor housekeeping skills was not as fortunate. When I last saw him, he was still clinging to the hope that his wife would recover from her alleged illness and send him the money he needed to enter South Korea under a false identity.

City Imo's family offers a glimpse into the pragmatics but also the cultural logic that motivates spouses, when possible, to migrate to South Korea in tandem, leaving their children behind in the care of a third party. Aside from the practical benefit of garnering two incomes and thereby curtailing the period of family separation that must be endured to reach a specific economic goal, migrating as a couple offers a way of preserving the stability of the marital relationship while also prioritizing the financial well-being of children. By choosing to migrate in conjunction with her husband, Imo imagined she would ward off the possibility that an extramarital affair might complicate or, worse, lead to the break up of her marriage as she had watched happen to so many of her relatives and neighbors. Based on my casual conversations with people and their evaluations of their own and others' decisions regarding how to split the family to take advantage of income-earning opportunities in South Korea, I learned that parents and children were considered better able to withstand long-term separations than were husbands and wives.

What is more, the willingness to migrate in order to give one's children a better future was considered the mark of a good parent. In the case of Imo and her husband, their decision to leave the children in the care of the maternal grandmother for seven years while they worked for Korean wages enabled them to buy a better apartment for their family as well as pay tuition and housing costs for their daughter as she pursued a graduate degree in Chinese medicine. While I was living with Imo in Mudanjiang, her frenzied efforts to enter South Korea a second time were driven by her single-minded determination to raise the money needed to launch her son on his future, yet-to-be-determined career path. Imo and her husband's hard work and sacrifice, as she put it, were entirely "for the children."

Such transnational family arrangements are not without emotional costs, however. Hondagneu-Sotelo and Avila report that Latina migrant workers in Los Angeles cited the inability to have daily contact with their children as a source of deep personal loss (2003, 332). Concerns about whether children are being properly cared for in the mother's absence, whether they will get into trouble during adolescence, and whether they will transfer their allegiance and affection to the surrogate parent were also anxieties that plagued the same migrant mothers. With the exception of the last concern, migrant Chosŏnjok parents voiced similar fears. I described in the previous chapter Imo's profound sense of sorrow in having missed out on the daily pleasure of witnessing firsthand the growth and development of her children. Imo personally expressed confidence both in her mother's ability to care for her children and in her children's ability to behave responsibly in her absence (indeed my impression was that her children conducted themselves with a striking combination of childlike innocence and maturity beyond their years). However, it was a widespread popular sentiment among the Chosŏnjok that the mass exodus of parents to South Korea had the effect of depriving almost an entire generation of children of adequate supervision and guidance. Adolescence in particular was considered a stage of childhood development when children were most in need of a parent's discipline.

I spoke with the principal of a Chosŏnjok elementary school on the outskirts of Mudanjiang City. He estimated that forty-eight percent of the students in his school had at least one parent working in South Korea at the time. Most of these children were being raised by their grandparents, a situation he described as having negative consequences for their moral and educational development. Grandparents as a group had a reputation for doting on their grandchildren and not disciplining them. In addition, the steady flow of spending money that migrant parents funneled to their children from abroad exacerbated the situation. Lack of discipline at home combined with the children's unrestrained spending power, in his opinion, constituted a pressing and widespread "social problem" (*shehui wenti*).

One eighteen-year-old girl I spoke with issued a similar critique. Of the fifty-four students in her high school class, she claimed that "the mother of every single one of them" had gone to Korea through a fake marriage.

In many families, she said, both parents had left. Alarmed by the situation, her teacher had reportedly appealed to the parents of her classmates to resist the urge to migrate to South Korea. "Early adolescence is a very risky time for a parent to leave," the girl explained. "Kids are most vulnerable at that time to turning bad." She then bemoaned the inadequacies of grandparents caring for teenage children: "It's simply not the role of a grandparent to be a disciplinarian. It's only natural that grandparents want to spoil their grandchildren."

It is important to note, however, that individual experiences do not necessarily conform to the stereotype of the overly indulgent grandparent. A friend of mine reflected with nostalgia and gratitude on the formative years she spent in the care of her maternal grandmother between the ages of eight and fifteen while her mother worked long hours at her day job. She claimed to have learned many practical skills from her grandmother whom she described as a very strict, intelligent, and capable woman. More research is needed to understand the way children feel about the quality of care grandparents (and other kin) provide for them in the absence of their migrant parents.

While the public perceives the proliferation of transnational households as creating something of a childcare crisis, I did not observe any attempt to cast blame on the individual parents who pursue transnational family strategies. The opposite is true in the Philippines, as noted, where women who leave their children behind to take up employment as domestic workers in the United States are vilified in the popular media and in state-level discourse as "bad mothers" who "abandon" their families and children (Parreñas 2001b, 2003).[11] Similarly, Hondagneu-Sotelo and Avila note that Latina nannies who bring their children with them to the United States frequently look upon migrant women who leave children at home as neglecting their motherly responsibilities (2003, 335). One reason for the greater acceptance of transnational motherhood in China, as I suggested earlier, may be found in a more expansive definition of motherhood that

---

11. Transnational families in the Philippines were not always equated with "broken homes." To the contrary, the Filipino government has enthusiastically touted migrant workers as "economic heroes" in recognition of their crucial contributions to the national economy. Only when women began to dominate the flow of migration in the late 1980s did public discourse about migrant mothers turn critical (Parreñas 2003, 51).

includes breadwinning alongside, rather than in opposition to, more traditional notions of caregiving.

Imo's seven-year separation from her children was looked upon by her friends and neighbors not as sacrificing maternal love but, to the contrary, as its ultimate expression. Imo's son and daughter themselves expressed appreciation that their mother had endured years of hard labor for their benefit and emphasized their filial obligation to succeed academically and professionally to repay her rather than highlighting the emotional losses they admittedly felt in growing up without daily contact with either parent.[12] Indeed, proof of the worthiness of Imo's long-distance mothering seemed to lie in the educational attainment of her children and the material acquisitions of her household. By the same token, public opinion could turn against those whose extended separations from family did not result in upward class or educational mobility for family members left behind. Recall, for example, the case of the forlorn househusband whose nonstudious son and materially bereft household spoke to others of the futility of his family's separation.

Far from feeling abandoned by their parents, some Chosŏnjok children have come to expect, even insist, that their parents migrate on their behalf. At a gathering of Imo's relatives, I listened with amazement as a fifteen-year-old girl instructed her mother to go to South Korea to make money for her education overseas. When asked whether she intended to study in South Korea, the girl announced with disdain that she had no desire to go *there* but rather had set her sights much higher on Canada, Australia, or the United States. Pointing out that her daughter's grades were not up to par, the mother retorted, "What makes you think you can test into such a school?" The daughter smugly replied that if she failed to test into a school, her parents should simply pay for her to attend. The surrounding guests gasped and laughed uneasily at the audacity of this young woman.

The sense of entitlement displayed by this young woman resonates with Yunxiang Yan's observations regarding what he calls the "demystification of parenthood" in postrevolution China (2003,188). In describing the collapse of the traditional notion of filial piety, Yan argues that

---

12. According to Parreñas, children in the Philippines also view the migration of their parents as a demonstration of love, contrary to the dominant imagery of migrant women as deserting their children. Parreñas suggests that viewing migration as a maternal sacrifice to be repaid later in life is one way children cope with the emotional insecurity of being left by their parents (2001b, 47).

intergenerational reciprocity is no longer based on the belief that children are indebted to parents for a lifetime simply for the gift of life, once considered the highest form of favor (*enqing*) one could give. Instead, intergenerational exchange, like other types of exchange, must be balanced and consistently maintained. According to this new logic, Yan writes, "If the parents do not treat their children well or are otherwise not good parents, then the children have reason to reduce the scope and amount of generosity to their parents" (178). In the absence of guaranteed old-age support from their children, parents feel compelled to do the best they can to secure the support of their children while building up savings for their retirement. Middle-aged Chosŏnjok parents talked about their migration to South Korea in precisely these terms, as a way of acquiring wealth to pass on to their children and ensure their own financial security in old age.

Migrating to South Korea was thus seen as a parental strategy for building stronger bonds, both emotional and material, with children. At the same time, the possibility that dispersing the family in order to make money would weaken or even dissolve family relationships was an ever-present danger. It was not uncommon for migrants or their spouses at home to jeopardize ties to their families by engaging in extramarital affairs. These were considered genuine cases of abandonment, and the children of these families were unanimously regarded as victims of transnational kinship strategies gone awry. Imo's brother's daughter, eight-year-old Yuna, for example, was being raised by Imo's mother alongside Imo's own children. But unlike Bongnam and Binmu, whose stay with their grandmother had been prearranged by their parents, Yuna was taken in by her grandmother as a last resort when her father moved in with his Chosŏnjok lover, severing ties to both his migrant wife in South Korea and the young daughter in his charge. Though she was earning money in South Korea, Yuna's mother sent her little financial support, much to the little girl's chagrin. Relatives quietly speculated that Yuna's mother might not ever return. I was at Imo's house one day when a package arrived from Yuna's mother. Yuna sullenly tore off the wrapping and then scowled at the contents—a backpack, a pair of sneakers, and a few trinkets—while Imo and Bongnam tried in vain to persuade her to view these small tokens as signs of her mother's unwavering affection. Though she received good marks in school, awards for her gymnastic ability, and ample affection from her extended family members, a gloomy expression remained stubbornly fixed upon her face. Imo shook her head in sorrow when contemplating Yuna and explained to me that her niece was just one of a large number of Chosŏnjok children whose sense of family and stability had been unhinged by Korea Wind.

The tendency to point to the larger forces of Korea Fever as the culprit in wrenching Chosŏnjok families apart may also have tempered the inclination to blame individuals for the emotional costs incurred by transnational parenting. People often talked about Korea Wind as an infectious and irresistible force sweeping across the northeastern provinces over which individual Chosŏnjok were presumed to have little control. Instead of parents, for example, being condemned for abandoning their children, public discourse more often targeted the impersonal forces of Korea Wind for "taking away" parents and spouses and generally wreaking havoc upon family relationships. In his ethnography of a Han village in northeastern China, Yunxiang Yan similarly writes about the importance of *cunfeng* or "village wind" (which he suggests translating as "village trend" or "village mood") in shaping the growth of a new fertility culture (2003, 212–13). While the power of community-wide norms to guide the actions and opinions of individuals is certainly not unique to China, I do think that naming various kinds of "winds" and according them a measure of independent agency is a culturally particular proclivity. Among the Chosŏnjok, the collective acknowledgment of the omnipotence of Korea Wind enabled them to view their transnational family practices as an inevitable accommodation to the times in which they were living.

Bargaining with Matrimony

The experiences of Chosŏnjok couples as they negotiate uncharted territories of transnational family making draw our attention to the nuanced and complex ways gender shapes and is shaped by migration. Here I have shown how decisions regarding the allocation of mobile versus stay-at-home family labor create culturally particular dilemmas about how to finesse and prioritize gender, conjugal, and parenting relationships.

In contemporary Chinese society where gender ideology dictates that married women divide their energies evenly between work and home, women who stay home to raise the children while their husbands earn money abroad are often seen as carrying out only half of the cultural expectations: they perform the domestic work but not the productive work associated with being an industrious and devoted wife and mother. We saw in the case of Fifth Sister-in-Law how a mother's decision to remain at home might be viewed as a waste of her productive potential, especially when extended family members are on hand to take over the task of caring for children. Mothers who migrated to South Korea, on the other hand, labored firmly within the frame of supporting the domestic realm and encountered criticism for traveling far from home only when it led to extramarital relationships and the siphoning of a woman's resources and loyalties away from her nuclear household in China.

In light of the fact that migrant mothers are seen as prioritizing their role as breadwinners over their role as daily caregivers, I wondered whether the reliance on extended family members for surrogate mothering was perceived as weakening the bonds between mothers and their children. To obtain the material comforts enjoyed by the large numbers of children with migrant parents in their midst as well as to better their life chances in an increasingly competitive and globalizing marketplace, children I spoke with in Mudanjiang appreciated the necessity of their mother's (and father's) money-making efforts overseas. As we saw in the case of one high school girl, children sometimes went so far as to insist that their mothers migrate on their behalf. Binmu and Bongnam viewed their mother's seven-year sojourn in South Korea as a form of maternal sacrifice that they would repay in the future through their own academic and material achievements. Thus, rather than weakening parent-child relations, acquiring wealth in South Korea and investing it in one's children became an important parental strategy for reinforcing intergenerational ties (see Yan 2003).

If migrant mothers presented no significant challenge to dominant Chosŏnjok models of motherhood, fathers who stayed behind to mind the domestic sphere were commonly perceived as transgressing into "female" territory. The sketches I presented of stay-at-home fathers illustrate the extent to which these men could become the butt of jokes and objects of pity. Perhaps it is too soon to tell, but the proliferation of housebound husbands did not seem to have led to any radical redefinition of Chosŏnjok fatherhood and masculinity to include primary responsibility for everyday household tasks and childcare. Instead, stay-at-home-husbands were perceived either as poor substitutes for their wives or as lacking the wherewithal to restore proper gender relations in their households.

In contrast to previous studies, which focused on the emotional difficulties and practical challenges of transnational parenting, I discovered that the emotionally charged site for Chosŏnjok couples was transnational conjugality. The separation of parents and children in the name of capital accumulation was considered both strategically imperative and culturally permissible. The separation of husbands and wives was generally perceived as more problematic. Not only did newly emergent ideals of conjugal intimacy and co-residency make it undesirable for spouses to spend extended periods of time apart from each other, but the real and perceived dangers of an extramarital relationship reinforced the notion that geographically separated spouses were taking enormous risks with their marriage. The risks were perceived to be greatest for newly married couples whose marital bonds had not been solidified by years of living together. Age was also considered an important factor. For middle-aged couples and younger, considered to be in the prime of their sexual lives, long-term separation was discouraged because of the presumed inevitability that separated spouses, particularly men, would look to satisfy their sexual desires through extramarital relationships.

In this context, Chosŏnjok dance halls lost their former innocence as places where men and women could spice up their everyday work and family lives, and came to symbolize instead the pervasiveness of marital instability and the hazards of extramarital romance. The readiness of so many Chosŏnjok couples to enact fake marriages and divorces in this climate of uncertainty points to a new morality in which marital relationships became bargaining chips in a game of transnational mobility. In a more positive light, these developments propelled the issue of a middle-aged wife's sexuality into public discourse, heralding the fact that a married Chosŏnjok woman is no longer bound by webs of obligation spun by her husband's family or by the terms of a wife's unquestioned fidelity. While I acknowledge the potentially emancipatory effects of these trends, I have concentrated here on the moral and emotional costs of Chosŏnjok transnational life strategies and what they reveal about the cultural expectations Chosŏnjok hold about gender and family. Cases of fake marriages unexpectedly turned real further underscore not simply the extreme flexibility of martial relationships under transnational conditions but, just as important, their extreme fragility.

6

A FAILED NATIONAL EXPERIMENT?

At the beginning of the 1990s, South Korea provided a source of dreams about life in a wealthy, developed nation, fostered new feelings of pan-ethnic pride, and held out the promise of recovering a lost sense of ethnic homogeneity through exchanges of kin and labor. Yet making kinship across the national divide, whether in the literal form of marriages and family reunions or the metaphorical sense of fostering ethnic solidarity through an idiom of blood, proved more complicated than any of the parties had imagined. Discriminatory treatment, artificially suppressed wages, clashing gender logics, and the criminalization of so-called runaway brides and undocumented workers tarnished the myth of ethnic homogeneity and exposed the contradictions at the heart of South Korea's transnational kin-making project. The widespread Chosŏnjok practice of faking kinship identities and forging genealogies as a means to enter South Korea further undermined the sanctity of kinship as a unifying force between South Koreans and the diaspora in China. One Chosŏnjok observer, C. Song, does not mince words in describing the upshot of these encounters: "The meeting of Korean-Chinese and South Koreans was the first experiment for national reunification and it completely failed" (C Song 2005, 9, quoted in H Kim 2010, 11).

Recent work on Korean transnational adoptees and their return visits to the country of their birth provides a useful point of comparison for the "repatriation" of Chosŏnjok migrants to South Korea. Eleana Kim (2007, 2010) expertly explores the ambiguities of adoptees' position in the Korean nationalist imaginary as both reminders of the pain of family separation, cultural loss, and the nation's past economic plights on the one hand and their resignification as "ambassadors" or "bridges" connecting Korea to the West on the other. Adoptees who travel to Korea must negotiate two sets of popular and official discourses, which variously position them as pitiable orphans returning to their "biological" roots and as potential national assets that will provide productive links to the global economy (506–9).

Kim describes the unanticipated feelings of alienation and inauthenticity with which many adoptees contend upon return to their country of birth. Amid the contradictions created by the official discourses that welcome adoptees into the national "family" while simultaneously defining them as a precious national resource, Kim argues that increasing numbers of adoptees are responding by making alternative claims to Koreanness based on a new form of transnational adoptee consciousness. Ultimately, these new definitions of what it means to be "Korean" disrupt dominant ideologies that conflate race, nation, culture, and kinship (Kim 2003, 2007, 2010).

Like adoptees, Chosŏnjok migrants have undergone a similar revaluation: from a reminder of the nation's difficult past and its struggle against colonial and imperialist forces to a symbol of national hope. Lacking the cultural and financial capital that "Westernized" adoptees are perceived to possess, Chosŏnjok migrants were understood as bridge builders of a different sort, their movement into South Korea signifying the imminence of national reunification with North Korea. If adoptees supplied the cultural capital needed to propel South Korea into the age of global capital, Chosŏnjok migrants supplied the unskilled labor that was equally necessary to advance the nation's competitiveness on the global stage. And like the adoptees, Chosŏnjok migrants commonly experienced feelings of disillusionment because of their negative experiences with Korean ethnocentrism, leaving many with feelings of "homelessness" and abandonment by the South Korean government.

Many Chosŏnjok I met spoke of their national status as being betwixt and between South Korea and China; they feel at home or treated equitably in neither country (more than one person invoked the metaphor of an orphan rejected by both parents, China and South Korea). Some remarked that unexpected feelings of attachment to China had surfaced as a result of their experiences in South Korea. It was common for Chosŏnjok brides I interviewed to express this transformation in terms of the teams they rooted for while watching televised soccer matches. Many claimed that for the first time in their lives, they found themselves cheering for China's soccer team rather than the Korean one.

Chosŏnjok migrants also sought to restore their sense of dignity as Chinese nationals by comparing what they saw as lacking in Korea to abundance found in China, especially in terms of food, leisure time, close interpersonal relations (*renqing wei*), hospitality toward guests (*haoke*), and gender equality. As one older migrant who had returned to China after working for several years in Korea remarked defiantly, "They [Koreans] think Chinese people are so desperately poor, but they don't realize how well we eat here. It's true we lack money, but we have an abundance of food. The rice they eat in Korea is what we would use for pig feed!" Such counterdiscourses and polarized characterizations of life in China versus South Korea suggest an attempt by the Chosŏnjok to reclaim a sense of dignity by reframing their experiences of exclusion as their own conscious decision not to belong.

Shifting Cartographies of Transnational Marriage

Chosŏnjok Brides Marry Upward

If at the turn of the millennium Chosŏnjok migrants were no longer secure in the belief of "one blood, one people [*minjok*]," they also began to question the wealth and power of the South Korean nation itself. When I arrived in the field, South Korea was reeling from the aftershocks of the 1997 Asian financial crisis and what would prove to be a short-lived but nonetheless epochal IMF bailout. To many Chosŏnjok men and women contemplating their next migratory move at this era-defining juncture, South Korea's position in the economic world order seemed in peril.

Real and perceived shifts in the global economy in the wake of the IMF's actions had dramatic effects on patterns of transnational marriage. Marriage brokers I interviewed in South Korea in 1998 and 1999 were struggling to drum up business and blamed the IMF crisis for its impact not only on South Korea's image abroad but on the ability of South Korean grooms to afford the high costs of a marriage tour to China. Instead of arranging marriages between Chosŏnjok maidens and South Korean bachelors, marriage brokers reported that the Chosŏnjok women who sought their services increasingly were women who had divorced their South Korean husbands and were looking to find marriage partners in Japan.

Thus, when I arrived in Harbin one year later, intending to interview brides bound for South Korea, I was not caught entirely off guard by the news with which my Chosŏnjok friend Hyejin greeted me at the airport. "It's becoming the trend now to marry to Japan, not South Korea," she informed me. In fact, Hyejin herself had switched her own marital sights in keeping with the new trend and was preparing for this change of plans by taking nightly Japanese classes at a local language school.

One year earlier when I first met Hyejin she had been midway through a two-year stint in Seoul, where her parents had sent her on a student visa to study the Korean language. Her parents hoped that in the process of studying and living abroad, their twenty-seven-year-old daughter, who was pushing the limits of marriageable age, would meet and marry a South Korean man. Hyejin's mother had financed her daughter's sojourn abroad out of wages she had previously earned as a migrant laborer in South Korea. She was thus profoundly disappointed when Hyejin returned home without a marriage proposal. Even so, she wasted little time devising a back-up plan.

Hyejin's mother would sell a piece of real estate (also purchased with wages earned in South Korea) to fund a second stint of study abroad for Hyejin, this time in Tokyo, where she hoped her daughter would be well situated to meet and marry a Japanese man. "Japan is even more developed than South Korea and salaries are higher. Why go to South Korea when you can go directly to Japan?" her mother reasoned. (Of course, it was not without a hint of sour grapes that Japan began to appear a promising hunting ground for a husband.) "Such a pretty girl," said her great-aunt, tapping Hyejin on the leg. "You should go to Japan and find yourself a nice man." "This is your final opportunity," her father admonished. Hyejin voiced reservations. "I couldn't relate to a South Korean man," she said, referring to her broken engagement to a South Korean construction worker. "How am I ever going to relate to a Japanese one?"

As news of South Korea's internal poverty and rigid gender norms trickled homeward to northeastern China, prospective migrant brides were understandably beginning to reevaluate their transnational possibilities. In the folk model of the world system that held sway among the Chosŏnjok, Japan was located a step above South Korea. Many ranked the nations in the top tier with mathematical precision, as Hyejin's great-aunt articulated: "The United States is number one. Japan is ten years behind the United States. South Korea is ten years behind Japan. And China is ten years behind South Korea. That makes China forty years behind the United States." Did Chosŏnjok women believe that by aspiring upward on the ladder of nations they would find superior marriage partners?

Extreme winter temperatures create icy spectacles on the windows of buildings and buses in Harbin.

Chosŏnjok brides who married to South Korea discovered firsthand that marrying into a nation with a higher gross national product (GNP) does not automatically result in upward mobility for the bride (nor could upward mobility always be measured in purely economic terms). Gendered constructions of family labor constrained the ability of Chosŏnjok brides to capitalize on their new geographic positioning and complicated their adjustment to conjugal life. In the case of Yunŏk, for example, her South Korean husband invoked conservative gender ideals to deter her from pursuing her entrepreneurial ambitions outside the home; Yŏnjae clashed with her in-laws over the right to manage her own income. Stories like these might have provided cautionary tales for the next wave of Chosŏnjok women looking to use transnational marriage as a means of upward mobility. Were the young women in Hyejin's Japanese class—many of whom, according to Hyejin, shared her matrimonial ambitions—not daunted by the prospect that gender inequalities in Japan might stand in their way of pursuing the cosmopolitan lifestyles and economic opportunities they envisioned?

With the permission of the Japanese language teacher, I circulated a written questionnaire among the students in Hyejin's class to explore their motivations for studying Japanese and their general attitudes toward Japanese society. While only a few women in the class professed to want to learn Japanese because they intended to marry a Japanese man (the vast majority of the forty-four students that I surveyed claimed to want to work or study abroad), nearly all of them described Japanese society as a place where men enjoyed higher status than women. In addition to adjectives such as responsible (*zeren xin hen qiang*), hardworking (*gongzuo nuli de jingshen*), and career-minded (*shiye xin qiang*), students (both male and female, Han and Chosŏnjok) commonly invoked the term "chauvinistic" (*da nanzihan/da nanzi zhuyi*) to describe Japanese men. By contrast, students posited Japanese women as subservient to men by using terms like gentle (*wenrou*), considerate (*you aixin*), and low status (*diwei hen di*).

In shifting their sights to Japan, Chosŏnjok marriage migrants, it seems, still looked to economic stature in the world economy as the primary measure of desirability when searching for a spouse, placing less importance on prevailing gender and family norms. As we contemplate how Chosŏnjok women could remain stalwart in their conviction that marrying up the ladder of nations represented their best available option for improving their life chances, we should recall not just the stories of downward economic mobility and disappointment suffered by Chosŏnjok brides in South Korea but also the degree of agency brides exercised in shaping their own social and economic circumstances. Some brides vowed to persevere despite their experiences of grinding poverty, the rigors of farm labor, and the rigid gender norms of their marital families. Others sought solace in the closeness of their marital bond. But many also used their marital potential in South Korea (and beyond) to expand their opportunities for social mobility. Yunŏk and Yŏnjae both succeeded in using the threat of divorce to overcome the inequalities of gender imposed by their marital families, while Juju and others resolved their differences with their marital families by searching for better marital opportunities in Korea, Japan, and beyond.

The modicum of control migrant brides exerted over their marital destinies—the ability to vote with their feet—may partly explain the continued confidence of Chosŏnjok women about matrimonial forms of "cross-border gambling" (Lan 2006), which had already proved to be quite risky. Their willingness take a leap in the dark is equally a testament to their sense of feeling stuck in a place that, at the turn of the millennium, had yet to catch up with the globalizing times. To refer again to Hyejin's great-aunt's schema (astoundingly out of date a mere ten years later), China—and northeastern China in particular—was nearly half a century "below" and "behind" the United States. Using marriage to move upward and outward toward an uncertain future seemed a more prudent course of action than staying in a place where the bleakness of the present appeared certain.

South Korean Grooms Marry Downward

A conversation with a farmer during the final phase of my fieldwork in South Korea suggested that "cartographies of desire"[1] were also shifting for South Korean men in the IMF era. I asked a farmer, who was taking a break from the summer heat in the shade of a pavilion, whether there were any Chosŏnjok brides living in his village. "There are a few," he replied, pointing off in the distance. "But," he quickly added, "there are

---

1. I borrow this term from Constable (2003a) who in turn borrowed it from Pflugfelder (1999) to signify the linkages between political economy and perceptions of desirability.

more Filipina women here now." He explained that Filipina women were thought to be "pure and innocent." The implication was that Chosŏnjok women were no longer thought of in these terms. In the case of his own recent (albeit failed) attempt to secure a Filipina bride through the assistance of a local South Korean minister, the lower costs and fewer bureaucratic obstacles involved in taking a marriage tour to the Philippines factored significantly into his choice of where to look for a foreign bride.

It is no coincidence that the geographic shift in the source of foreign brides occurred at roughly the same time as the dominant popular image of the Chosŏnjok bride changed from submissive, virginal, and virtuous to insubordinate, conniving, and self-serving. As Abelmann and Kim observed in the course of documenting a South Korean mother's (failed) attempt to secure a Filipina bride for her disabled, rural son through the Unification Church, "a pure, 'traditional,' rural Filipina girl is posed in contradistinction to a scheming Korean Chinese girl" (2005, 112).

"With the 'marriage pipeline' between South Korea and China temporarily and partially clogged by increased state regulation" (Lim 2010, 67–68) and the reputation of the Chosŏnjok bride tarnished by well-publicized accounts of fake and runaway brides, marriage brokers in South Korea sought to revive their businesses by promoting Southeast Asian women as a more affordable and reliable model of the ideal "traditional" bride. As in Taiwan's ethnically stratified market in domestic labor, in which labor recruitment agencies manipulate ethnic and nationality-based stereotypes to promote Indonesian domestic workers over Filipinas (Lan 2006, see chapter 2), so marriage brokers in South Korea implicitly market Southeast Asian brides over Chosŏnjok ones with claims that the former are "too immature, naïve and docile to run away" (M Lee 2008, 70). South Korean marriage brokers go so far as to back their claim that Southeast Asian brides are less likely to abscond by offering "in-warranty services," guaranteeing the replacement of a runaway bride with a new one for a period of six to twelve months after marriage (HM Kim 2007, 111–12).

The contingent nature of these ethnicized constructions of the ideal migrant bride is revealed by the shifting locus of their referent. When the reputation of Filipina women became tainted as a result of their work in the South Korean sex industry (Abelmann and Kim 2005, 110), the popularity of Vietnamese women surged. Here too a comparison to the racialized stereotyping of domestic workers in Taiwan is instructive. Lan describes the serial transference of the imagery of the "runaway" domestic worker from Filipina domestic workers onto first Indonesian and later Vietnamese women, as rates of workplace abandonment climbed progressively higher for each successive group (Lan 2006, 79). The rotating discourse of "runaways" and the rising rates of divorce and abandonment currently reported among the second wave of foreign brides suggest that neither the discursive nor the empirical aspects of the runaway bride phenomenon are unique to Chosŏnjok brides. Rather, it stems from the Orientalizing myths of femininity, docility, and virginity ascribed to the category of the "poor migrant bride," independent of her national or ethnic origins, and the often patent refusal of the brides themselves to passively submit to these patriarchal stereotypes.

Family Making to Serve the State

Scholars have begun to speculate about the implications of the racial diversity these so-called multicultural families inevitably bring to a nation that has staunchly advocated ethnic endogamy and ethnic homogeneity as its defining characteristics. South Korean men's willingness to take a Filipina or Vietnamese bride might indicate that definitions of kinship and national belonging are becoming more flexible. As I have argued throughout this book, the unexpected conflicts and tensions that South Korean men experienced in bringing Chosŏnjok brides who shared the "same blood" into their households served to unsettle the primacy of blood in South Korean conceptualizations of kinship and ethnonationalism. Is the newer trend among South Korean farmers to look for brides in Southeast Asia to some degree driven by the realization that kinship and ethnic solidarity are more than simply a matter of blood ties?

Abelmann and Kim caution us against such an interpretation. They suggest we should view Filipina-South Korean marriages as a "contingency of strategy rather than an attempt to exceed the national or ethnic" (2005, 112). Prevailing assimilationist perspectives on international marriage in South Korea, they argue, posit "traditional" women from "less developed" foreign nations as easily molded into "Korean" wives and citizens and thus preserve the continuity of the Korean patriline (Abelmann and Kim 2005, 108–11). Research on the discursive and legislative dimensions of this new trend supports their view that at the heart of this new family-making project is an old cultural logic and nation-building strategy. That strategy relies on a moralistic vision of the patriarchal family, and women's central role within it, to support the economic development of the South Korean nation. It is a pattern particularly pronounced in times of crisis.

Jesook Song (2009), for example, documents how the restoration of normative (patriarchal) family life was promoted as the best way to restore order and productivity to South Korean society in the wake of the IMF financial crisis. South Korean mothers were singled out for their pivotal role in preserving the stability of the family by serving their breadwinning husbands and pledging their commitment to the domestic sphere. Song shows how so-called responsible mothers were rewarded with not only public praise but concrete legal privileges, as the notion of "moralistic maternalism" was used as the key criterion for distinguishing deserving from undeserving welfare recipients. At the same time, a discourse on "irresponsible mothers" was also deployed with unprecedented transparency during the IMF crisis—a correlate to the discourse on the "runaway" foreign bride—to vilify homeless women and others accused of abrogating their duty to the patriarchal family and, by extension, the nation (Song 2009, 51–52).

The family focus of the government's current array of multicultural initiatives targeting foreign brides is evident. Welfare resources and support services are made available only to "dutiful" migrant brides who remain in the homes of their marital families. Foreign brides who divorce or abandon their families for reasons of domestic abuse, discriminatory treatment, or marital incompatibility are legally excluded from receiving government support (HM Kim 2007, 109). Moreover, a close examination of the kinds of support services offered to exemplary foreign brides—support programs for childrearing, legal and financial aid, employment counseling, language and cooking lessons, and a host of other family-oriented programs—reveals an underlying concern with turning Asian brides into "Korean" mothers and wives and anchoring them within the confines of the Korean patriarchal family. Without denying the sincerity of the stated goal of these policies, to help migrant brides acquire the practical skills and resources they need to adjust to daily life in South Korea, Mary Lee asserts, "The value of foreign women is clearly interpreted within the framework of Korean ethno-racial nationhood, and the policies that target them solicit their subordination to patriarchal family structure and to raising their children to become as Korean as possible in terms of language and cultural attitudes" (2008, 77).

It remains to be seen how this second wave of migrant brides will respond to practices of inculcating Koreanness and conservative family norms that disregard the cultural logics of family, gender, and nationness[2] they bring from their diverse countries of origin. Research is needed to explore in depth the ways foreign brides grapple with and negotiate the normative subjectivities they are encouraged to embody by policymakers, social workers, commercial marriage brokers, and, perhaps most important, their marital family members.

Nicole Newendorp (2008) describes the disjunctures that result from social workers' attempts to socialize mainland immigrant wives into local ideologies of national and familial belonging in post-1997 Hong Kong. As she shows, mainland wives selectively embrace, challenge, and resist various aspects of the normative ideologies imposed on them to suit their own culturally particular ideals and aspirations. Such findings, as well as the agency exercised by the Chosŏnjok brides featured in this book, make it unlikely that non-Korean foreign brides will prove willing to remain within the bounds of essentializing ethnic and kinship constructions—let alone within actual marital relationships—unless South Korean family members, social workers, and government officials become more attuned to the personal desires and culturally particular ways of foreign brides.

Faking Kinship and the Limits of State Sovereignty

South Korea's extreme familist stance toward migrant brides coexists with an equally extreme antifamilist stance toward migrant workers. Migrant workers for the most part have been legally prohibited from bringing their

---

2. Borneman (1992) makes an important, often-overlooked distinction between "nationalism" and what he calls "nationness." While nationalism connotes a "subjective devotion to the nation" on the part of longtime members and newcomers alike, "nationness" is defined by Borneman as "a subjectivity, not contingent on an opinion or attitude but derived from the lived experience within a state" (352 fn1). According to this definition, Chosŏnjok and South Koreans, while they might share nationalistic sentiments, would inevitably have different orientations toward "nationness" as a result of having lived under different state regimes.

own family members to South Korea, denied the right of permanent settlement (Seol and Skrentny 2009), and because they fall outside the boundaries of normative (South Korean) families, "they receive little or no attention
within the imaginative space of the multiculturalism initiatives" (M Lee,
2008, 76). In practical terms, as we saw in the case of the Chosŏnjok, restrictive immigration laws and the lack of governmental support do not
stop migrant workers from staying in the country for as long as ten years.
But migrant workers live in constant fear of deportation and must negotiate the complexities and moral dilemmas of managing split transnational
family lives.

Recruiting migrant workers as a disposable workforce and migrant
brides as a permanent one has had both practical and symbolic advantages
for the South Korean state. But the ambiguities between the official South
Korean rhetoric of inclusion based on shared blood and the realities of
Chosŏnjok workers' legislative exclusion from the national family could
not be suppressed for long. I have shown how the South Korean government selectively opened its doors and extended benefits to various categories of migrants, based on their presumed potential to contribute to the
economic well-being of the nation-state and/or its "imagined community"
of citizens bound by blood or kinship. This combination of criteria was
used to determine who was awarded citizenship or citizenship-like benefits (Chosŏnjok brides, overseas Korean foreign investors from developed
nations, first-generation emigrants to China); who was eligible for temporary visitation rights only (visiting relatives and wage laborers); and who
was denied entry altogether (those without ties of genealogy, capital, or
labor). The discriminatory treatment embodied in these policies made it
clear to the Chosŏnjok that definitions of ethnic homogeneity and kinship
are contingent upon the bureaucratic and territorial interests of the South
Korean state.

Chosŏnjok responded by learning how to manipulate the kinship categories sanctioned by South Korea's restrictive immigration legislation.
Arranging a fake marriage to a South Korean man, traveling in the guise
of a parent of a married-out bride, and posing as a "separated family member" (*isan kajok*) in search of long-lost kin in South Korea were all common
ways of taking advantage of South Korea's open-door kin policies. These
tactics of faking kinship, though common to disenfranchised migrants
worldwide, took on heightened subversive power since they struck at the

heart of South Korean definitions of national identity. Such acts of fakery further revealed the instrumentality of relationships that by definition were supposed to be about the primacy of blood above all else. Faking kinship, it turned out, was a more expedient means of entering South Korea than relying on real genealogies and the assistance of actual blood relatives, rendering the dividing line between welcome kin and unwanted stranger even more unstable and contradictory than it had been at the outset of Chosŏnjok–South Korean encounters. Through acts of faking kinship, Chosŏnjok migrants bypassed the nation's borders and turned the South Korean state's own rhetoric of blood and genealogy on its head, exposing the limits of both the territorial and the discursive boundaries of the South Korean nation-state.

Faking, Unmaking, and Remaking Kinship

Most Chosŏnjok migrants felt little or no compunction in committing these legal and social transgressions. In faking kinship, ordinary Chosŏnjok mothers and fathers across the socioeconomic spectrum asserted what they saw as their rightful, collective claim as overseas "compatriots" to share, if only temporarily, in the prosperity of South Korea, even when they could not claim a literal, genealogically backed kinship relation to a specific South Korean citizen. Migrant mothers and fathers also felt morally compelled to fake kinship as a way of advancing the interests of their families, particularly their children. Parents explained the urgency of working (illegally) in South Korea as the only available means of improving their children's future life chances, and by extension their own old age security, in an increasingly competitive and capitalist marketplace. And despite the inherent pain of family separation and the potential that extended absences would result in permanent abandonment of children and spouses, children often acknowledged the necessity of their parents' masquerading as someone else's kin, and even of faking marriage and divorce, so that one or both parents could labor abroad on their behalf.

Though split transnational families and bartering with real and fake kinship relations became normal practice in northeastern China, people intensely debated the merits and demerits of various transnational family formations. Couples tried out different ways of allocating the roles of overseas breadwinner and stay-at-home family caretaker and then grappled with the complexities of gender and the difficulties of sustaining family relations across time and space. While transnational couples across the globe are faced with similar dilemmas, Chosŏnjok mothers, fathers, and children invoked culturally particular ideas about gender, conjugality, and parenthood to evaluate various patterns of family dispersal and localization. Specifically, I noted moralizing discourses that praised mothers for privileging their productive over reproductive roles in the family and conjugal over parent-child togetherness. The ideal, responsible mother was one who could secure the future of her children by earning economic capital in South Korea, if possible alongside her husband, leaving the daily social and emotional care of her children to a capable third party.

The normalization of extramarital relationships among "living widows and widowers" in China and the well-known potential for fake divorces and fake marriages to turn real reinforced the notion that split transnational couples took enormous risks with their marriages. Against the main grain of the literature that has emphasized the resilience of cross-border relationships despite the strain of prolonged separation, these practices of infidelity that I described invite explorations of the moral dilemmas and high-risk stakes involved in the making (and breaking) of split transnational families. Though denied the excitement and risks of foreign travel, nonmigrant husbands and wives sought to create their own fashionable urbanite pleasures in the dance halls of Mudanjiang. The figure of the left-behind wife engaged in dance hall dalliances overturns two familiar oppositions: the binary of active male migrant worker versus his patient supportive and supported wife, and the "gambler migrant" engaged in a global adventure versus the risk-averse, nonmigrant spouse who is stuck in place. Based on this view from the Chinese side, I suggest we take a broader view of transnational mobility and see movers and nonmovers alike as actively negotiating the risks and opportunities involved in transnational family projects.

From Korea Wind to China Boom

Recent developments suggest that those who stayed behind in China may in fact have been the true winners in this game of transnational gambling.

Many Chosŏnjok I spoke with in the year 2000 expressed an awareness of China's potential to surpass South Korea in the not-too-distant future and many fantasized about a day when South Koreans would be compelled to seek employment opportunities as well as husbands in China.[3] As Hyejin's great-aunt predicted triumphantly, "In ten to twenty years, China will surpass the Korean economy. At that time China will be a better place to live than South Korea." Ten years have passed since my conversation with Hyejin's great-aunt and, true to her prediction, signs do indeed point to a shift in the center of gravity from South Korea to China. In a world of "polycentric global capitalism" (Ong 1997, 14), not only are the divisions between "core" and "peripheral" nations becoming increasingly difficult to distinguish but the speed of technological and cultural innovation accentuates the potential for rapid reconfigurings or even reversals in the global ranking of nations.

Upon completing extensive fieldwork among the Chosŏnjok in Yanbian, June Hee Kwon reports that many recently returned migrants now feel they may have gambled unwisely by venturing to South Korea. Migrant laborers returning from ten-year sojourns in South Korea reportedly express acute feelings of alienation amid the dramatic socioeconomic changes in China. While returnees struggle to regain their social and economic bearings in a radically transformed, capitalist China, they observe that many who resisted or failed to follow the popular tide to South Korea a decade earlier are now better off. They cultivated local networks and the know-how to succeed in China's radically altered social and economic milieu. When Chosŏnjok people greet each other on the streets today, they no longer ask: "When are you going to South Korea?" Instead they quip with disapproval, "You're going to South Korea, *again*?" (June Hee Kwon, personal communication, March 14, 2010).

The rising costs of living in China coupled with the soaring value of the yuan also contribute to Chosŏnjok people's dampening enthusiasm for dirty, dangerous, and difficult labor in South Korea. Many question why they should endure the indignities of unskilled labor in South Korea if the wages can no longer purchase several decades' worth of comfortable

---

3. While marriages between South Korean women and Chinese men do exist, they occur in small numbers and are almost exclusively "love marriages" (*yŏnae kyŏrhon*), according to the Korean definition of the term as couples who meet without the assistance of a third party.

living in China. According to a recent news article, "Korean Chinese No Longer Willing to Do Dirty Work,"[4] Chosŏnjok workers in South Korea have become much choosier about the jobs they are willing to perform, taking into consideration factors such as cleanliness of work environment and drudgery of the labor involved. In addition, the recent liberalization of South Korea's restrictive immigration policies now makes it possible for Chosŏnjok migrant workers to bring family members with them to South Korea. Migrant mothers and fathers with children in tow prefer jobs that afford them leisure time to spend with family and are less willing to take up employment outside metropolitan areas (ibid.).

Another related twist in migratory patterns involves the exodus of over one hundred thousand middle-class migrants from South Korea into China. In the context of escalating social stratification and class anxiety brought on by the social and political changes in the wake of the 1997 Asian financial crisis, these middle-class immigrants are driven not by the allure of a "China dream" so much as by fears of losing their middle-class liveli-hoods and lifestyles in South Korea (Seo 2007). In the enclosed condomin-ium communities of Wangjing in suburban Beijing, the site of a growing Koreatown since the mid-1990s, South Koreans enjoy a higher standard of living than would have been possible for them in South Korea (484).

But even in Wangjing, South Koreans' middle-class status remains on uncertain ground. Some lack the financial and social network capital needed to survive in Beijing and even resort to selling their South Korean passports on the Chinese black market (Seo 2007, 491). They are counter-parts to the growing numbers of "stateless" Chosŏnjok women in South Korea whose South Korean citizenship has been revoked for contracting putatively fake marriages. Having given up their Chinese passports in mar-rying to South Korea, these women are "living like ghosts," in the words of one South Korean reporter (*Living Like Ghosts*, April 8, 2008). Instead of achieving the status upgrade they initially bargained for, these stateless Chosŏnjok and South Korean migrants are legally and socially trapped in an underground, liminal space, each in the other's country of citizenship. Their strategies for keeping apace with the globalizing times have back-

---

4. Korean Chinese No Longer Willing to Do Dirty Work. *Digital Chosunilbo*. April 9, 2010. Available at: http://english.chosun.com/site/data/html_dir/2010/04/09/2010040900288.html.

fired and they are closed off indefinitely from future transnational travel and acts of cross-border gambling.

Chosŏnjok and South Koreans alike are forced to negotiate with deep uncertainty amid the ever-globalizing and what some scholars call the neoliberalizing forces in the post-IMF era. As they travel in opposite directions in search of economic security and as they set up transnational households of the split-transnational, fully intact, or cross-border-marriage variety inside one another's national territories, they experience firsthand the empirical social, cultural, and political differences that underlie longcherished ideological constructions of ethnoracial homogeneity. Rather than relinquish racialized and patriarchal definitions of Korean national identity, South Koreans instead are giving name to new types of intraethnic difference—though without jettisoning underlying ideals of ethnic unity. Multiculturalism is one such construction. The term "New Chosŏnjok" (*sin Chosŏnjok, xinxianzu*), the term used to demarcate and elevate South Korean migrants in China from the general Chosŏnjok population (Seo 2007, 491–92), is another. Both constructions support a racialized worldview in which South Korea is separate from and superior to its diasporic and other counterparts in Asia.

At the same time, the Chosŏnjok have responded to the subtle and not-so-subtle discursive and legal forms of inequality they experienced by honing their tactics of bureaucratic subversion and negotiating around the constraints that stood in the way of achieving the transnational mobility they desired. These tactics have further problematized the formerly takenfor-granted linkages between kinship/blood and nationality/ethnicity. The story of making and faking kinship thus points to the complexity of interrelations between gender, family, and nation; between ideologies and genealogies; between state bureaucracies and transnational migration. In thinking through these complexities, it will be useful to remember that the state's own idioms of kinship can easily backfire when those "kin" whose membership in the national family is in dispute take charge of their own projects of making and faking kinship.

References

Abelmann, Nancy. 1997. Narrating Selfhood and Personality in South Korea: Women and Social Mobility. *American Ethnologist* 24(4): 784–812.

———. 2003. *The Melodrama of Mobility: Women, Talk, and Class in Contemporary South Korea.* Honolulu: University of Hawai'i Press.

Abelmann, Nancy, and Hyunhee Kim. 2005. A Failed Attempt at Transnational Marriage: Maternal Citizenship in a Globalizing South Korea. In *Cross-Border Marriages: Gender and Mobility in Transnational Asia,* ed. Nicole Constable, 101–23. Philadelphia: University of Pennsylvania Press.

Abelmann, Nancy, and Jiyeon Kang. Forthcoming 2011. Defending South Korean Education Migration Mothers and Humanizing Global Children: Memoir/Manuals of Pre-College Study Abroad. *Global Networks: A Journal of Transnational Affairs.*

Adelman, Jacob. 1999. Top U.N. Official Says N.K. Refugees' Situation "Serious." *Korea Herald* (Internet version), October 14.

Adrian, Bonnie. 2003. *Framing the Bride: Globalizing Beauty and Romance in Taiwan's Bridal Industry.* Berkeley: University of California Press.

Ahn, Byong Man, and William W. Boyer. 1988. The Dilemma of Tenant Farming in South Korea. *Korean Studies* 12:1–13.

Anderson, Benedict. 1983. *Imagined Communities: Reflections on the Origins and Spread of Nationalism.* London: Verso Press.

Bak, Sangmee. 1997. McDonald's in Seoul: Food Choices, Identity, and Nationalism. In *Golden Arches East,* ed. James L. Watson. Stanford: Stanford University Press.

Borneman, John. 1992. *Belonging in the Two Berlins: Kin, State, Nation.* Cambridge: Cambridge University Press.

Brennan, Denise. 2001. Tourism in Transnational Places: Dominican Sex Workers and German Sex Tourists Imagine One Another. *Identities: Global Studies in Culture and Power* 7(4): 621–63.

Burgess, Chris. 2004. (Re)constructing Identities: International Marriage Migrants as Potential Agents of Social Change in a Globalising Japan. *Asian Studies Review* 28:223–42.

Carsten, Janet. 2004. *After Kinship.* Cambridge: Cambridge University Press.

Chalfin, Brenda. 2010. *Neoliberal Frontiers: An Ethnography of Sovereignty in West Africa.* Chicago: University of Chicago Press.

Chee, Maria W. L. 2003. Migrating for the Children: Taiwanese American Women in Transnational Families. In *Wife or Worker? Asian Women and Migration,* ed. Nicola Piper and Mina Roces, 137–56. Lanham: Rowman and Littlefield.

Cho Haejoang. 2002. Living with Conflicting Subjectivities: Mother, Motherly Wife, and Sexy Woman in the Transition from Colonial-Modern to Postmodern Korea. In *Under Construction: The Gendering of Modernity, Class, and Consumption in the Republic of Korea,* ed. Laurel Kendall. Honolulu: University of Hawai'i Press.

Cho Hyungrae. 1999. Life Is Hard for North Koreans in Yenji. *Digital Chosunilbo.* January 8.

Cho, John (Song Pae). 2009. The Wedding Banquet Revisited: "Contract Marriages" between Korean Gays and Lesbians. *Anthropological Quarterly* 82(2): 401–22.

Cho Uhn, 2005. The Encroachment of Globalization into Intimate Life: The Flexible Korean Family in "Economic Crisis." *Korea Journal* 45:8–35.

Chŏng Sinch'ŏl. 1995. Chungguk Chosŏnjok in'gu punp'oŭi pyŏnhwa t'ŭkching e kwanhayŏ [On the changing population distribution of Chinese Chosŏnjok]. *Chosŏn Hak* [Chosŏn studies]: 217–26.

Choo, Hae Yeon. 2006. Gendered Modernity and Ethnicized Citizenship: North Korean Settlers in Contemporary South Korea. *Gender and Society* 20:576–604.

Chung, Byung-Ho. 2008. Between Defector and Migrant: Identities and Strategies of North Koreans in South Korea. *Korean Studies* 32:1–27.

Clark, Constance D. 2001. Foreign Marriage, "Tradition," and the Politics of Border Crossings. In *China Urban: Ethnographies of Contemporary Culture,* ed. Nancy N. Chen, Constance D. Clark, Suzanne Gottschang, and Lyn Jeffery, 104–122. Durham, NC: Duke University Press.

Constable, Nicole. 2003a. *Romance on a Global Stage: Pen Pals, Virtual Ethnography, and "Mail-Order" Marriages.* Berkeley: University of California Press.

———. 2003b. A Transnational Perspective on Divorce and Marriage: Filipina Wives and Workers. *Identities: Global Studies in Culture and Power* 10(2): 163–180.

———. 2005. Introduction: Cross-Border Marriages, Gendered Mobility, and Global Hypergamy. In *Cross-Border Marriages: Gender and Mobility in Transnational Asia,* ed. Nicole Constable. Philadelphia: University of Pennsylvania Press.

Croome, John. 1995. *Reshaping the World Trading System: A History of the Uruguay Round.* Geneva: WTO.

Deuchler, Martina. 1992. *The Confucian Transformation of Korea: A Study of Society and Ideology.* Cambridge, Mass.: Council on East Asian Studies, Harvard University.

Dorrow, Sara K. 2006. *Transnational Adoption: A Cultural Economy of Race, Gender, and Kinship.* New York: New York University Press.

Ehlert, Meilan Piao. 2008. Multilingualism and Language Practices of Minority Language Background Youths in China. Master's thesis, Simon Fraser University.

Ehrenreich, Barbara, and Arlie Russell Hochschild. 2003. *Global Woman: Nannies, Maids, and Sex Workers in the New Economy.* New York: Metropolitan Books.

Em, Henry H. 1999. Minchok as a Modern and Democratic Construct: Sin Ch'aeho's Historiography. In *Colonial Modernity in Korea,* ed. Gi-Wook Shin and Michael Robinson. Cambridge, Mass.: Harvard University Press.

Epstein, Stephen. 2009. The Bride(s) From Hanoi: South Korean Popular Culture, Vietnam and "Asia" in the New Millennium. 2009 KSAA Proceedings. http://sydney.edu.au/arts/korean/about/proceedings.shtml (and then select Epstein) (accessed 4/21/11).

Evans, Harriet. 2002. Past, Perfect or Imperfect: Changing Images of the Ideal Wife. In *Chinese Femininities, Chinese Masculinities,* ed. Susan Brownell and Jeffery Wasserstrom. Berkeley: University of California Press.

———. 2008. Sexed Bodies, Sexualized Identities, and the Limits of Gender. *China Information* 22(2): 361–86.

Fabian, Johannes. 1983. *Time and the Other: How Anthropology Makes Its Object.* New York: Columbia University Press.

Fan, C. Cindy, and Youqin Huang. 1998. Waves of Rural Brides: Female Marriage Migration in China. *Annals of the Association of American Geographers* 88(2): 227–51.

Farrer, James. 2000. Dancing through the Market Transition: Disco and Dance Hall Sociability in Shanghai. In *The Consumer Revolution in Urban China,* ed. Deborah S. Davis. Berkeley: University of California Press.

Foley, James A. 2003. *Korea's Divided Families: Fifty Years of Separation.* London: Routledge.

Fouron, Georges, and Nina Glick Schiller. 2001. All in the Family: Gender, Transnational Migration and the Nation-State. *Identities: Global Studies in Culture and Power* 7(4): 539–82.

Franklin, Sarah, and Susan McKinnon. 2001. Introduction. In *Relative Values: Reconfiguring Kinship Studies,* ed. Sarah Franklin and Susan McKinnon. Durham: Duke University Press.

Freeman, Caren. 2005. Marrying Up and Marrying Down: The Paradoxes of Marital Mobility for Chosŏnjok Brides in South Korea. In *Cross-Border Marriages: Gender and Mobility in Transnational Asia,* ed. Nicole Constable. Philadelphia: University of Pennsylvania Press.

Friedman, Sara. 2006. *Intimate Politics: Marriage, the Market, and State Power in Southeastern China.* Cambridge, Mass.: Harvard University Press.

Gardner, Katy. 1995. *Global Migrants, Local Lives: Travel and Transformation in Rural Bangladesh.* Oxford: Clarendon Press.

Gates, Hill. 1996. Buying Brides in China—Again. *Anthropology Today* 12(4): 8–11.

Gilmartin, Christina, and Lin Tan. 2002. Fleeing Poverty: Rural Women, Expanding Marriage Markets, and Strategies for Social Mobility in Contemporary China. In *Transforming Gender and Development in East Asia,* ed. Esther Ngan-ling Chow. New York: Routledge.

Gilot, Louie. 1998. Irish Farmers Calendar Is Aiming to Cultivate Women's Affections. *International Herald Tribune,* October 20.

Glick-Schiller, Nina, Linda Basch, and Cristina Blanc-Szanton, eds. 1992. *Towards a Transnational Perspective on Migration: Race, Class, Ethnicity, and Nationalism Reconsidered.* New York: New York Academy of Sciences.

Glick-Schiller, Nina, Linda Basch, and Cristina Szanton Blanc. 1994. *Nations Unbound: Transnational Projects, Postcolonial Predicaments, and Deterritorialized Nation-States.* Langhorne: Gordon and Breach.

Greenhalgh, Susan. 2003. Planned Births, Unplanned Persons: "Population" in the Making of Chinese Modernity. *American Ethnologist* 30(2): 196–215.

Grinker, Roy Richard. 2000. *Korea and Its Futures: Unification and the Unfinished War.* London: Macmillan Press.

Gupta, Akhil, and James Ferguson. 1992. Beyond "Culture": Space, Identity, and the Politics of Difference. *Cultural Anthropology* 7(1): 6–23.

Hogarth, Hyun-Key Kim. n.d. Matrifocality in Korean Society: Hindrance or Help Towards Gender Equality? The Royal Anthropological Institute: 104–114. http://sydney.edu.au/arts/korean/downloads/KSAA2009/Global_KoreaProceed ings_104-114_Hogarth.pdf.

Hondagneu-Sotelo, Pierrette, and Ernestine Avila. 2003. "I'm Here, but I'm There": The Meanings of Latina Transnational Motherhood. In *Gender and U.S. Immigration: Contemporary Trends,* ed. Pierrette Hondagneu-Sotelo. Berkeley: University of California Press.

Jacobson, David. 1997. *Rights across Borders: Immigration and the Decline of Citizenship.* Baltimore: Johns Hopkins University Press.

Jager, Sheila Miyoshi. 2003. *Narratives of Nation Building in Korea: A Genealogy of Patriotism.* Armonk: M. E. Sharpe.

Janelli, Roger L., and Dawnhee Yim Janelli. 1982. *Ancestor Worship and Korean Society.* Stanford: Stanford University Press.

Kang Hae Sun. 1998. Chung-han sŏboe hon'in ŭi silt'ae wa chŏnmang [The current and future outlook for marriages between China and Korea]. Paper read at the *Che 11 hoe han'guk kajŏng pokchi chŏngch'aek semina* (11th Korean Family Welfare Policy Seminar), November 17, Yŏsŏng Kaebalwŏn kukche hoeŭijang (Women's Development Institute, International Conference Center), Seoul.

Kang, Jiyeon, and Nancy Abelmann. 2011. The Domestication of South Korean Pre-College Study Abroad (PSA) in the First Decade of the Millennium. *Journal of Korean Studies* 16(1): 89–118.

Kelsky, Karen. 2001. *Women on the Verge: Japanese Women, Western Dreams.* Durham: Duke University Press.

Kendall, Laurel. 1996. *Getting Married in Korea: Of Gender, Morality, and Modernity.* Berkeley: University of California Press.

———. 2002. Introduction. In *Under Construction: The Gendering of Modernity, Class, and Consumption in the Republic of Korea,* edited by Laurel Kendall. Honolulu: University of Hawai'i Press.

Kim Chaeguk. 1996. *Han'gukŭn ŏpda* [There is no Korea]. Seoul: Minyedang.

Kim, Choong Soon. 1988. *Faithful Endurance: An Ethnography of Korean Family Dispersal.* Tucson: University of Arizona Press.

Kim, Eleana. 2003. Wedding Citizenship and Culture: Korean Adoptees and the Global Family of Korea. *Social Text* 21(1): 57–81.

———. 2007. Our Adoptee, Our Alien: Transnational Adoptees as Specters of Foreignness and Family in South Korea. *Anthropological Quarterly* 80(2): 497–531.

———. 2010. *Adopted Territory: Transnational Korean Adoptees and the Politics of Belonging.* Durham: Duke University Press.

Kim, Hye-jin. 2010. *International Ethnic Networks and Intra-Ethnic Conflict: Koreans in China.* New York: Palgrave McMillan.

Kim, Hyun Mee. 2007. The State and Migrant Women: Diverging Hopes in the Making of Multicultural Families in Contemporary Korea. *Korea Journal* 47(4): 100–122.

Kim Ji-soo. 1999. Ethnic Korean Chinese Take Issue with New Bill They Say Unfairly Excludes Them. *Korea Herald,* September 2.

Kim Kwang-ok, ed. 1998. *Chungguk Hŭngnyŏnggangsŏng Hanin tongp'o ŭi saenghwal munhwa* [The life and culture of Korean compatriots in China's Heilongjiang Province]. Seoul: National Folklore Museum [Kungnip minsok pangmulgwan].

Kim, Nan. 2010. Impossible Returns: The Temporary Border-Crossings of Separated Korean Family Members. Presentation at Crossing the Divide: Migration and Disruptions of Identity among North Koreans and South Koreans. Annual Meeting of the Association for Asian Studies, Philadelphia, Pennsylvania, March 27.

Kim, Samuel S. 2000. Korea's *Segyehwa* Drive: Promise versus Performance. In *Korea's Globalization,* ed. Samuel S. Kim. Cambridge: Cambridge University Press.

Kim, Seung-Kyung, and John Finch. 2002. Living with Rhetoric, Living against Rhetoric: Korean Families and the IMF Economic Crisis. *Korean Studies* 26:120–39.

Kim Sŏngsu. 1994. Nongŏch'on ch'ŏngso'nyŏn munje e kwanhayŏ [On the problems of rural youth]. Paper read at UR sat'aelŭl kulbokhagi wihan nong'ŏch'on pokchi semina [Rural welfare seminar on how to overcome the Uruguay Round situation]. February 24, Chŏn'guk nong'ŏp kisulcha hyŏphoe hoeŭijang [National Association of Agricultural Engineers Conference Hall].

Kim, Suki. 2010. The System of Defecting: Stories from the North Korean Border. *Harper's Magazine* July:48–55.

Kim, Wang-Bae. 2010. Nostalgia, Anxiety and Hope: Migration and Ethnic Identity of Chosŏnjok. *China Pacific Affairs* 83(1): 95–114.

Kwon Mee-yoo. 2010. Police Clamp Down on Marriage Brokers. *Korea Times.* July 8. http://www.koreatimes.co.kr/www/news/nation/2010/07/113_69698.html.

Lan, Pei-Chia. 2003. Among Women: Migrant Domestics and Their Taiwanese Employers across Generations. In *Global Woman: Nannies, Maids, and Sex Workers in the New Economy,* ed. Barbara Ehrenreich and Arlie Russell Hochschild. New York: Metropolitan Books.

———. 2006. *Global Cinderellas: Migrant Domestics and Newly Rich Employers in Taiwan.* Durham: Duke University Press.

Lavely, William. 1991. Marriage and Mobility under Rural Collectivism. In *Marriage and Inequality in Chinese Society,* ed. Rubie Watson and Patricia Buckley Ebrey. Berkeley: University of California Press.

Lee, Chae-Jin. 1987. The Korean Minority in China: A Model for Ethnic Education. *Korean Studies* 11:1–12.

Lee, Chae-jin. 2000. South Korean Foreign Relations Face the Globalization Challenges. In *Korea's Globalization,* ed. Samuel S. Kim. Cambridge: Cambridge University Press.

Lee, Ching Kwan. 1997. Factory Regimes of Chinese Capitalism: Different Cultural Logics in Labor Control. In *Ungrounded Empires: The Cultural Politics of Modern Chinese Transnationalism,* ed. Aihwa Ong and Donald M. Nonini. New York: Routledge.

———. 1998. *Gender and the South China Miracle: Two Worlds of Factory Women.* Berkeley: University of California Press.

Lee, Hye-Kyung. 2006. International Marriage and the State. Paper read at International Conference of International Marriage. http://www.cct.go.kr/data/acf2006/multi/multi_0303_Hye%20Kyung%20Lee.pdf.

———. 2007. Cross-Border Marriages between Korean Men and Migrant Women and Their Marital Satisfaction. Population Association of Korea (PAK)/the Institute of Population and Aging Research (IPAR) Conference on International Marriage Migration in Asia, Seoul: September 13–14.

Lee, Jean Young. 2001/2002. Ethnic Korean Migration in Northeast Asia, 118–40. http://gsti.miis.edu/CEAS-PUB/200108Lee.pdf.

———. 2002. Ethnic Korean Migration in Northeast Asia. In *International Seminar: Human Flows across National Borders in Northeast Asia,* ed. Tsuneo Akaha. Monterey: Center for East Asian Studies, Monterey Institute of International Studies.

Lee, June J. H. 2002. Discourses of Illness, Meanings of Modernity: A Gendered Construction of Sŏnginbyŏng. In *Under Construction: The Gendering of Modernity, Class and Consumption in the Republic of Korea,* edited by Laurel Kendall. Honolulu: University of Hawai'i Press.

Lee Kwang-kyu. 1997. *Korean Family and Kinship.* Seoul: Jipmoondang Publishing Company.

Lee, Mary. 2008. Mixed Race Peoples in the Korean National Imaginary and Family. *Korean Studies* 32:56–85.

Lee, Michelle, and Nicola Piper. 2003. Reflections on Transnational Life-Course and Migratory Patterns of Middle-Class Women: Preliminary Observations from Malaysia. In *Wife or Worker? Asian Women and Migration,* ed. Nicola Piper and Mina Roces. Lanham: Rowman and Littlefield.

Lee, Yean-Ju, and Hagen Koo. 2006. "Wild Geese Fathers" and a Globalised Family Strategy for Education in Korea. *International Development Planning Review* 28(4): 533–53.

Leean, Jiyoung. 2010. A Review of Commercialized International Marriage Brokers in Korea. Migrant Women Human Rights Forum, South Korea. March 10. http://

www.arenaonline.org/xe/?document_srl=1889&mid=mmia_info&sort_index=last_
update&order_type=asc.

Lett, Denise Potrzeba. 1998. *In Pursuit of Status: The Making of South Korea's "New"
Urban Middle Class.* Cambridge, Mass.: Harvard University Asia Center.

Lie, John. 1998. *Han Unbound: The Political Economy of South Korea.* Stanford: Stanford University Press.

Lim, Timothy. 1999. The Fight for Equal Rights: The Power of Foreign Workers in
South Korea. *Alternatives: Social Transformation and Humane Governance* 24:1–30.
http://instructional1.calstatela.edu/tclim/articles/fight.pdf.

———. 2002. The Changing Face of South Korea: The Emergence of Korea as a "Land
of Immigration." *Korea Society Quarterly* 3:16–21.

———. 2010. Rethinking Belongingness in Korea: Transnational Migration, "Migrant
Marriages" and the Politics of Multiculturalism. *Pacific Affairs* 83(1): 51–71.

Linger, Daniel T. 2001. *No One Home: Brazilian Selves Remade in Japan.* Stanford: Stanford University Press.

Liu, Xin. 1997. Space, Mobility, and Flexibility: Chinese Villagers and Scholars Negotiate Power at Home and Abroad. In *Ungrounded Empires: The Cultural Politics
of Modern Chinese Transnationalism,* edited by Aihwa Ong and Donald M. Nonini.
New York: Routledge.

Long, Lynellen D., and Ellen Oxfeld, eds. 2004. *Coming Home? Refugees, Migrants and
Those Who Stayed Behind.* Philadelphia: University of Pennsylvania Press.

Louie, Andrea. 2004. *Chineseness across Borders: Renegotiating Chinese Identities in China
and the United States.* Durham: Duke University Press.

Mahler, Sarah J. 2001. Transnational Relationships: The Struggle to Communicate
Across Borders. *Identities: Global Studies in Culture and Power* 7(4): 583–619.

Mahler, Sarah J., and Patricia R. Pessar. 2001. Gendered Geographies of Power: Ana-
lyzing Gender Across Transnational Spaces. *Identities* 7(4): 441–59.

Mair, Victor H. 1991. What Is a Chinese "Dialect/Topolect"? Reflections on Some Key
Sino-English Linguistic Terms. *Sino-Platonic Papers* 29:1–31. Philadelphia: Department of East Asian Languages and Civilizations, University of Pennsylvania.

Massey, Doreen. 1994. *Space, Place and Gender.* Minneapolis: University of Minnesota
Press.

Mills, Mary Beth. 1999. *Thai Women in the Global Labor Force: Consuming Desires, Contested Selves.* New Brunswick: Rutgers University Press.

Min, Han, and J. S. Eades. 1995. Brides, Bachelors and Brokers: The Marriage Market
in Rural Anhui in an Era of Economic Reform. *Modern Asian Studies* 29(4): 841–69.

Mintz, Sidney W. 1985. *Sweetness and Power: The Place of Sugar in Modern History.* New
York: Viking Penguin.

Modell, Judith. 1994. *Kinship with Strangers: Adoption and Interpretations of Kinship in
American Culture.* Berkeley: University of California Press.

———. 1998. Rights to the Children: Foster Care and Social Reproduction in Hawai'i.
In *Reproducing Reproduction: Kinship, Power and Technological Innovation,* ed. Sara
Franklin and Helena Ragone. Philadelphia: University of Pennsylvania Press.

Moon, Katharine H. S. 1997. *Sex among Allies: Military Prostitution in U.S.—Korea Relations.* New York: Columbia University Press.

———. 2000. Strangers in the Midst of Globalization: Migrant Workers and Korean Nationalism. In *Korea's Globalization,* ed. Samuel S. Kim. Cambridge: Cambridge University Press.

Na Chongkŭn. 1997a. Nongŏch'on e kajŏng pokchinŭn inŭn'ga? IMF ihu'ŭi nongŏch'on [Is there family welfare in farm and fishing villages? post-IMF farm and fishing villages]. Seoul: Han'guk Nongch'on Pokchi Yŏn'guhoe [Research Association for the Welfare of Korean Farm and Fishing Villages].

———. 1997b. Nongch'ŏn ch'onggak kyŏrhon taech'aek sokhi sewŏya [Countermeasures to Help Rural Bachelors Marry Must Be Taken Immediately]. *Donga Ilbo,* October 13, 31.

Nelson, Laura. 2000. *Measured Excess: Status, Gender, and Consumer Nationalism in South Korea.* New York: Columbia University Press.

Newendorp, Nicole Dejong. 2008. *Uneasy Reunions: Immigration, Citizenship, and Family Life in Post-1997 Hong Kong.* Stanford: Stanford University Press.

Olivier, Bernard Vincent. 1993. *The Implementation of China's Nationality Policy in the Northeastern Provinces.* San Francisco: Mellen Research University Press.

———. 1995. Korean Contribution to the Development of Heilongjiang/Hŭngnyŏnggang. *Korea Journal* 35:54–71.

Ong, Aihwa. 1997. Chinese Modernities: Narratives of Nation and of Capitalism. In *Ungrounded Empires: The Cultural Politics of Modern Chinese Transnationalism,* ed. Aihwa Ong and Donald M. Nonini. New York: Routledge.

———. 1999. *Flexible Citizenship: The Cultural Logics of Transnationality.* Durham: Duke University Press.

Pae Yŏnggi. 2007. *Han'guk sasang gwa sahoe yulli* [Korean Ideology and Social Ethics]. Seoul: Han'guk Haksul Chŏngbo.

Pak Hyeran. 1994. Kusulsalŭl t'onghae pon Chungguk Chosŏnjok yŏsŏng ŭi sam [A look at Chinese Chosŏnjok women's lives through their oral history]. *Yŏsŏnghak nokchip* [Women's Studies Review] 11:11–54.

Pak Kwangik. 2000. Tot po i nŭn "saenggwabu" [An exceptional "living widow"]. *Hŭngyŏnggang sinmun* [Heilongjiang News]. March 23.

Park, Chai Bin, and Nam-Hoon Cho. 1995. Consequences of Son Preference in a Low-Fertility Society: Imbalance of the Sex Ratio at Birth in Korea. *Population and Development Review* 21(1): 59–84.

Park, Han Shik. 1987. Political Culture and Ideology of the Korean Minority in China. *Korean Studies* 11:13–32.

Park, Heh-Rahn. 1996. Narratives of Migration: From the Formation of Korean Chinese Nationality in the PRC to the Emergence of Korean Chinese Migrants in South Korea. PhD diss., University of Washington.

Park, Hyun Ok. 2004. Democracy, History, and Migrant Labor in South Korea: Korean Chinese, North Koreans, and Guest Workers. Paper presented at Center for Korean Studies Colloquium, University of California at Berkeley, December 3. http://iis-db.stanford.edu/pubs/20790/Democracy,_History,_and_Migrant_Labor_in_South_Korea_by_Hyun_Ok_Park.pdf (accessed 4/21/11).

———. 2005. *Two Dreams in One Bed: Empire, Social Life, and the Origins of the North Korean Revolution in Manchuria.* Durham: Duke University Press.

Park, So Jin. 2006. The Retreat from Formal Schooling: "Educational Manager Mothers" in the Private After-School Market of South Korea. PhD diss., University of Illinois at Urbana-Champaign.

Parreñas, Rhacel Salazar. 2001a. *Servants of Globalization: Women, Migration and Domestic Work*. Stanford: Stanford University Press.

———. 2001b. Mothering from a Distance: Emotions, Gender, and Inter-Generational Relations in Filipino Transnational Families. *Feminist Studies* 27(2): 361–90.

———. 2003. The Care Crisis in the Philippines: Children and Transnational Families in the New Global Economy. In *Global Woman: Nannies, Maids, and Sex Workers in the New Economy,* ed. Barbara Ehrenreich and Arlie Russell Hochschild. New York: Metropolitan Books.

———. 2005. *Children of Global Migration: Transnational Families and Gendered Woes.* Stanford: Stanford University Press.

Pe-Pua, Rogelia. 2003. Wife, Mother, and Maid: The Triple Role of Filipino Domestic Workers in Spain and Italy. In *Wife or Worker? Asian Women and Migration,* ed. Nicola Piper and Mina Roces. Lanham: Rowman and Littlefield.

Pessar, Patricia R. 2003. Engendering Migration Studies: The Case of New Immigrants in the United States. In *Gender and U.S. Immigration: Contemporary Trends,* ed. Pierrette Hondagneu-Sotelo. Berkeley: University of California Press.

Pflugfelder, Gregory M. 1999. *Cartographies of Desire: Male–Male Sexuality in Japanese Discourses, 1600–1950.* Berkeley: University of California Press.

Piper, Nicola, and Mina Roces. 2003. Introduction: Marriage and Migration in an Age of Globalization. In *Wife or Worker? Asian Women and Migration,* ed. Nicola Piper and Mina Roces. Lanham: Rowman and Littlefield.

Pribilsky, Jason. 2004. "Aprendemos A Convivir": Conjugal Relations, Co-parenting, and Family Life among Ecuadorian Transnational Migrants in New York and the Ecuadorian Andes. *Global Networks* 4(3): 313–34.

Ri Sŭngmae. 1994. Yŏnbyŏn Chosŏnjok yŏsŏngdŭl ŭi sŏpwae honin munje e kwanhayŏ [On the problems surrounding Chosŏnjok women's international marriages]. *Yŏsŏng yŏn'gu* [Women's research] 1:200–217.

Roth, Joshua Hotaka. 2002. *Brokered Homeland: Japanese Brazilian Migrants in Japan.* Ithaca: Cornell University Press.

Rouse, Roger. 1991. Mexican Migration and the Social Space of Postmodernism. *Diaspora* 1(1): 8–23.

———. 1995. Questions of Identity: Personhood and Collectivity in Transnational Migration to the United States. *Critique of Anthropology* 15(1): 351–80.

Sadiq, Kamal. 2009. *Paper Citizens: How Illegal Immigrants Acquire Citizenship in Developing Countries.* Oxford: Oxford University Press.

Sassen, Saskia. 1991. *The Global City: New York, London, Tokyo.* Princeton: Princeton University Press.

———. 1998. *Globalization and Its Discontents.* New York: New Press.

———. 1999. *Guests and Aliens.* New York: New Press.

———. 2003. Strategic Instantiations of Gendering in the Global Economy. In *Gender and U.S. Immigration: Contemporary Trends,* ed. Pierrette Hondagneu-Sotelo. Berkeley: University of California Press.

Seo, Jungmin. 2007. Interpreting Wanjing: Ordinary Foreigners in a Globalizing Town. *Korea Observer* 38(3): 469–500.

Seol, Dong-Hoon, and John D. Skrentny. 2009. Ethnic Return Migration and Hierarchical Nationhood: Korean Chinese Foreign Workers in South Korea. *Ethnicities* 9(2): 147–74.

Shin, Yong-bae. 1998. Government Approves Bill to Ease Rules on Ethnic Koreans with Foreign Citizenship. *Korea Herald* (Internet version), December 18.

Shipper, Apichai W. 2010. Introduction: Politics of Citizenship and Transnational Gendered Migration in East and Southeast Asia. *Pacific Affairs* 83(1): 11–29.

Sim, Jae-yun. 1999. Number of "Illegal Migrants" Sharply Increases. *Korea Times,* September 27.

Sin Hwawu, and Hwang Tongsim. 1997. "Katcha lihon" = chintcha lihon ["Fake divorce" = Real divorce]. *Hŭngnyŏnggang sinmun* [Heilongjiang News], November 22.

Smith, Michael Peter, and Luis Eduardo Guarnizo. 1998. *Transnationalism from Below.* New Brunswick, N.J.: Transaction Publishers.

Solinger, Dorothy J. 1999. *Contesting Citizenship in Urban China: Peasant Migrants, the State and the Logic of the Market.* Berkeley: University of California Press.

Song, Changzoo. 2005. Brothers Only in Name: Korean Chinese Migrants in South Korea. Paper presented at the Conference for the Center for Comparative Immigration Studies at the University of California, May 20–21, San Diego, California.

Song, Jesook. 2006. Family Breakdown and Invisible Homeless Women. *positions: east asia cultures critique* 14(1): 37–65.

———. 2009. *South Koreans in the Debt Crisis: The Creation of a Neoliberal Welfare Society.* Durham: Duke University Press.

Sorensen, Clark W. 1988. *Over the Mountains Are Mountains: Korean Peasant Households and Their Adaptations to Rapid Industrialization.* Seattle: University of Washington Press.

Sørensen, Ninna Nyberg, and Finn Stepputat. 2001. Narrations of Authority and Mobility. *Identities* 8(3): 313–42.

Tsuda, Takeyuki. 2003. *Strangers in the Ethnic Homeland: Japanese Brazilian Return Migration in Transnational Perspective.* New York: Columbia University Press.

Wallerstein, Immanuel. 1974. *The Modern World-System I: Capitalist Agriculture and the Origins of the European World-Economy in the Sixteenth Century.* New York: Academic Press.

———. 1980. *The Modern World System II: Mercantilism and the Consolidation of the European World-Economy, 1600–1750.* New York: Academic Press.

———. 1989. *The Modern World System III: The Second Era of Great Expansion of the Capitalist World Economy, 1730–1840s.* San Diego: Academic Press.

Wang, Danyu. 2004. Ritualistic Coresidence and the Weakening of Filial Practice in Rural China. In *Filial Piety: Practice and Discourse in Contemporary East Asia,* ed. Charlotte Ikels. Stanford: Stanford University Press.

Weston, Kath. 1991. *Families We Choose: Lesbians, Gays, Kinship.* New York: Columbia University Press.

Wolf, Eric R. 1982. *Europe and the People without History.* Berkeley: University of California Press.

Yan, Yunxiang. 2003. *Private Life under Socialism.* Stanford: Stanford University Press.

Yngvesson, Barbara. 2005. Going "Home": Adoption, Loss of Bearings and the Mythology of Roots. In *Cultures of Transnational Adoption,* ed. Toby Alice Volkman. Durham: Duke University Press.

Yoon, Hyungsook. 1989. Rethinking Traditional Marriage in Korea. *Korea Journal* 29:17–27.

Yoon, Soon-Young S. 1990. Super Motherhood: Rural Women in South Korea. In *Structures and Strategies: Women, Work and Family,* ed. L. Dube and R. Palriwala. New Delhi: Sage.

Zhang, Li. 2001a. *Strangers in the City: Reconfigurations of Space, Power, and Social Networks within China's Floating Population.* Stanford: Stanford University Press.

———. 2001b. Migration and Privatization of Space and Power in Late Socialist China. *American Ethnologist* 28(1): 179–205.

Zheng Xinzhe. 1998. Chaoxianzu renkou liudong jiqi shehui wending wenti yanjiu [Research on Chosonjok population mobility and the problem of social stability]. *Manzu Yanjiu* [Manchu research] 4(53): 74–85.

Index

Note: Page numbers for illustrations are set in *italics*.